Eisenhower's Nuclear
Calculus in Europe

Eisenhower's Nuclear Calculus in Europe

The Politics of IRBM Deployment in NATO Nations

GATES BROWN

McFarland & Company, Inc., Publishers
Jefferson, North Carolina

LIBRARY OF CONGRESS CATALOGUING-IN-PUBLICATION DATA

Names: Brown, Gates M., author.
Title: Eisenhower's nuclear calculus in Europe : the politics of IRBM deployment in NATO nations / Gates Brown.
Other titles: Politics of Intermediate-range ballistic missiles deployment in NATO nations | Politics of IRBM deployment in NATO nations
Description: Jefferson, North Carolina : McFarland & Company, Inc., Publishers, 2019 | Includes bibliographical references and index.
Identifiers: LCCN 2018047645 | ISBN 9781476669502 (softcover : acid free paper) ∞
Subjects: LCSH: Eisenhower, Dwight D. (Dwight David), 1890–1969. | Intermediate-range ballistic missiles—Europe—History—20th century. | North Atlantic Treaty Organization—History—20th century. | United States—Foreign relations—1953–1961. | Europe—Foreign relations—1945– | Europe—Defenses. | Nuclear weapons—Government policy—United States—History—20th century. | Nuclear warfare—Government policy—United States—History—20th century. | National security—United States—History—20th century. | Cold War.
Classification: LCC E835 .B688 2019 | DDC 327.73009/04—dc23
LC record available at https://lccn.loc.gov/2018047645

BRITISH LIBRARY CATALOGUING DATA ARE AVAILABLE

ISBN (print) 978-1-4766-6950-2
ISBN (ebook) 978-1-4766-3474-6

© 2018 Gates Brown. All rights reserved

No part of this book may be reproduced or transmitted in any form or by any means, electronic or mechanical, including photocopying or recording, or by any information storage and retrieval system, without permission in writing from the publisher.

Front cover images: Jupiter IRBM on its launch pad (U.S. Army Redstone Arsenal); Dwight D. Eisenhower (photograph by *The New York Times*, 1954, Library of Congress)

Printed in the United States of America

McFarland & Company, Inc., Publishers
  Box 611, Jefferson, North Carolina 28640
     www.mcfarlandpub.com

To Marty, Anna, and Garrison,
you bring more to my life than
I could ever return. Thank you.

Acknowledgments

This book required the support and patience of many people.

Adrian Lewis was instrumental in helping this project from its inception by providing a lot of valuable criticism and advice on how to improve not only the quality of the research but of the writing.

Ted Wilson ensured that I focused on the people who make policy.

Nick Sambaluk provided insightful critiques and friendship, which made this project easier to complete.

Jonathan House was always able to identify where I could improve the work and was gracious enough to do so often.

I would not have had the ability to write this book or to study history without Jim Willbanks.

Two anonymous readers provided helpful feedback on an early draft.

Archival support was key to make this project a reality: Christopher Abrams at the Eisenhower Presidential Library was fundamental in helping me navigate my way through their holdings.

Because of the help of those listed above and that of many others, this project was successful; any errors or mistakes are mine.

Table of Contents

Acknowledgments vi
Introduction 1

1. Creating the New Look: Project Solarium and the Intellectual Foundation of the New Look Defense Policy 11
2. Many Strands into One Rope: Creating a Unified Defense Policy 28
3. Resistance to Massive Retaliation: The Arguments Against Massive Retaliation and the Deficiencies in Eisenhower's National Security Policies 37
4. The Development of IRBMs 55
5. The Suez Crisis and Bermuda Conference Reconciliation 83
6. A European Solution to an American Problem: Eisenhower's Initial Reaction to the Soviet Launch of Sputnik 106
7. U.S-U.K. IRBM Agreement 129
8. Unintended Consequences 148

Conclusion 162
Chapter Notes 169
Bibliography 184
Index 195

Introduction

President Eisenhower faced many security threats during his administration. One of the most dangerous was the constant threat of thermonuclear war with the Soviet Union. He and his Soviet counterpart, Nikita Khrushchev, had the ability to level weapons of previously unimaginable power. Understanding how Eisenhower dealt with this security threat is important to understanding his New Look defense policy, written in 1953, and his views on how to wage war in the atomic age. A fundamental part of his approach to this problem was putting more emphasis on technologically advanced atomic weapons. One of the primary weapons systems Eisenhower focused the nation's research efforts on was the Intercontinental Ballistic Missile (ICBM). However, in the mid–1950s, the most hopeful estimate for readiness for these weapons was in the middle of the next decade. The president had to have a more immediate response to the ever-growing Soviet military threat. Intermediate Range Ballistic Missiles (IRBMs) provided a stop gap solution. The problem with IRBMs was that they did not have ability to destroy Soviet targets from the continental United States; they required European launch sites to reach the Union of Soviet Socialist Republics (U.S.S.R).

The primary security concerns that motivated President Eisenhower to deploy IRBMs were domestic. The Soviet launch of the *Sputnik* satellite raised security concerns for many U.S. citizens. Although the Soviet launch was a pivotal moment, it did not cause President Eisenhower to change his administration's New Look defense policy. He saw this event as proof that the United States required missiles in addition to its manned bomber atomic force. The ICBM was not ready for deployment, however. The only missiles close enough for production that could carry large atomic warheads were the IRBMs but these required European bases in

Introduction

order to be able to hit Soviet targets. Because of this, European cooperation was vital. In order to gain this cooperation, the Eisenhower administration had two frameworks for offering these weapons to its European allies. One, the British offer, was British-owned missiles with U.S.–owned but jointly controlled warheads and the promise of the opportunity to purchase IRBMs for use with British nuclear warheads that were under the sole control of the British government. The British offer was unique because the British had an independent nuclear weapons program. The second framework, which was available to other North Atlantic Treaty Organization (NATO) allies was missiles with U.S.–owned and jointly controlled warheads. There was no offer of sales to non-nuclear NATO allies. The differences between the two frameworks frustrated French leaders, especially Charles de Gaulle, who wanted France to have a more important role in the alliance.

In order to better understand the implications of the New Look defense policy and the decision to deploy IRBMs, this work discusses the concerns of U.S. Army leaders, such as Chiefs of Staff Generals Matthew Ridgway and Maxwell Taylor, regarding the New Look and the administration's decision to consolidate the IRBM program under the U.S. Air Force. The discussion shows that the Eisenhower administration did not deviate from the New Look defense policy throughout Eisenhower's term in office, as Campbell Craig argued in *Destroying the Village*.[1] In this way, this work is in agreement with Peter Roman's *Eisenhower and the Missile Gap*, which argues for the consistent presence of Massive Retaliation throughout Eisenhower's administration.[2] This book expands upon the work done in Philip Nash's *The Other Missiles of October*,[3] which looks at how John F. Kennedy's administration used the Jupiter missiles in Turkey as a bargaining chip in the Cuban Missile Crisis. This work provides a more detailed explanation of why Eisenhower decided to deploy IRBMs to Europe and the impacts of that policy. This project also provides an expansion on the discussion of nuclear strategy in the Eisenhower administration. Works such as Edward Kaplan's *To Kill Nations* effectively discuss the role of the U.S. Air Force in the late 1940s and 1950s in the formation and execution of U.S. atomic strategy.[4] One of the purposes of this book is to provide a similar argument about U.S. Army leaders' efforts to increase the importance of the ground service in these plans. This book

Introduction

also discusses the implications of the deployment of IRBMs on the Franco-American relationship. It is in agreement with Frederic Bozo's *Two Strategies for Europe: De Gaulle, the United States, and the Atlantic Alliance* but seeks to provide a more U.S.–focused interpretation of these events to highlight the reasons why Eisenhower and his administration's decision ran into resistance from the French.[5]

President Dwight Eisenhower's decision to deploy IRBMs to Western Europe in the late 1950s had strategic, military, and political objectives. These weapons were important in their own right, even though they had a short operational life. The missiles, which were active from 1959 through 1963, were inaccurate, took a long time to launch, and once deployed were already obsolete because of the success of the Navy's Polaris solid-fueled IRBM program and the unanticipated success in the ICBM research efforts. However, the military value of these weapons was only one component of the decision to deploy them to Western Europe.

The IRBMs influence on the North Atlantic Treaty Organization (NATO) alliance and American security concerns outweighed their relatively limited military value. As a result of the IRBM deployment, the Anglo-American relationship improved. With this missile deployment, President Eisenhower hoped to begin the process to move America's commitment to NATO away from ground forces and toward missile and strategic bomber forces. He also used their deployment to calm domestic fears after the Soviet launch of *Sputnik* in 1957. However, not all of the effects of this decision were positive. The establishment of IRBMs in Western Europe solidified a two-tiered alliance in NATO between nations with nuclear weapons—the U.S. and the U.K.—and those without them. Finally, the deployment of IRBMs contributed to the French exit, under Charles de Gaulle, from the military component of the NATO alliance.

Deploying IRBMs was a single part of President Dwight D. Eisenhower's New Look defense policy, which sought to weave fiscal and national security into one strategy. In order to do this, Eisenhower had to find different solutions to the serious defense challenges faced by the nation. Atomic weapons seemed to provide a way to deliver maximum deterrence and protection at the lowest possible cost. By the mid–1950s, decreases in the size of nuclear warheads, improvements in guidance systems, and more effective propulsion methods made it possible for missiles

Introduction

to strike the Soviet Union from Western Europe. IRBMs offered a new way for the United States to protect its European allies that did not require sustaining numerous Army divisions far away from the United States. The problem for Eisenhower was integrating these weapons into the American and NATO defense structures; a corollary to this issue was determining how much control each individual nation would have over the use of these missiles.

IRBMs were part of the new focus on nuclear warfare under Eisenhower. The controversy over atomic weapons and their use in defending Western Europe also stirred animosity in the U.S. defense community. The Army, which lost its IRBM missile program to the Air Force, saw its budget and manpower levels erode after the Korean War. In contrast, the Air Force received almost half of the national defense budget for many years in Eisenhower's administration. The deployment of IRBMs to Europe represented the dominance of airpower and the decline of ground forces in national security. The struggle over which service should control long-range missile research and development had political and budgetary implications that went beyond the control of specific programs. Again, looking at the IRBMs only in terms of their military value clouds their real influence on the struggle between service branches to determine the direction of national defense under the New Look defense policy.

This clash between the Army and the Air Force took place in the new paradigm of atomic warfare. President Eisenhower had the capability to destroy nations with a large arsenal of thermonuclear weapons. The United States tested its first fusion weapon, otherwise known as a hydrogen bomb, in 1952. The Soviet Union tested its first atomic bomb in 1949 and its first hydrogen bomb in 1953. Britain also developed fusion nuclear weapons during the early 1950s. President Eisenhower was the first president to preside in an era when both superpowers had the capability to wage thermonuclear war. Examining Eisenhower's decision to deploy IRBMs from a military and political perspective explains how he intended to combat the Soviet threat, maintain a viable nuclear deterrent, and balance military spending in the thermonuclear era.

During the 1950s, Great Britain and the United States were the only two nations in the NATO alliance with independent nuclear arsenals. By the end of the decade, nuclear weapons provided a barometer for judging

Introduction

a nation's standing in the alliance. France, which did not have an independent nuclear weapons arsenal at the time, was not in the same tier as Britain and the United States. This influenced the character of the IRBM deployment agreements offered to Britain and then to other NATO nations.

Charles De Gaulle, France's president from 1959 to 1969, thought France deserved recognition for its importance to the alliance with an IRBM deal similar to the one offered to Great Britain. He believed the U.S. offer of IRBMs held under joint U.S. and French control was insufficient. He did not believe Washington would sanction the use of IRBMs to defend French national interests if it did not align with American security needs. Because of this, France, in de Gaulle's opinion, required independent control of the missiles in order to best use these weapons for its own protection. He also wanted the United States to offer technological assistance in addition to national ownership of IRBMs for France, both of which Britain received. However, President Eisenhower did not want the number of nuclear nations to increase. He wanted the deployment of IRBMs to Europe to offer the protection of atomic weapons without the problems of nuclear proliferation. Eisenhower hoped that this plan would forestall the creation of an independent French nuclear arsenal in favor of a unified European nuclear umbrella under NATO auspices. The roots of this decision are evident in the New Look defense policy. However, looking at the missiles from a military perspective leaves aside the discussion of issues like national control of these weapons and why certain nations, like Britain, received more generous terms than other nations, like France. This book, by including the political aspects of Eisenhower's decision to deploy these missiles, illustrates the importance of these weapons to the NATO alliance and the security of Western Europe.

In addition to the two-tier atomic structure, personality differences played a role in diplomatic relations between NATO senior member states. President Eisenhower, while Supreme Allied Commander in World War II, worked with both Charles de Gaulle and Harold Macmillan. His relationship with Macmillan, who would later serve as prime minister while Eisenhower was president, improved the Anglo-American alliance. De Gaulle, however, was a frustration for Eisenhower during World War II and this continued when de Gaulle became the French premier. These

Introduction

personal differences colored diplomatic interactions between these three important NATO nations. Interpersonal conflicts do not receive sufficient attention when considering only the military aspects of the deployment of IRBMs. The addition of political perspectives shows how interpersonal and political issues influenced the military decision to deploy IRBMs in the early Cold War period.

Underlying the reliance on nuclear weapons was the doctrine of Massive Retaliation, an evolution of the United States' policy on the use of atomic weapons. The term, coined by Secretary of State John Foster Dulles in a speech to the Council of Foreign Relations in 1954, formed the basis for President Eisenhower's views of deterrence. The doctrine stated that the U.S. did not consider itself bound to limit its response to the scale of the Soviet attack or intervention. The focus on atomic warfare influenced the NATO alliance in terms of military planning and political prestige.

Nuclear weapons were just as much a political barometer of power as they were a measure of military might. President Eisenhower's defense policy's focus on nuclear weapons made them paramount. The possession of an independent nuclear capability had a direct influence on the IRBM agreement offered to the United Kingdom. France did not receive the same offer of cooperation, in part, because of its lack of such a program. The Franco-American agreement came under NATO auspices, whereas the Anglo-American agreement was outside of the NATO alliance. Although these were military agreements, they revealed the political importance of being a nuclear nation.

The New Look defense policy focused defense spending on nuclear weapons and the ability to launch nuclear assaults on the Soviet Union. Part of this emphasis included improving the United States' bomber and missile capability. ICBMs and IRBMs represented two different ways to strike the Soviet Union. IRBMs played an important role in the New Look and defense planning for Western Europe.

These missiles would provide NATO forces the ability to withstand and destroy a Soviet invasion. Eisenhower did not want to increase America's ground forces in the region and he believed that without an increase of manpower or IRBMs, NATO could not stop a determined Soviet attack. IRBMs provided the alliance the ability to destroy a significant amount of invading Soviet forces, making it possible for a reduced ground force to

Introduction

fight and prevail. The missiles, in most cases, were under the control of the host nation. However, it required NATO's Supreme Allied Commander in Europe (SACEUR) in coordination with the host nation's political leadership to approve of a launch. Officially, American forces controlled the nuclear warheads and only transferred them to the missiles in preparation for launching.

The first generation IRBMs were liquid fueled rockets with an inertial guidance system. There were two different models: the Jupiter and the Thor. The Army developed the Jupiter missile, which it intended to use with a mobile launcher, as this allowed forces on the ground to hide the weapons when they were not in use. The Army lost control of the program to the Air Force in 1956, however, which ended the mobile launcher concept. The Air Force design used fixed launch sites with hardened bunkers that housed the missiles. However, because hiding these facilities was impossible, they were obvious targets in the opening salvo of a conflict.

Another drawback of IRBMs was that they were unable to launch quickly in response to a Soviet attack. The liquid oxygen could not remain in the missiles on the launch pad for a prolonged period. In the event of an alert, the launch teams required almost an hour to fuel and prepare the missile for action. This lag between alert and ability to fire raised many questions in host nations about the viability of these weapons as a real second-strike option. These were not the only doubts nations had concerning the IRBM deployment.

Eisenhower's understanding of warfare in the atomic age affected his view of the place of nuclear weapons in national defense. During his second term, he continued to see warfare in the post–World War II period as atomic in character. Eisenhower often talked about balance in national defense and decried favoring only one type of weapon to protect the nation, but his actions tell a different story. During the late 1950s, the Army continued to suffer budget and force reductions while the Air Force's missile and strategic bombing programs continued to receive significant funding. Massive Retaliation was not just a doctrine Dulles created, it also represented the vision Eisenhower had of future conflicts. This understanding of the changing character of warfare made national control of nuclear weapons a matter of political importance and not only a military planning concern.

Introduction

President Eisenhower believed in the effectiveness of Massive Retaliation because of his understanding of Carl von Clausewitz's *On War*. He intended this policy to increase the cost of starting a conflict for the Soviet Union to such a level as to make it impossible for any political goal to justify it. This connection between politics and warfare was a fundamental part of Clausewitz's work and the New Look defense policy used this to inform its stance on nuclear weapons. Eisenhower wanted to make it clear that the United States intended to fight a total nuclear war with the Soviet Union in the hopes that this would prevent the Soviet Union from risking such a conflict. This made reliance on nuclear weapons seem like a viable option. These weapons, in the paradigm of Massive Retaliation, provided a superior level of security and deterrence than conventional forces. Massive Retaliation did not protect against the full range of possible conflicts, however. Limited wars, like the Korean War or Communist insurgencies were a poor fit for such a black-and-white policy approach to warfare.

Eisenhower's view of war in the age of thermonuclear weapons shaped his decision to deploy these missiles in the late 1950s. IRBMs and their role in Western Europe were a part of this understanding of how nuclear weapons changed warfare. These weapons helped accomplish the political objective of preventing a general war with the Soviet Union. Their importance was not their specific military capabilities but rather what they represented to the Soviet Union and Eisenhower's commitment to the doctrine of Massive Retaliation.

The Cold War pervaded every security concern Eisenhower faced during his presidency. His first defense priority was preventing a general conflict with the Soviet Union. Of almost equal importance was maintaining the alliance against the U.S.S.R., which required keeping a viable deterrent and ensuring that America's allies felt that an alliance with the U.S. provided more benefits and security than neutrality. Eisenhower had to address both the military and political tensions in the alliance. IRBMs became a tool to offer security to allies in Western Europe. They also became a way to repair relations with Great Britain after the Suez Crisis of 1956 caused a rift between the U.S., the UK, France and Israel.

The Suez Crisis had serious implications for NATO and the defense of Western Europe. President Eisenhower chose not to support U.S. allies, preferring instead to use diplomatic pressure to keep the Soviet Union

Introduction

out of the fight. In the aftermath of the conflict, the relationship between France, Great Britain, and the U.S. deteriorated. Although Eisenhower intended to repair the connections with both nations, he chose two different approaches to do so.

Thus, Great Britain received an offer of IRBMs and technological assistance in nuclear research. The Bermuda Conference in 1957, between President Eisenhower and Prime Minister Anthony Eden, provided a venue for Eisenhower to mend relations with the United Kingdom. Vital to this was the offer of not only the IRBMs, but also the promise of future collaboration and the sharing of nuclear research technology and information. Although President Franklin Roosevelt promised full cooperation with the British in atomic research, President Harry Truman changed American policy to make it much more restrictive and, in effect, broke the accord establishing the joint Anglo-American nuclear program. Investigating how these weapons worked to address this political problem in the NATO alliance demonstrates their political importance.

In contrast to Britain, France did not receive such a generous offer of cooperation in nuclear research or of IRBMs. Although the administration offered the missiles to France in 1958, it did so under the control of NATO. When President Charles De Gaulle took charge of France, he expected America to provide some technological aid to shorten the time for France to achieve its own nuclear program, as a sign of France's position in the alliance. Because of Eisenhower's opposition to an increase in the number of nations with atomic weapons, this placed France in a decidedly junior position relative to Britain and the United States, a position that maintained its World War II and post–World War II status.

The deployment of IRBMs to Europe did not have the effect that Eisenhower intended. It divided the three largest members of the alliance and created suspicion in other nations about the true nature of the U.S. commitment to NATO. This work shows how the offer of these weapons to Britain and France fit into Eisenhower's conception of atomic warfare and national security. Understanding Eisenhower's conception of atomic warfare is important because it sheds light on why the New Look defense policy was so consistent. This work discusses how the Army fared during the late 1950s under decreasing manpower and budget allocations, under a growing Communist threat in Europe and Asia. Eisenhower's

Introduction

understanding of nuclear war influenced not only the New Look but the NATO alliance as well.

The book begins with a discussion of the formation of the New Look defense policy, including how President Eisenhower created the policy and what he expected it to achieve. The second chapter outlines Eisenhower's views on war in the atomic age and its impact on U.S. defense strategy. The next chapter discusses the criticism of Massive Retaliation both from within and outside the Department of Defense. The fourth chapter outlines the development of guided missiles with a specific focus on this history of IRBMs. Chapter five analyzes the impact of the Suez Crisis on the U.S.-U.K. relationship and details the Bermuda Conference of 1957. The Soviet launch of *Sputnik* and how it changed the perception of security is the subject of the sixth chapter. The following chapter covers the specifics of the Anglo-American IRBM agreement, while the final chapter outlines the impact of the deployment of IRBMs on the NATO alliance.

1

Creating the New Look
*Project Solarium and the
Intellectual Foundation of
the New Look Defense Policy*

President Eisenhower assumed office during a turbulent time. The Korean War increasingly looked like an intractable conflict, showing the impotence of the Free World to defeat a determined Socialist invasion. In addition to the problems in Korea, atomic warfare reached a new and incredibly more deadly stage with the creation of hydrogen bombs. These new atomic warheads were vastly more destructive than those used in World War II. Although the United States was the first nation to possess hydrogen weapons, the Soviet Union quickly caught up. Only four years after the Soviets detonated their first atomic bomb in 1949, they perfected a hydrogen weapon. Now large cities like New York faced instant annihilation in a nuclear war with the Soviet Union.[1]

President Eisenhower's difficulties with the Korean War extended past Communists battlefield capability. He also had to contend with a problematic ally in South Korean President Syngman Rhee. Rhee wanted to expand the scope of the conflict and destroy North Korea. It was understandable why President Rhee sought the destruction of North Korea but for Eisenhower this represented an unacceptable risk. Also, making the elimination of North Korea a war objective destroyed any hope of a peace deal to stop the fighting. However, Eisenhower understood that he could not continue to fight the Korean War for an indefinite amount of time. In his memoir of his first term of office, *Mandate for Change*, he saw little use of maintaining the status quo in Korea. He wrote, "My conclusion as I left Korea was that we could not stand forever on a static front and continue to accept casualties without any visible results. Small attacks on small hills would not end this war."[2]

Communist incursion was nothing new to Eisenhower. He saw the Soviet Union as an expansionary force that had no problem with using for to achieve its objectives.[3] Even though the Korean War was over by 1953, Eisenhower was under no delusions about future relations between the Soviet Union and the United States. He also felt an obligation to make it clear that the Free World was the hope for newly independent people to maintain their freedom.[4]

Eisenhower's success in avoiding another conflict with the Soviet Union did not come about because of ambivalence towards the Soviets. Rather, his ability to maintain peace came from his understanding of the horrors of war and what war in the nuclear era meant for the United States. Eisenhower's diary, which he kept intermittently from his time in the Philippines in the 1930s through 1967, sheds some light on his views of warfare. Understanding how President Eisenhower approached war is important because of its influence on the development of his national security policy:

Brutality of war: In May 1942, Eisenhower struggled to advance the planning of Operation Bolero, the name for the buildup of troops in Britain in World War II. In his diary, he expressed frustration at those who thought they could "buy victory." He wrote that "not one man in twenty in the government (including the war and navy departments) realizes what a grisly, dirty tough business we are in." War was destructive and was something to be avoided, unless the threat of not going to war was more dangerous than fighting it.[5]

If the nation was going to fight, it should do so completely: At the initiation of the Korean War, Eisenhower went to Washington, D.C., to see some of his old friends and discuss preparations for the oncoming conflict. He worried that those in charge of preparing the nation for war did not understand the necessity of preparing for all-out war, even if they hoped it would be limited. Eisenhower did not think "that an appeal to force cannot, by its nature, be a partial one." He continued by writing that "in a fight we (our side) can never be too strong." America had to be ready for any eventuality "even if it finally came to the use of the A-bomb (which God forbid.)" War could not be something that a state could put artificial

1. Creating the New Look

limits on in the beginning of a conflict. This was another reason why Eisenhower was hesitant to use force as president, there was no reliable way to ensure that a limited war would remain limited.[6]

Four pillars of future strength: Eisenhower thought future global wars would be "ideological" conflicts. He wrote that the United States people, in order to be victorious in such a struggle, had to maintain: their dedication to democracy and capitalism, a solid economic base, moral character, and adequate military power. Eisenhower wrote this entry in 1946 but the four pillars of strength influenced the formation of his defense policy as president.

Importance of maintaining parity with the Soviet Union in military technology, specifically guided missiles: Long-range ballistic missiles became a threat during World War II. Eisenhower saw their destruction first hand while he was in Britain during World War II; his headquarters was in line with the flight path of many V-2 rockets that Hitler launched in the final years of World War II.[7] There was little defense against such weapons. By the time Eisenhower was president, guided missiles and smaller atomic warheads combined to make it possible to use such weapons to launch a nuclear attack across thousands of miles. He understood that the American people considered these to be the "ultimate" weapon. In his diary in 1956, Eisenhower wrote that people had "a picture of guided missiles raining out of the skies in almost uncounted numbers, it is extremely important that the Soviets do not get ahead" of the United States "in the general development of these weapons."[8] This became a significant problem for Eisenhower after the Soviet launch of *Sputnik*.

Effect of atomic weapons on future wars: Eisenhower saw atomic weapons as a fact of future wars. He also believed that there were benefits to this new paradigm. Concentrating defense spending on atomic weapons allowed for reductions in conventional troops.[9] However, this meant that any future conflict would be nuclear in nature. Any atomic conflict would be incredibly destructive, especially if it escalated into an unlimited atomic war between the Soviet Union and the United States. In his memoir of his first term in office, Eisenhower wrote that "modern global war would be catastrophic beyond belief." This made him realize that the U.S. needed a military to deter wars not just a force to fight them.[10]

Nuclear weapons were not going away and neither was the Soviet

Eisenhower's Nuclear Calculus in Europe

Union. Eisenhower had to balance the threat of war with the necessity to continue to maintain peace. The president knew that he could not unilaterally contain war once it began. He learned this from his experience in the military and his study of Carl von Clausewitz's work *On War*, which he read three times while a junior officer serving in Panama under General Fox Conner.[11] Although Eisenhower knew he could not control war if it broke out, he was very effective in controlling the threat of war, which was what he intended to do with his defense policy as president.

Eisenhower's defense policy, nicknamed the New Look, came out of the Project Solarium conference held in the summer of 1953. He intended this project to provide recommendations for developing his administration's defense policy. Eisenhower wanted to avoid large budget deficits as well as provide an effective deterrent to prevent future conflicts equal to or greater than the Korean War. President Eisenhower struggled with these competing interests of national defense and establishing a solid economy throughout his two terms in office.

The New Look defense policy offered a constructive way to balance these two, at times conflicting, ends. The president's defense policy focused America's national defense assets towards a massive nuclear response capability and less towards large ground forces to fight a conflict similar to the Korean War. Eisenhower intended this reliance on nuclear capacity, known as the doctrine of Massive Retaliation, to deter communist aggression. By focusing on nuclear weapons, Eisenhower hoped to concentrate U.S. defense allocations primarily on air power. In the early 1950s, building air power assets was cheaper than maintaining large ground forces deployed to defend Western Europe, Korea, and Japan. If the New Look policy proved effective, Eisenhower hoped to realize economic stability through balanced budgets, made possible by relatively cheap air power. Eisenhower wanted to build a solid economic foundation in order to create a viable long-term defense structure that wouldn't bankrupt the nation.

Although called the New Look, this name was misleading. It was not a dramatic shift from Truman's defense policy or subsequent Cold War defense policies that followed it. National security policies throughout the Cold War generally were variations on a theme and not markedly different. Containment, as espoused by National Security Council (NSC)-

1. Creating the New Look

68 under President Truman, continued to be the dominant paradigm for combating the Soviet Union and the People's Republic of China. Although some of the details changed, the core idea did not. The U.S. Army remained forward deployed under President Eisenhower, albeit in smaller numbers. Nuclear weapons, the central component of Eisenhower's policy, remained the main deterrent throughout the Cold War, with differing emphasis depending on the particular administration. Alliances formed a critical element of the New Look policy but they continued to be important in all administrations' Cold War defense programs. Foreign and military aid provided a way for Cold War U.S. presidential administrations to garner influence with nations around the world and hopefully limit the need for U.S. ground forces. Finally, scientific research to provide the best weapons technology continued to be important for U.S. strategy throughout the conflict.

The differences between Presidents Eisenhower and Truman's defense policies stemmed from the focus on atomic weapons. By leveraging this new technology, Eisenhower sought to provide an effective military deterrent at a reduced cost. Eisenhower's concern for fiscal security did not stem purely from his conservative political roots. He thought that the economic health of the nation directly influenced its ability to continue to fight communism. Another guiding experience was Eisenhower's time in the army through the Great Depression. He saw the damage that an economic crisis could bring to national defense.

Eisenhower played an active role as president in contrast to the popular perception of his preference for golfing rather than working. He delegated significant authority to his subordinates, just as he did when he was the Supreme Commander of Allied Forces in World War II. This delegation process increased the public profile of subordinates in the government, creating the impression that Eisenhower did little in his own administration. Although Eisenhower allowed his subordinates much leeway within their portfolios, he did not delegate his responsibility when issues grew beyond the scope of one individual department or grew so large that they demanded his attention.

Eisenhower observed that the economic problems Truman faced were serious but the previous president's solutions did not capitalize of the nation's free market economic system. Eisenhower believed that people depended on an effective economy to spur them to work hard and earn a return on their labor. If the economy did not provide the encouragement for strong production, Eisenhower felt it could invite more state control. This regimentation represented a reduction in the freedoms that the U.S. system provided. Eisenhower wanted to ensure the prosperity of the free market by keeping it free from government enforced economic regulations.[12]

President Harry Truman was also a fiscal conservative; however, he had to contend with the necessary military buildup to fight the Korean War. Truman, when he took office, worried that the Soviet Union "was trying to scare the United States into spending itself into bankruptcy."[13] Truman was just as cautious and concerned about deficit spending as Eisenhower was but the Korean War demanded immediate and drastic action to combat. The economic conundrum that the Korean War caused troubled Eisenhower as well but Eisenhower did not have to contend with the conflict as long as Truman did.

President Eisenhower had to strike a compromise between economic prosperity and national defense by reducing government spending while still protecting the United States. He wanted to decrease the cost of government in order to make it fiscally responsible, as he understood the term. The U.S. had to be able to resist the Soviet Union for an untold number of years. To provide this defense, the U.S. economy had to remain robust. If the economy lost its vigor, Eisenhower worried that America's free market economy would not survive.[14]

In his final budget, President Truman authorized an $11 billion deficit. Within his first six months in office, Eisenhower decreased this amount by half. He also cut the amount of federal spending by $13 billion out of a $74 billion budget.[15] Much of this savings came because of decreased defense appropriations following the cessation of hostilities in Korea. Balancing the federal budget consumed much of Eisenhower's thoughts during this time. The president wanted to balance the nation's budget quickly, which required maintaining the high tax rate. He did not agree with the majority of Republicans who wanted to reduce taxes for political purposes and increase the amount of time necessary to balance the federal budget. Eisenhower did not want to sacrifice the economic vitality of the nation for short-term political pay-off.[16]

Eisenhower's desire to decrease the deficit did have limits. He realized

1. Creating the New Look

that finding the proper balance between fiscal conservatism and a strong defense required time. On July 29, 1953, Eisenhower received a memo from Secretary of the Treasury George Humphrey requesting an increase in the national debt above the $275 billion limit set by Congress. Humphrey, the former president of the M.A. Hanna Steel Company, served in the administration from 1953 until 1957. Secretary Humphrey argued that raising the debt limit to $290 billion provided the ability of the government to meet Congressional authorizations and maintain some fiscal freedom of movement. This also would force the administration to begin to reconcile its expenses with revenue and balance the budget. By doing so, America could provide a firm economic foundation to lead the defense of the non-communist world.[17]

Taxes, deficits, and other economic factors all influenced national defense in multiple ways. For Eisenhower, these critically important issues were not mutually exclusive. Cutting taxes had to wait until the United States was secure against the Soviet threat. In order to achieve this end, the U.S. needed a sound perimeter of allies close to the Soviet Union. In order to create such an alliance, Eisenhower knew he needed to provide military and economic aid to partner nations. If the U.S. cut taxes, defense budgets could suffer, as well as the outposts that provided security. Eisenhower hoped "that nothing will happen to damage irreparably the progress toward unified strength and collective security that we have been trying so laboriously to build up."[18]

Technology, especially nuclear weapons, provided an attractive means of reducing defense budgets but not military capacity. With the Korean War cease-fire recently signed, Eisenhower had an opportunity to reduce military spending; however, he had to create a national security strategy that ensured that these budget cuts did not endanger the U.S. This required determining which weapons systems and military formations were vital and what their size and role in national defense should be. Project Solarium was one way that Eisenhower began to solve this complex problem.

Atomic weapons complicated national defense issues, not only because of their economic impact, but because of their increasingly powerful warheads. Public discourse concerning these new weapons coalesced around the nuclear fusion warhead. These new warheads could destroy large cities, such as New York, in one strike. Any attack using such a weapon, even if targeted at military units or industrial sites, would destroy the surrounding urban infrastructure. This meant that leaders knew that the decision to employ such weapons meant the destruction of civilians. The continuous increase in the lethality of nuclear weapons increased the moral cost of their use.[19]

The United States had to face the possibility of nuclear warfare, because many felt it had no other option. The consensus was that the Soviet Union had the capability to put more soldiers on the battlefield and that the U.S. However, the Soviet Union did not have the advanced air or nuclear assets that the United States possessed at time, although the Soviet Union was quickly closing the gap between the two nations. Due to the disparity of manpower between the Soviet and the U.S. Army, the United States, had to compete with assets and weapons that mitigated the manpower discrepancies between the two blocs. Central to this was the use of atomic weapons.[20]

One fact undercutting the manpower difference rationale for nuclear weapons was that the population difference was not that substantial. The population differential between the U.S. and the U.S.S.R. during the 1950s was about 30 million, or about a 20 percent difference between the two populations. This combined with the population of Europe put the two forces on much more equal footing but arguments focusing on the manpower asymmetries permeated the strategic discussion of the 1050s. American national security experts, including President Eisenhower, continued to believe that the Soviet Union's military forces greatly outnumbered those of the U.S. and its allies.[21]

Overcoming the superior manpower of the Soviet Union was not the only concern. Ensuring that the U.S. economy could support the military necessary to protect against and deter attack from the Soviet Union was also a vital issue Eisenhower had to face. Truman faced a deteriorating economic situation in 1949. He had to deal with shifting the nation to a peacetime economy and providing a way for the returning servicemen to integrate themselves into the labor market, this was not an easy process. His Director of the Budget, Frederick Lawton, recommended reducing military expenditures for fiscal year 1951, in order to reduce the deficit.[22] Truman's economic problems were not only a product of deficit spending;

1. Creating the New Look

in 1949, the economy was in the midst of a recession, largely due to the removal of government purchases of war material. Although Truman's Secretary of the Treasury, John Snyder, thought that the economy was on its way to recover by the end of the year without significant help from the government, the economic outlook at the end of the 1940s was not particularly good.[23]

In the face of this economic downturn, Truman had to increase the military spending that he previously decreased in order to combat the Korean War. This conflict also gave more aggressive policy makers in the Truman administration, such as Paul Nitze, the director of policy planning for the State Department from 1950 through 1953, the opportunity to influence the strategic policy debate.[24] One of Ntize's major contributions was the policy document NSC-68. This paper, written prior to the outbreak of the Korean War incorporated George Kennan's idea of containment but with a military emphasis. NSC-68 centered on preparing for a year of maximum danger, 1954. By this time, under the planning assumptions in the document, the Soviets would possess enough nuclear weapons to deal a devastating blow to the United States. Although, at the time of its drafting, the fears of NSC-68 concerning Soviet nuclear power were projections, these soon became a reality.[25]

When Eisenhower entered office, he saw two major problems with Truman's defense policy. First, he thought that the concentration on a year of maximum danger was unsound. Eisenhower also believed that Truman's policies were too rigid in their estimation of the Soviet threat. He concluded that the policies under Truman did not offer the needed flexibility to operate in a changing world. Apart from the policies lack of military vigor, Eisenhower believed that they relied too much on manpower, which was expensive. Eisenhower said, "Today three aircraft with modern weapons can practically duplicate the destructive power of all the 2,700 planes we unleashed in the great breakout attack from the Normandy beachhead." He hoped to replace soldiers with technology and make it economically feasible to provide a powerful military for the long conflict with the Soviet Union. This effort to shift the burden of defense from manpower to technology pervaded Eisenhower's defense policy.[26]

In his first State of the Union address in 1953, Eisenhower outlined what he thought were the major problems confronting his administration.

Eisenhower's Nuclear Calculus in Europe

First was balancing defense and economic concerns. If he concentrated on defense spending with too little focus on economic issues, Eisenhower worried he would be solving one problem while creating another. He wanted to move away from manpower metrics as the best judge of military power., In his speech, Eisenhower explained that he wanted a leaner military that provided significant deterrence but at a reduced cost.[27]

In his address, Eisenhower discussed the threat that the Soviet Union posed. He mentioned how the Communist world was encroaching on free people in Korea, Indochina, and Malaysia. Communism and the Soviet Union were synonymous in the inaugural address.[28] President Eisenhower expressed what many American believed about the expansionist tendencies of the Soviet Union. A Gallop Poll, released in 1953, shows that almost 80 percent of respondents felt that the Soviet Union wanted to rule the world. The American public did not cynically receive the rhetoric of the Cold War. They interpreted the threat as real and dire.[29]

Prior to Project Solarium, the United States made a significant advance in making atomic weapons more useful and easier to deploy. When used in World War II, the only way to deploy a nuclear weapon was by loading it in a strategic bomber and dropping the ordinance. However, in May 1953, about a month prior to the start of conference, the Atomic Energy Commission (AEC) successfully tested an atomic shell fired from a field gun. This 280-millimeter weapon broadened the spectrum of atomic weapons. It made it possible to envision their use in limited conflicts and not just a total war.[30]

Understanding the scale of the Soviet threat is difficult because of the knowledge of how the Cold War ended. However, President Eisenhower did not have the benefit of this. In an NSC meeting on July 30, 1953, the council heard from the director of the Central Intelligence Administration (CIA) Allen Dulles about the growing Soviet threat. Dulles stated that the Soviet economy was growing and was closing the gap between it and the United States. Also, both the U.S. and the U.S.S.R. were building incredibly destructive weapons further eroding U.S. security. Although the building Western European military strength helped offset Soviet advances, there was no clear victory in sight. The stakes of the Cold War were very high and it was not just a matter of winning militarily, President Eisenhower had to wage a long conflict.[31]

1. Creating the New Look

In constructing his defense policy, Eisenhower expected Project Solarium to supply a definitive direction for his administration. The project came out of the need to explore different foreign and defense policy courses of action. His intent for the project was to provide varied recommendations, from which he would choose the best way to proceed.[32] Eisenhower expected this new program to give him the tools to cut defense spending, while maintaining sufficient defense forces. Each of the three Task Forces had separate planning assumptions that drove their investigations. The Task Forces would report their findings to the president and the NSC. While each Task Force created a useful report, making a unified defense policy from these three recommendations proved difficult.

Task Force A, chaired by George Kennan, advocated a program similar to the containment policy under President Truman.[33] George Kennan, a State Department official, who served in the Soviet Union during the mid–1940s, played a fundamental role in Cold War defense policy. His insights into Soviet behavior, as explained in his long telegram and "Roots of Soviet Conduct" published in *Foreign Affairs* in the 1947, gave the intellectual framework for the containment policy of the Cold War.[34] Kennan wrote that his course of action, Alternative A, preserved armed forces capable of securing the United States and providing assistance to its allies for a prolonged time. This required the U.S. to continue to support the free world with military and economic aid. Finally, the U.S. should exploit Soviet weaknesses in the social, political, and economic realms. This effort should not significantly increase the tensions between the Soviet Union and the United States. If carried out successfully it would avert another world war.[35]

Based on the assumptions Kennan used to shape his Task Force's findings, the risk of war was not high. In response to this decreased risk, his plan recommended the reduction of defense allocations. However, Kennan warned that to reduce the nation's defense at the same rate as the post–World War II defense cuts raised the risk of Soviet aggression due to a diminished U.S. readiness to counter Soviet actions.[36]

Kennan proposed a strategy centered on three areas, the United States, its allies, and the Soviet Union's sphere of influence. Kennan identified two contradictions in the Soviet system, they were its authoritarian state and its controlled economy. These contradictions meant that the

Soviet government was unable to provide a national defense and a strong military alliance supported by the Soviet economy while still maintaining a robust consumer-based economy for its own citizens. If the U.S. focused its efforts in these areas towards exacerbating these contradictions then, Kennan argued, the Soviets had to accept some form of peace with the West. Eventually, if put under enough pressure, the Soviet system demanded too much of the people and the system would fall. He further warned in the report, that the risk of war could not distract the U.S. from completing its objective of preventing the Soviet Union from increasing its hegemony. Kennan stressed that his Task Force's recommendations provided the ability to curb, not stop, Soviet expansion if the administration followed its provisions.[37]

The Korean War ended just as Project Solarium started. Ensuring that the U.S. avoided another conflict was vitally important for Task Force A, as well as President Eisenhower. Kennan understood this fact and the report contains a section explaining how to proceed during peacetime. The Soviet Union could easily misinterpret American actions, if the president chose Alternative A, as provoking war and not averting it. The U.S., under Alternative A, intended to reduce Soviet territory to that of imperial Russia. This confinement, Kennan's group argued, would discredit the Soviet Union, and cause its failure through contradictions in the Soviets' ideology, economy, and politics.[38]

One problem with Kennan's task force was its assumption that its recommended course of action would lead to the Soviet Union's demise. If this were true, it was wishful thinking to argue that the Soviet Union would willingly accept this state of affairs. The U.S.S.R would, if faced with its imminent defeat, strike out in order to reverse its decline. Kennan's group did not adequately address the problems with this fundamental assumption in their report.

Kennan encouraged Eisenhower to ensure that his foreign policy had a sense of consistency and predictability. The U.S. should be the solid foundation of the free world and of its resistance to the Soviet Union. Eisenhower, in Kennan's opinion, had to ensure his government acted with one accord, and was consistent in its policy with its allies and the Soviets. This reduced the chance that the Soviets would misconstrue changes in policy as aggressive actions.[39]

1. Creating the New Look

America's position in relation to the Soviet Union was advantageous in Kennan's opinion. However, there were dangers that could undermine the U.S. He encouraged Eisenhower to build alliances, ensure that U.S. allies understood the stakes of the conflict, and took on their fair share of the burden. In the end, Kennan's Task Force recommended a continuation of the containment policy, with a few changes. These changes included the assumption of a strategic offensive against the Soviet Union, as opposed to the general defensive nature of Truman's containment policy. Soviet Premier Josef Stalin's death, in February 1953, was an important turning point in Kennan's analysis; he thought that the U.S. could use this to start reducing the Soviet Union's power over its satellites. However, he proposed to do this through ideological and economic means, not through military confrontation. Finally, Kennan cautioned Eisenhower to avoid focusing solely on communism. The U.S. policy, though oriented to bring about the eventual defeat of the Soviet Union, should not imply that the only U.S. concern was the elimination of the Soviet system. The Task Force closed its report by acknowledging the fact that though they did not choose the policy they researched; they thought it could not "be safely rejected."[40]

Kennan's strategy did not advocate specific reductions or realignments of defense forces. However, it did imply that strategic forces would be more critical to U.S. defense than tactical units in the long-term against the Soviet Union. This policy, as with the other two policies presented in Project Solarium, only provided broad outlines. The specifics came after President Eisenhower chose how to translate these recommendations into a defense policy.

While the members of Project Solarium worked on their reports, the Soviets continued making progress in their military capabilities. In August, the Soviets announced through a scientific paper that they now possessed deuterium, a key ingredient in the research and production of hydrogen bombs. This announcement was further proof of the rising stakes of the Cold War and the increasingly destructive capacity of both the U.S. and the U.S.S.R. Although this event wasn't a part of any specific task force report, Soviet power was a key concern for all the task forces.

Task Force B, chaired by Major General James McCormack, advocated a more aggressive position than Kennan's group.[41] General McCormack served as the director of the Division of Military Application of the

Atomic Energy Commission in the early 1950s.⁴² Alternative B had three stages. First, the United States would draw a line outside of which it would not allow the Soviet Union to expand. If the Soviet Union tried to expand outside of this line, then the U.S. would respond with a full-scale military reprisal. Second, U.S. leaders had to ensure that their Soviet counterparts understood the serious implications of continued Soviet expansion. Finally, McCormack's policy proposal stressed the need for "freedom of action" if communism expanded through revolutions. In this case, he thought the U.S. needed to do what was necessary to restore non-communist leadership. Task Force B provided primarily a military-based proposal.⁴³

McCormack identified several problems with the legacy of Truman's containment policy. By trying to stop Soviet expansion, the U.S. surrendered its ability to shape the conflict between the two nations. This allowed the Soviet Union to assume the strategic offensive, while relegating the U.S. to playing a defensive role. Trying to stop all Soviet expansion did not allow the U.S. to concentrate its resources where they were most effective. McCormack thought that eventually this would push the conflict beyond what the U.S. economy could bear.⁴⁴ His team's alternative took back the offensive from the Soviet Union, allowing the U.S. to dictate the terms of the struggle between the two superpowers.⁴⁵

If Eisenhower chose to continue President Truman's version of the containment policy, McCormack warned that it escalated the arms race. He wrote that within 5 to 10 years the American atomic arsenal would be of sufficient size that the numbers would not be as important as the strategy for their use. Once the U.S. reached this "age of atomic plenty," it had sufficient atomic capability to ensure the destruction of the Soviet Union. Unfortunately, the Soviet Union would not allow its nuclear program to remain in second place. This would create a nuclear standoff between the two nations, each having the capability to destroy the other. McCormack believed that Alternative B diverted the emphasis from atomic weapons in national defense and avoided such a future.⁴⁶

Again, the devil was in the details of this proposal. As with Kennan's policy the fundamental assumption of Soviet passivity was problematic. McCormack assumed that the Soviet Union would accept a state of affairs that ceded the strategic initiative to the United States. Arguing that this policy halted the escalation in nuclear arms presumed that the Soviet

1. Creating the New Look

Union would agree to act in the way that U.S. planners dictated. Also, McCormack's proposal proposed a very stiff penalty for Soviet expansion, one difficult to justify enforcing.

The pivotal part of McCormack's proposal was the line of defense, or the construction of Soviet and U.S. spheres of influence. This line, his committee argued, acted as barrier to Soviet expansion, because the U.S. would interpret any effort to expand beyond this line as an act of aggression. Similar to the Monroe Doctrine, McCormack defined certain parts of the world as under U.S. influence and others under Soviet influence. Constructing the line proved more difficult than anticipated. The line had to encompass the foreign land bases, sea-lanes, and airfields that allowed the U.S. to attack the Soviet Union. This required drawing the line well outside the territorial boundaries of the United States and its European and Asian allies. The line, as envisioned by McCormack, confined the Soviet Union to Eastern Europe, north of the Middle East, no farther south than South Korea, and China as its eastern limit.[47]

One of the benefits of this policy, in McCormack's estimation, was the elimination of peripheral wars. Wars like Korea, which took place outside of American and Soviet strategic interests, McCormack's group argued were too costly for the Soviet Union to contemplate supporting under this plan. As the U.S. nuclear threat grew, so did the cost of instigating such limited wars, since small-scale wars could escalate. Increasing the cost of aggression, especially for small-scale war, became a fundamental aspect of Eisenhower's New Look defense policy, even though this policy bore little resemblance to the enforcement of the Soviet sphere of influence as McCormack's task force proposed.[48]

Deterring conflicts of any size decreased the likelihood of the Soviets supporting peripheral wars. McCormack's alternative required a large international alliance supported and led by the United States. Under his recommendation, U.S. military power formed the main deterrent to Soviet aggression. It reduced the doubts of U.S. allies and made clear that the intent of U.S. aid was to prepare other nations to fight their own limited wars. Shifting the burden of fighting limited wars to allies created the opportunity for the U.S. to focus precious defense resources on deterring a direct conflict with the Soviet Union. McCormack argued that because his policy prevented Soviet expansion through limited wars, allied nations did not have to waste their own defense assets combating small-scale Soviet supported conflicts.[49]

By concentrating on preparing for general war against the Soviet Union, McCormack believed his policy alternative effectively delineated the roles of U.S. forces and laid out a strategy that used them in an economically efficient manner. If the U.S. tried to win the smaller-scale conflicts, it could not create the forces necessary to defeat the Soviet Union in a general war between the two superpowers. This put the nation "in mortal danger." McCormack offered a policy that U.S. citizens could support. His proposal he argued, if adopted, reduced the likelihood of the U.S. having to fight future limited wars that wouldn't lead to a comprehensive peace with the Soviets.[50]

The implications of McCormack's policy proposal were too aggressive for Eisenhower. The first problem was the fact that any Soviet military offensives meant a major war between the U.S. and the Soviets. McCormack's committee argued that this policy made such military actions and any direct conflict between the two states unlikely. However, this policy made any confrontation catastrophic. Although McCormack did not think that the Soviet Union wanted war, he thought it was still possible. Another large-scale conflict could arise from the escalation of several peripheral wars or from inaccurate Soviet perceptions of America's limitations on Soviet expansion. This policy's concentration on military force meant that it was not a viable option for President Eisenhower.[51]

Task Force C, chaired by Admiral Robert Connolly, differed dramatically from the positions adopted by the other two committees.[52] Connolly recommended a policy that would sow chaos and confusion within the Soviet Union and its allies. This course of action was the most offensively minded of those advocated by the three task forces. Connolly's group argued that increasing the pressure on the Soviet Union was the best way to prevent communism from spreading. Their course of action, Connolly argued, forced the Soviet Union to focus on maintaining its sphere of influence and not on expanding to new nations. A major drawback of Connolly's policy was the increased risk of world war.[53]

In order to decrease the threat of general war breaking out, Connolly advocated several different strategies. The first was the elimination of the Soviet-Chinese alliance. In order for this to occur, the U.S. had to remove the communist government from China, depriving the Soviets of a major ally. Once this occurred, the U.S. could concentrate its efforts on stripping away the allegiance of the Soviet satellite states. Finally, the U.S. had to stop communist expansion in Vietnam and Korea. Connolly argued that these courses of action were an effective way to weaken the power and international prestige of communism, which the Soviet Union relied on to maintain its global offensive.[54]

Soviet advances in nuclear weapons brought a sense of urgency to Connolly's report. The assessment of the Soviet nuclear threat led his task force to conclude that in five years the Soviet Union's nuclear arsenal would be roughly equivalent to that of the United States. Due to the increased military threat the Soviet Union posed in near future, Connolly stressed that initiating his recommended course of action was vital. Waiting too long, he argued exposed the U.S. to the anticipated increased Soviet nuclear response.[55]

Connolly stated that his Task Force's plan benefited the United States by quickly resolving the Cold War, something neither of the other proposals promised.[56] Although the policy risked general war; it was the only alternative recommending an indirect offensive against the Soviet Union. Alternative C, in Connolly's opinion, was a reasonable recommendation for achieving U.S. objectives in the Cold War. He wrote that the best way to prevent general war was to end the current conflict with the Soviets quickly. Bringing closure to the Cold War required the U.S. to confront and defeat the threat that the Soviet Union posed. Although Connolly claimed his course of action would bring the struggle to a close, it was more likely that such an offensive would spur a war with the Soviet Union rather than end the Cold War.[57]

The task forces completed their work after six weeks. However, this was not the end of Project Solarium. One of the expected outcomes of the project was a clear recommendation for President Eisenhower's national security strategy. President Eisenhower wanted a unified view of national security policy to create a shared vision for his administration. However, the recommendations were too different to easily form one policy.[58]

2

Many Strands into One Rope
Creating a Unified Defense Policy

Although each of the three groups involved in Project Solarium expected one of their proposals to carry the day, this was not the case. After the groups drafted their reports, they presented them to Eisenhower and the NSC. Each task force attempted to sway the NSC to adopt their recommended course of action. Andrew Goodpaster, the staff secretary to Eisenhower, saw that each task force presented a different version of the containment strategy. Although there were similarities with Truman's containment policy, there were some notable differences, such as a stronger focus on disseminating pro–U.S. information in Soviet territories, Eastern Europe, U.S. allies, and neutral nations, including Egypt, India, and Yugoslavia.[1]

Eisenhower, after the Solarium groups' presentations, explained his general concerns about national defense. He did not want to trade a free society in order to defeat the Soviet Union. President Eisenhower also did not know what the U.S. would do with the old communist state if it defeated and destroyed the Soviet Union. Eisenhower explained that Americans "have demonstrated their reluctance after a war ... to occupy the territory conquered in order to gain our legitimate ends." Connolly's aggressive rollback policy created more problems than it solved.[2]

Eisenhower wanted the task forces to continue their work, but with a significant change. He wanted a joint meeting of all the groups to discuss creating a plan that unified the salient points of their proposals. Eisenhower wanted the three proposals merged into one program that the NSC could adopt.[3]

After Eisenhower made his comments and left the conference, the individual groups explained their disagreements with the competing plans.

2. Many Strands into One Rope

Although the president saw many commonalities between the three plans, the task forces did not agree. Admiral Connolly, spokesman for Alternative C, and George Kennan, spokesman for Alternative A, explained that the two groups could not compromise to create one policy. Both argued that their groups' estimates of Soviet objectives and capabilities were too far apart to unify. Even if the three groups could write one policy, Connolly and Kennan, were sure that such a policy would eviscerate the essential recommendations of each group. Neither Kennan nor Connolly thought their groups would approve a single policy crafted out of the remains of the three recommendations.[4]

After Eisenhower learned from Robert Cutler, the Special Assistant to the president for National Security Affairs from 1953 to 1955 and 1957 to 1958, that the task forces could not reach a consensus, he told Cutler to proceed as he deemed best. Cutler determined that the Special Staff of the National Security Council should summarize the major conclusions each group presented in their presentations to the president. Once representatives from each task force approved these summaries, the NSC would review them. Cutler hoped to highlight the similarities between each recommendation in this review and allow the NSC to proceed and create one unified policy. Cutler wanted the task force members who could to participate in the NSC planning board's review.[5]

The approved Basic National Security Policy, NSC 162/2 compiled by James Lay, the executive secretary of the National Security Council, contained the compromised policies of Project Solarium and presented them as one coherent defense strategy. It outlined how the U.S. would respond to the Soviet threat during Eisenhower's administration. The document explained the importance of developing the assets of an effective defense that focused on nuclear weapons. The U.S. and its allies had to be able to deploy their forces quickly, in response to Soviet aggression. This was crucial if the free world were to maintain its influence and its alliances throughout the world. In case of a general war, the U.S. had to have the ability to produce a large number of soldiers and munitions to fight such a conflict. In order to achieve these goals, the U.S. needed a firm economic foundation for building national security.[6]

Kennan's containment policy comes through in the NSC 162/2. The paper stated that the U.S. should use all means, covert and overt, to weaken Soviet control over its satellites and China. U.S. propaganda efforts needed to target the internal contradictions and complications of the Soviet

Union. By showing Soviet allies how untrustworthy and problematic and alliance with the Soviet Union was, President Eisenhower hoped to limit Soviet ability to demand loyalty from its allies and prospective allies.[7]

The Basic National Security Policy (NSC 162/2) became the foundation of the New Look defense policy. This new defense policy contained what became known as the doctrine of Massive Retaliation. John Foster Dulles, the Secretary of state from 1953 to 1959, first articulated this doctrine in January 1954, three months after NSC 162/2 was written. This doctrine, as explained by Andrew Goodpaster, who served as the Defense Liaison to President Eisenhower relied on the ability to use atomic weapons however the United States deemed appropriate. Goodpaster believed that this gave Eisenhower the capacity to withstand Soviet political or social subversion. He continued by stating that if military conflict did arise then the doctrine of Massive Retaliation provided a framework to stop such action at a low level. He thought that John Foster Dulles' interpretation of Massive Retaliation stressed the threat of atomic warfare, not its implementation.[8]

Part of the appeal of the doctrine of Massive Retaliation was its potential to allow decreases in defense spending. In a conversation Eisenhower had with Secretary of State John Foster Dulles and Secretary Wilson, concerning the defense budget for fiscal year 1955, they discussed methods to realize reduced defense allocations. Secretary Dulles argued for the redeployment of manpower from Korea back to the United States. Such reductions emphasized American naval and air assets in the region, allowing for significant reductions in ground forces.[9] The meeting concluded with the agreement that America's forces in "Europe could be somewhat skeletonized." The group decided that the Army would not get the 1.5 million soldiers it requested in 1955, unless the strategic situation deteriorated. Eisenhower also wrote that atomic weapons provided the ability to reduce American reliance on conventionally armed units.[10]

The corollary to this decision was the fact that, at the time, the U.S. could only launch nuclear weapons capable of hitting Soviet targets using long-range bombers. This required the use of overseas air bases since aerial refueling was not possible until the introduction of the KC-135 in 1957. The Army and Navy were equally incapable of taking a prominent role in this new strategy, neither had the force projection capability. As a result, both the Army and Navy saw their allocation of defense spending decrease in Eisenhower's first term.

2. Many Strands into One Rope

The Air Force was also the branch that most U.S. citizens thought would play the largest role in future conflicts. Almost 80 percent of the respondents to a Gallup Poll taken in October 1953 said that the Air Force was the most important defense asset in a future global war.[11] The policy of Massive Retaliation reinforced the confidence that most people in the U.S. placed in the Air Force. The Air Force represented the modern method of warfare, strategic bombing and, in the near future, missiles.[12]

The U.S. public generally supported the idea of using nuclear weapons in a war with the Soviet Union. When asked in 1954 if they thought the U.S. should use the hydrogen bomb immediately in a conflict with the Soviet Union or wait for the Soviets to escalate the conflict to the nuclear stage, 57 percent of respondents said the U.S. should escalate the conflict first. Nuclear conflict pervaded many people's perception of what war with the Soviet Union meant. In the same survey, most respondents thought that the hydrogen bomb made a future conflict less likely. Also, many agreed that improving the U.S. nuclear arsenal provided some form of deterrent. Much of this stems from the fact that a majority of those surveyed thought that a future conflict with the Soviet Union was inevitable.[13]

Eisenhower's understanding of Clausewitz also contributed to his choice of Massive Retaliation as a means of deterrence.[14] Clausewitz theorized, in his seminal work *On War*, about the nature of warfare. Clausewitz explained that all military goals should stem from the overall political objectives of the conflict.[15] Eisenhower's main goal was political; he wanted to craft a policy that reduced the threat of conflict and allowed the U.S. to focus on building its economy, at minimal cost. In order to do this, he raised the potential cost of war exponentially, using military means. The New Look defense policy rested on the assumption that, to the Soviet Union, no political objective was worth the cost of combating a cataclysmic nuclear war.

One of the first crises that tested the New Look defense policy was the French fighting in Indochina. President Eisenhower did not let the immediacy of the conflict override his focus on the strategic goal of staying out of limited and peripheral wars, over the objections of several senior officials. John Foster Dulles and Admiral Arthur Radford supported intervention, in some form. However, General Matthew Ridgway, Chief of Staff of the Army from 1953 to 1955, and Eisenhower did not want to enter another Korean-style conflict.[16] This decision, even though it was controversial, was an example of the policy's strength. Since the political goal of retaining French hegemony in Indochina, later Vietnam, was not worth the risk of general war, the rubric of the New Look defense policy mandated that the U.S. stay out of the conflict. Eisenhower supported the South Vietnamese in their opposition to the communist North Vietnamese with military advisors and aid, but not with combat troops. This was part of the New Look's emphasis on supporting allies and increasing their ability to wage limited war. While the New Look defense policy did not solve the problems that led to the Vietnam War, Eisenhower's dedication to his strategy did avoid significant American involvement in the early stages of the conflict. The president also avoided a large-scale war in Vietnam during his administration, largely by not forcing a decisive engagement with the Viet Minh.

Concentrating on waging nuclear war was not a panacea. In a discussion about the need for a 1,500-mile missile during an NSC conference on August 4, 1955, President Eisenhower and Secretary of State Dulles talked about the implications of larger atomic forces on warfare. The secretary said that as the Soviets and the U.S. focused on waging large wars, smaller conflicts became more important. However, President Eisenhower disagreed. He responded that small wars could escalate into big ones. He reminded the secretary that the president and his administration criticized those who acted to keep the Korean War limited.[17]

Project Solarium did not provide President Eisenhower with a single course of action recommendation for a defense policy. It is also doubtful that it greatly changed the ideas that he came into office with concerning defense issues. However, the project did provide Eisenhower with the ability to take stock of a range of ideas concerning how to combat the Soviet threat. The recommendations of the three groups influenced what became the New Look defense policy and the president continued to use this strategy as the bedrock of national security policy throughout his administration.

Ramifications of the New Look Defense Policy Through the 1950s

The implications of this policy and its influence on manpower and fiscal resources of the military is important to understanding the New Look and its focus on deterring warfare and limiting American involve-

2. Many Strands into One Rope

ment in future conflicts. When President Eisenhower took office, there were over 3.5 million active duty personnel. In the aftermath of the Korean War, there was a peace-time reduction so that, by the end of the decade, the total number of active duty personnel was approximately 2.5 million. The Army absorbed the majority of this decrease. It declined from its wartime high of 1.6 million soldiers to less than 900,000 by 1960. This was a 46 percent reduction in the active force.[18]

The Army's drop in manpower was not the only indication of Eisenhower's influence on defense policy. By 1961, the year he left office, the Army and Air Force had roughly the same percentage of the overall force structure, in terms of manpower. The table below shows the differences between the services in the years 1953 and 1961. The Army took the brunt of the decreases in manpower. The Air Force maintained approximately the same number of personnel as it had during the war.[19]

The Air Force clearly won the manpower and budget struggle under President Eisenhower's leadership. It grew 6 percent during under the New Look policy while the Army decreased 8 percent from its Korean War level. Some of this was due to the transition from wartime to peacetime reductions. It is informative to look at President Truman's force allocation prior to the Korean War in 1950. The table below shows that, prior to the war, the Army was the largest force in the Department of Defense. Compared to the force structure of 1961 the Army shrank by 6 percent and the Air Force grew by 5 percent. This was a force that had a total of 1.5 million men in uniform. The table below shows the changes in manpower through the end of the Truman administration and the entire Eisenhower administration.[20]

The forces deployed to Europe also provide insight into the New Look defense policy. During the 1950s the Army personnel deployed in Europe did not radically change, as the chart below shows. Although there were several realignments of forces in the Army's European command (USAEUR) the basic formation was two corps headquarters, one with three divisions and the other with two. These units fell under the overall command of 7th Army.[21]

United States Army Europe maintained about 200,000 soldiers through Eisenhower's eight years in office. He did not change the deployment numbers very much from Truman's initial deployment in response to the Korean War. Although the Army as a whole continued to face severe reductions in manpower, USAEUR maintained its wartime footing. However, the number

Eisenhower's Nuclear Calculus in Europe

Year	Total	Army	Navy	Marine Corps	Air Force
1950	1,459,462	593,473	380,739	74,279	411,277
1951	3,249,371	1,531,774	736,596	192,620	788,381
1952	3,635,912	1,596,419	824,265	231,967	983,261
1953	3,555,067	1,533,815	794,440	249,219	977,593
1954	3,302,104	1,404,598	725,720	223,868	947,918
1955	2,935,107	1,109,296	660,695	205,170	959,946
1956	2,806,441	1,025,778	669,925	200,780	909,958
1957	2,764,761	997,994	676,071	200,861	919,835
1958	2,599,518	898,925	639,942	189,495	871,156
1959	2,503,631	861,964	625,661	175,571	840,435
1960	2,475,438	873,078	616,987	170,621	814,752
1961	2,482,905	858,622	626,223	176,909	821,151
1962	2,805,603	1,066,404	664,212	190,962	884,025

of American personnel deployed to defend Western Europe along with European forces was not sufficient to defeat a Soviet offensive without the help of atomic weapons. Although the numbers look impressive when compared to present military force levels, Eisenhower understood that if the Soviets invaded NATO member nations it required the use of nuclear weapons to stop the assault.

Even though Eisenhower did not reduce forces in Europe after the Korean War, this did not mean that they were adequate for the task assigned to them. At the height of the Korean War almost 300,000 Army soldiers fought in that theater, this figure does not include allied nations contributions or the number of South Korean soldiers who fought in the conflict.[22] Comparing the two forces shows that in order to fight a similar conflict in Western Europe against a fully mobilized Soviet force would require significantly more than 200,000 troops, especially if Eisenhower intended to fight the conflict without nuclear weapons. However, this was

2. Many Strands into One Rope

not the case; nuclear weapons would be part of any conflict with the Soviet Union in Western Europe in addition to significant troop contributions from NATO member states.

The New Look defense policy did not completely focus on economic issues. Although reducing the fiscal burden of military spending was important, maintaining a solid, credible defense against Soviet aggression was paramount for Eisenhower. For this reason, nuclear weapons provided an effective solution. They offered a counter to Soviet manpower at a reduced expense.

The scale of the threat of atomic warfare was clear for Eisenhower. In a diary entry on January 23, 1956, the president wrote of his reactions to a report about the impact of a full-scale atomic war between the Soviets and the U.S. If this occurred, according to the report, about 65 percent of

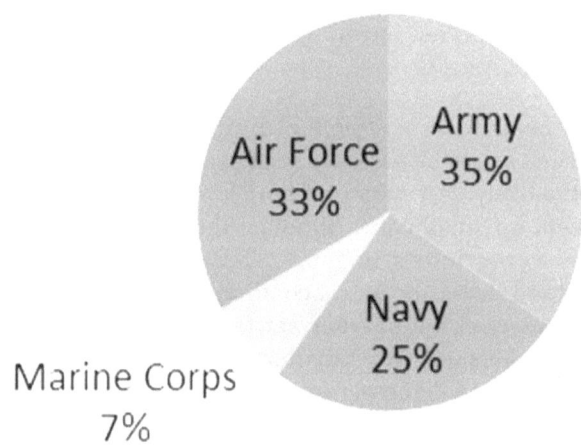

This chart shows the distribution of forces at the end of President Eisenhower's administration. The Army and the Air Force are almost equal in terms of manpower. This was evidence of the New Look defense policy that prioritized airpower over land forces in the nation's strategy for deterring and, if necessary, fighting war.

1953 Force Allocation

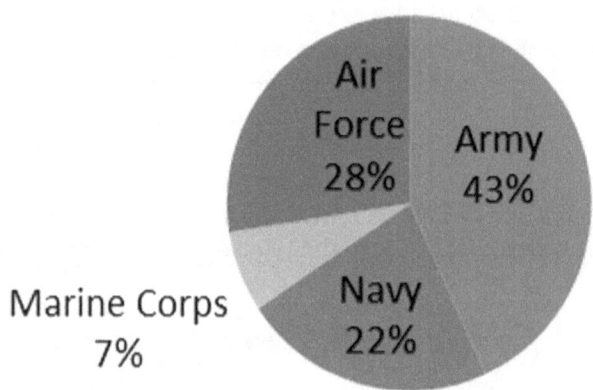

This chart shows the distribution of forces in the United States military at the start of the Eisenhower administration. The Army was the primary force in terms of manpower, which was not surprising given the Korean War was still ongoing.

U.S. citizens would need medical attention. Despite this clear need for medical care after such an attack access to such care would be impossible for many. Due to the likely destruction of port facilities shipping would be nonexistent except for small craft. Although the Soviet Union would receive three times as much destruction, there was little to celebrate. Eisenhower understood that after such a conflict, "it would literally be a business of digging ourselves out of ashes, starting again." There were no winners in such a war. This was why Eisenhower dedicated his administration and defense policy to deterring and preventing such a conflict. It also explains why he was willing to assume risk with limited wars.[23]

3

Resistance to Massive Retaliation

The Arguments Against Massive Retaliation and the Deficiencies in Eisenhower's National Security Policies

On May 24, 1956, the Joint Chiefs of Staff met with President Eisenhower to discuss national military strategy. General Maxwell Taylor, Chief of Staff of the Army, requested the meeting to determine the guiding principles of U.S. military strategy in the future. He felt that the Joint Chiefs were in two different camps, the Army and Marines were advocating for a more flexible policy and the Air Force and the Navy taking the position that "all planning must be based on the use of atomic weapons." General Taylor argued that the presence of large thermonuclear arsenals made general nuclear war between the Soviet Union and the United States less likely. Since big wars were less likely, Taylor wanted to be able to plan for small-scale conflicts.[1]

General Taylor stated that his main concern was the assumption that nuclear weapons would be a part of any conflict, large or small. He did not think that strategy reflected "the principle of 'flexibility' which [had] been worked into NSC papers." Such an assumption could lead to the concentration of nuclear weapons while neglecting the resources required for limited conflicts. President Eisenhower countered that he understood Taylor's position but he thought that the Army Chief of Staff operated from a flawed premise concerning potential Soviet actions in a conflict. President Eisenhower did not think that the Soviets had an aversion to destruction like the United States. He continued by stating that if war came, the Soviets had very little to restrain them from using atomic weapons. This belief in Soviet willingness to use nuclear weapons was a foundational assumption for the president and it influence his defense policy.[2]

The president and General Taylor's lack of consensus was an example of the friction between the two. The root cause of their disagreement was the difference between Taylor and Eisenhower's conception of war in the atomic age. General Taylor wanted the Army ready for the myriad of small-scale conflicts he thought possible because of the deterrence of thermonuclear weapons. However, Eisenhower saw the potential for atomic weapons even in limited conflicts.

General Taylor discussed his initial reaction to the possibility that atomic weapons brought to warfare in his book *The Uncertain Trumpet*, which he wrote after he left military service in 1959. He saw the promise of atomic weapons as a way to prevent war from occurring in the future. However, Taylor soon realized the errors of his initial reaction to nuclear weapons. In his book, he wrote of this deterrence view as a "Great Fallacy." General Taylor's and President Eisenhower's views on nuclear deterrence were very different. Taylor saw Massive Retaliation as a policy that created a significant security vulnerability for the United States.[3]

The president, in the conference on May 24, told General Taylor that he did not think it would be possible to deploy large ground units to fight in the future. The Army, according to President Eisenhower, needed to focus on providing security and stability in the continental United States. Eisenhower was sympathetic to the fact that his strategy did not provide the Army with a "great role in the first year of war" relative to the other branches of the military.[4]

In relation to small wars, President Eisenhower firmly stated that peripheral conflicts detracted U.S. forces readiness to wage war with the Soviets. Eisenhower saw the U.S. responsibility in these wars as providing support through mobility assets and weapons, not soldiers fighting on the ground. He continued that, in order to bolster "critical points," he could see the need to deploy "several battalions" but was adamant that such a deployment would not grow any larger. The president and General Taylor were of two dramatically different minds concerning small-scale wars as well as how to create a national military strategy that dealt with both the threat of thermonuclear war and limited wars, at the same time.[5]

General Taylor countered that it was important to be ready to fight a broad spectrum of warfare. If the U.S. concentrated only on thermonuclear war, Taylor doubted this could limit defense requirements. First, the

3. Resistance to Massive Retaliation

nation should determine what was necessary to deter conflicts, and then define what it needed to fight small-scale wars, and then the rest of the defense resources could go to preparing for a general atomic war with the Soviets. Eisenhower did not agree, he stated that air assets were vital for the early stages of a conflict. The president ordered his senior military commanders to continue to plan their strategy "on the basis of the use of tactical atomic weapon against military targets in any small war in which the United States might be involved." General Taylor, just like Chief of Staff of the Army General Matthew Ridgway before him, faced an uphill battle in convincing President Eisenhower about the need for a large Army to combat limited wars.[6]

The Army wasn't the only institution struggling with the impact of atomic weapons. In the 1950s, the pace of change in the yield and range of these weapons grew exponentially. In the beginning of the decade, strategic bombers were the only weapon system capable of projecting an atomic strike into the Soviet Union, using foreign air bases. By the end of the 1950s, the Intercontinental Ballistic Missile (ICBM) was a reality, although still in its infancy. The growth of missiles provided a new way to protect European allies and project U.S. power. It was a modern way to fight a war. In addition, missiles were relatively inexpensive, especially, when compared to large ground forces, namely U.S. Army divisions.

Missiles became more important in the New Look defense policy throughout the 1950s. Although the emphasis was on the ICBM, in the early years of Eisenhower's administration no one foresaw the rapid success of the research program for these weapons. ICBMs, and to a lesser extent IRBMs, offered a way to project power without vulnerable air bases or putting pilots and crew in danger while flying over enemy territory. Missiles fit well with Eisenhower's and the U.S. people's conception of future conflicts; they represented a more efficient and technologically sophisticated way of war. Throughout the decade, missiles became more prominent in the nation's deterrent forces. This required more money for research and development. During this time, the Air Force used its position as the proponent for long-range missile technology to increase its share of defense dollars, at the expense of the Army. Also, the Navy began to develop submarines capable of launching nuclear missiles in order to expand its role in national security.

Eisenhower was consistent in his application of the doctrine of Massive Retaliation. Throughout the 1950s, Eisenhower's defense budget continued to emphasize strategic nuclear forces.[7] The mid–1950s were a continuation of, not a retreat from, Massive Retaliation. Eisenhower's decisions concerning military budgets show that his emphasis did not shift from nuclear weapons. As a result of this emphasis on atomic warfare, national defense fiscal allocations continued to center around a robust U.S. nuclear arsenal through the entirety of his administration.

President Eisenhower's speeches, National Security Council (NSC) meeting minutes, and diary entries shed light on his views of warfare and other defense issues. However, his words only give part of Eisenhower's understanding of how atomic weapons influenced national security. Budget projections and fiscal decisions indicate the importance Eisenhower placed on these weapons in his national security policy. Although Eisenhower referenced balance and flexibility many times when discussing national defense, his actions showed that the idea of atomic supremacy permeated his military planning principles.

President Eisenhower's public addresses also revealed the influence of nuclear weapons on his defense policy and give insight into his vision of modern warfare. In his 1955 State of the Union message, given on January 6, he discussed the essential functions of government as well as defense issues. He stated that the essential function of government was to "support freedom, justice and peace."[8] Secondary to this was the preservation of a sound economy. Eisenhower discussed how the United States could maintain peace with the Soviet Union in his address. He stated that the U.S. ability to respond to a Soviet attack quickly and forcefully ensured that the Soviet Union would not start a nuclear war. He continued by saying that this produced a "world stalemate." However, this condition, Eisenhower explained, provided opportunities for the free world to work for an ultimate peace.[9]

Eisenhower, in that State of the Union message, also said it was important for the nation to maintain "balance and flexibility" in its weapons program. He stated that, "undue reliance on one weapon or preparation for only one kind of warfare simply invites an enemy to resort to another."[10] However, during this period the majority of funding went to the Air Force. Eisenhower advocated the necessity of a balanced military; however, his conception of balance was not equality. When he used these terms, he was talking about a defense structure built on nuclear deterrence and a small land force, responsible for domestic security in case of an attack. This was a product of Eisenhower's conception of modern warfare. Eisen-

3. Resistance to Massive Retaliation

hower thought that nuclear war was the most dangerous threat, if not the most likely, he wanted to protect the nation against this type of threat.

The 1955 State of the Union message continued with a reference to research and development programs in the defense sector. Eisenhower stated that his budget for that year improved airpower in three services, the Air Force, Navy, and Marine Corps. The budget also focused on developing weapons with greater "striking power." He stated that this ensured "the maintenance of effective, retaliatory forces as the principal deterrent to overt aggression."[11] The deterrent force Eisenhower referenced was the United States' nuclear arsenal, which gave strength to the doctrine of Massive Retaliation. The retaliatory forces were those forces capable of inflicting a swift nuclear response to a Soviet attack. The only forces capable of doing so without being forwardly deployed were Air Force elements. Although Eisenhower discussed the necessity of balance and flexibility in the armed services, his actions showed his preference for a national security program based on nuclear weapons.

Eisenhower then covered his success in decreasing the defense budget. He pointed out that "national security programs [consumed] two-thirds of the entire Federal budget." He touted his success of cutting defense spending by "concentrating on essentials."[12] Unsaid was the fact that these decreases came mainly from the Army's and Navy's budgets. Eisenhower's words, interpreted through his actions as president, indicate how the primacy of nuclear weapons shaped his view of defense matters.[13]

Eisenhower described his defense budget as one that reflected the "realities of [his] time." He said that he personally directed the areas of emphasis in the defense budget. Eisenhower believed that this budget gave the United States a defense program suited to the necessities of the world stage. He continued by stating that the focus on nuclear weapons had to continue because of the Soviet stubbornness in refusing armament limitation agreements. As long as the Soviet Union continued its obstinacy, America had to continue to build and maintain a large nuclear arsenal capable of deterring and responding to a Soviet attack.[14]

The assumption of the supremacy of nuclear weapons was part of a framework that interpreted defense issues through a new conception of war in the atomic age. This framework influenced budgetary and strategic decisions. America's defense program during the 1950s relied heavily on atomic weapons to cut the expense of ground and naval forces.

Eisenhower's Nuclear Calculus in Europe

Nuclear weapons formed the backbone of Eisenhower's defense policy.[15] Although these weapons were expensive, by using them as the foundation of national defense, Eisenhower sought to decrease U.S. ground forces and shift that burden to its allies. In the 287th meeting of the National Security Council (NSC) in June 1956, one of his regularly scheduled weekly NSC appointments, President Eisenhower encouraged smaller Asian allies to build their ground forces. He stated that this allowed them to concentrate their defense resources on assets that the United States was not planning on supplying. He wanted the United States to supply air and naval aid, including an atomic umbrella for strategic security. Eisenhower preferred to support U.S. allies by providing assets they could not such as aircraft or nuclear weapons, not with large combat forces.[16]

There were two prongs in the defense of Western Europe. One was the military capacity of the conventional forces deployed to protect the region. The other was the superiority of the U.S. nuclear deterrent compared to Soviet atomic capability. Eisenhower's idea of the new paradigm of future wars focused on the nuclear capacity of the United States and framed its effectiveness in bomb yields and operational ranges, not in conventional power metrics like soldiers on the ground.

The pervasive threat of Soviet nuclear attack was one reason why Eisenhower offered an atomic umbrella to U.S. allies. In 1956, the Soviet Union's atomic capability was growing. Admiral Arthur Radford, Chairman of the Joint Chiefs of Staff, alerted the president, in an NSC meeting, to the fact that the Soviet Union would have a multi-megaton weapon sooner than the United States previously thought. This multi-megaton weapon was on par with the United States' hydrogen bomb.[17] Eisenhower's offer of atomic protection, instead of ground troops, bolstered its European allies against a Soviet atomic strike. This strategy fit with the paradigm of providing strategic support for allies in order to avoid a long-term limited conflict fought with U.S. ground forces.

As part of the effort to design a nuclear age military, Eisenhower integrated these weapons into the U.S. defense system. The United States' official policy concerning the use of nuclear weapons in 1956 stated that the administration considered these weapons a critical part of its arsenal and planned to use them in general and limited warfare, as the situation required. This understanding concerning the use of nuclear weapons suffused Eisenhower's defense and budgetary policies. Eisenhower did not see atomic weapons as a separate part of the defense arsenal. In a conflict,

3. Resistance to Massive Retaliation

the president wanted the Soviets to know, that the United States expected to use nuclear weapons.[18]

In order for the doctrine of Massive Retaliation to be effective, the United States had to have the ability to survive an initial Soviet strike. The basic national security policy stated in NSC document 5501, approved in January 1955, focused the United States' defense assets toward creating an effective atomic capacity to respond to Soviet attacks and surviving the opening stage of an all-out nuclear war.[19] This retaliatory capability was part of the doctrine of Massive Retaliation. In order to maintain the efficacy of this deterrent, the U.S. needed to continue to research and develop new weapons systems. This ensured that the United States could strike back at the Soviet Union and offset any growing Soviet nuclear capability. The U.S. could not rely on the assets that won World War II, large ground divisions, it had to be ready to fight the Soviets immediately.

Ground forces did not support a national defense policy that required a quick response. Compared to nuclear weapons and guided missiles, Army divisions seemed quaint. NSC 5501 explained that the role of U.S. forces was to suppress hostilities quickly using atomic weapons before a conflict escalated. Atomic weapons offered the possibility of quickly ending limited or peripheral conflicts.[20] In the context of New Look defense policy, the duty of deterring local aggression fell mainly to U.S. allies. By 1957, the Basic National Security Policy NSC 5707/8, which superseded NSC 5501, made the reliance on nuclear weapons more explicit; in this policy, these weapons were the "main" deterrent force.[21]

The nuclear battlefield was a relatively new feature in the 1950s. However, not all security analysts agreed with Eisenhower about the likelihood of a future nuclear conflict. Robert Osgood, who served as dean of the Johns Hopkins University School of Advanced International Studies, was one of the more vocal civilian critics of Massive Retaliation. His book *Limited War*, published in 1957, described the necessity of preparing for small-scale conflicts. He granted that there was a need to deter general war and that Massive Retaliation effectively did this. However, it was unsuccessful in restraining lesser conflicts.[22]

Bernard Brodie was another academic critic of the president's defense policy. His work, *Strategy in the Missile Age*, published in 1959, explained the strategic gap created by Massive Retaliation. The policy deterred large-scale conflicts but did not prevent or prepare the nation to combat limited war. Brodie argued that the Soviet Union could continue to pursue regional objectives and the U.S. had little recourse outside of atomic retaliation, which was an unlikely response to small-scale aggression. The U.S. faced great difficulty in answering these challenges, using the doctrine of Massive Retaliation.[23]

The New Look defense policy rested on premise that the central threat to the U.S. was the Soviet Union and that deterring this threat protected the U.S. economy and its essential ideals.[24] The New Look defense policy assumed that that the U.S. atomic threat inhibited the Soviet Union from launching "local aggression."[25] This differed markedly from the argument for limited war made by Brodie and Osgood. The belief in the efficacy of atomic deterrent across the full range of possible conflicts was a fundamental part of Eisenhower's notion of the supremacy of atomic weapons. The effects of decolonization and future wars of national liberation, supported by the Soviet Union, strained the assumptions of the New Look defense policy.

Osgood, Brodie, and Eisenhower agreed on the necessity of countering small-scale conflicts but they disagreed about the best way to accomplish this. For Brodie and Osgood, the answer lay in a robust ground force that could quickly stop limited wars on the perimeter of America's area of influence. Eisenhower wanted to shift the burden of ground warfare to America's allies, allowing this U.S. to concentrate on its main threat, the Soviet Union. His defense policy put the onus on the Soviets for stopping their client states from starting conflicts. In the 1950s, few questioned the ability of the Soviet Union to control the actions of its client states in Eastern Europe and Asia. So, for Eisenhower, creating a defense policy with the main goal of stopping the Soviet Union from entering into limited conflicts made sense during Eisenhower's administration. It is important to remember that Khrushchev did not announce the policy of supporting wars of national liberation until 1961, publicly stating what Soviet actions previously implied.[26]

Before Brodie and Osgood began criticizing the New Look policy, General Matthew Ridgway grew frustrated under the New Look's focus on the Air Force. He did not think that the policy allocated enough funding or manpower for the Army to accomplish its mission. Ridgway asked for more resources but felt that his military opinion did not sway what he perceived as the politically motivated conclusions of Eisenhower's security policy. This friction led to his termination as Chief of Staff after two years, in contradiction of the normal renewal of the initial two-year term for a

3. Resistance to Massive Retaliation

second two-year term. He made his concerns about the New Look program public in an article in the *Saturday Evening Post* in January 1956.[27]

In his article, General Ridgway described the three reasons the administration gave him to justify the cuts to the Army's budget: the fact that new atomic weapons were more destructive, the new Army reserve system made rapid mobilization easier, and the creation of a West German military reduced manning requirements from other NATO member states. The Army Chief of Staff did not think that these were valid reasons for the cuts. Ridgway pointed out that the Army, during the middle of the decade, only had 30, 280-millimeter atomic howitzers in addition to a few Corporal missiles and Honest John rockets to defend a 400-mile front. He did not see how these resources were adequate, especially if the administration continued to decrease the number of troops deployed to Western Europe. General Ridgway argued that telling the U.S. public that atomic weapons could make up for troop cuts was disingenuous.[28]

Concerning the new reserve system, the second justification of troop and budget cuts, the outgoing Chief of Staff was similarly skeptical of these soldiers' ability to quickly join an atomic war. He claimed that ground forces had to be ready to fight well before the initiation of hostilities. Otherwise the United States and its allies were at great risk. As to the addition of West German troops to make up for American decreases he found that recommendation wanting as well. Ridgway pointed out that by the beginning of 1956 there were 6,000 of the planned half-million West German troops in uniform. He argued that West Germany needed another three and a half years to be ready.[29]

Another difference between General Ridgway and President Eisenhower was in the estimation of the Soviet threat. Although both understood that the Soviets possessed a large ground force, Ridgway concluded that the Soviets were more likely to use conventional forces in order to prevent a nuclear war. This required the U.S. to establish a similarly powerful conventional force to meet the Soviet threat. He did not think that the U.S. would be able to justify using atomic weapons if the Soviets did not use them first. If the Soviets refused to use atomic weapons it took the teeth out of Massive Retaliation. He also argued that there were too many reciprocal defense agreements that Ridgway felt bound the nation to use force to protect its allies. Ridgway warned that the U.S. might not have the military power on hand to fulfill its side of the numerous security pacts it signed, if it were unable to use atomic weapons in a conflict.[30]

Eisenhower's Nuclear Calculus in Europe

Matthew Ridgway summarized his concerns by outlining the problems he felt that the United States and its military faced in the coming years, if it continued with the New Look defense policy. He cited Soviet improvements in atomic weapons that dealt "critical damage on the United States' war-making potential." He wrote that the Soviet air defenses degraded "the nuclear-air superiority which the United States" possessed in the late 1950s. In addition, the general did not see that the U.S. and its allies' forces could fight as a coordinated whole against a Soviet assault. He wrote that the myriad units deployed to fight the Soviet Union were "military detachments only." He summed up his argument by stating that the U.S. military had to be able to fight conflicts that ranged from a full nuclear war to a limited conflict. Ridgway did not see how the current forces and the planned organizational changes of the New Look created a military prepared to combat the full range of conflict.[31]

General Ridgway was not the only Army leader to bristle under the restrictions of the New Look defense policy. The next Army Chief of Staff, General Maxwell Taylor, also did not subscribe to the arguments of Massive Retaliation or the supremacy of atomic warfare. Neither of these Army leaders accepted Eisenhower's paradigm of warfare in the atomic age or his focus on preventing nuclear war in the belief that doing so prevented limited wars as well.

General Maxwell Taylor, Chief of Staff of the Army from 1955 through 1959, wanted to create an Army that could fight limited wars. In a speech to the Executives' Club of Chicago in 1955, he stated that U.S. needed a weapon that allowed for nuance in a way that atomic weapons did not.[32] He took issue with people who thought that the next war would be short and devastating. Taylor said that as the nuclear arsenals of both America and the Soviet Union grew in power it made the possibility of a general nuclear conflict much less likely. This left limited wars as the only viable alternative.[33]

The Army under the New Look defense policy faced severe budget cuts. General Maxwell Taylor explained the severity of the Army's fiscal situation in his first speech to the Army staff after he assumed the duties of the Chief of Staff of the Army in 1955. He also used this opportunity to talk about his unease with the New Look policy and Massive Retaliation. General Taylor outlined his concerns for the Army in the immediate future about the lack of resources available for the Army to complete its mission. Referring to the recent budget cuts, he stated that "your heads be bloody

3. Resistance to Massive Retaliation

but certainly unbowed."[34] These funding cuts decreased the ability of the Army to meet its commitments effectively.

Under the New Look defense policy, limited warfare was the responsibility of America's allies. Eisenhower did not want to send U.S. troops to combat every small conflict. The U.S. would support its allies in these conflicts with air and naval forces, if necessary. He worried that if small skirmishes became too frequent, the U.S. had to force a larger war because continuous small war would waste U.S. strength.[35] Eisenhower did not see limited hostilities as contributing to the overall security of the United States. Limited warfare was something that detracted from the U.S. ability to wage general warfare.

This was not to say that the United States under President Eisenhower did not invest in military and financial aid to its allies in order to help bolster their defense forces. Rather, the focus for Eisenhower was not in creating a large conventional standing military force ready to combat limited wars in foreign lands, he wanted to concentrate U.S. military assets towards deterring the most dangerous threat, a conflict with the Soviet Union.

General Taylor also advocated for other forms of deterrence, outside of nuclear weapons. He said that the Army, with sufficient weapons systems and manpower, was an effective deterrent to future conflict. The Army's ability to deter wars, according to General Taylor, extended beyond the immediate location of its troops. His conception of deterrence did not shift the requirement of local security to indigenous forces, as Eisenhower hoped to do. This difference of opinion arose because General Taylor and the president had different ideas about the influence of atomic weapons on warfare.[36]

General Taylor did not think that atomic weapons made ground forces obsolete or overly vulnerable. He believed that ground forces still had an important place in the nation's deterrence program. When Taylor discussed future conflicts, as shown above, he argued that smaller campaigns better suited the Soviet Union because it allowed the Soviets to avoid general war. He did not ascribe to Eisenhower's view that warfare, at least as it concerned the U.S., was increasingly becoming an all or nothing proposition. Much of this came from the emphasis that the New Look defense policy placed on atomic weapons. The doctrine of Massive Retaliation did not leave much room in policy options for responding to any incursion of U.S. security perimeter other than a full-scale nuclear conflict.

Eisenhower's Nuclear Calculus in Europe

This was not a policy oversight; it was a fundamental part of the effort to preclude rising tensions with the Soviet Union.

As part of General Taylor's efforts to improve the ability of the Army to fight and survive on a nuclear battlefield, he created the Pentomic division. This was a short-lived experiment that pushed nuclear weapons down to the tactical level, defined as the division level and below. Its intent was to disperse troop formations yet still give them enough firepower to stop any attacking Soviet ground forces. Instituted in the late 1950s; by the early 1960s, the Army stopped its atomic transformation and shifted its emphasis to more conventional force structures.[37]

Eisenhower and Taylor also differed on how best to support U.S. allies, although both agreed on the importance of doing so. When faced with the decision to support allies with ground forces, Eisenhower declined. The preferred method for supporting U.S. allies was with a nuclear umbrella. Eisenhower encouraged U.S. Asian allies to supply their own conventional forces and allow the U.S. to provide the strategic assets. General Taylor's position required the deployment of conventional ground forces to provide deterrence. The difference between the two leaders concerning their view of future conflicts was stark.

The Army continued to bear the burden of shrinking defense budgets in Eisenhower's second administration. Although the Army required $14 billion to complete its modernization program, it received less than of half of what it needed. It did not have enough manpower to support its worldwide responsibilities and was, by its own projections, approximately 50,000 personnel short of its manning needs. Another area slighted in the Army's budget was it missile program. It did not receive adequate funding for its surface-to-air missile program, the Nike Hercules. This project was part of the Army's effort to combat the Soviet bomber threat to the continental United States. Finally, the Army did not receive enough funding for its research program for the Nike Zeus. This program tried to develop an anti-missile missile. However, these initiatives suffered because of the Army's decreased funding.[38]

Army leaders tried to improve its budgetary position by researching and developing new weapons systems, such as the Nike Zeus. However, the Army could not match the Air Force's capability to conduct nuclear warfare in accordance with how Eisenhower understood it. These new weapons systems, in addition to the Pentomic experiment, exhibited the lengths that Army leaders went to in order to change their organization

3. Resistance to Massive Retaliation

to fit the new paradigm. These programs also revealed how hard Army leaders tried to demonstrate their service's ability to protect the nation from a Soviet nuclear attack. Eisenhower's fiscal decisions demonstrated that Army leaders could not translate these new projects into increased funding or a greater role in national defense.

In contrast to Army leaders' efforts to justify their service's budget, Air Force leaders did not face the same struggle. Vice Chief of Staff of the Air Force, General Thomas White argued that air power, specifically nuclear weapons, were vital to protecting the U.S. in "an age of danger."[39] General White was not alone in thinking that the Air Force was the number one defense asset that the United States had. Over half of the respondents in a Gallup public opinion poll in 1952, believed that the Air Force should receive more funding.[40] The Air Force, for many in the U.S., represented the new way to wage war. It was an atomic age force. As General White explained, the Air Force was the only branch of service that could "bring greater forces to bear on an enemy at less exposure of United States personnel than ... any other military force available to the United States."[41]

The fiscal implications of focusing more resources on the Air Force initially seemed benign. John von Neumann, a professor of mathematics at the Institute for Advances Studies at Princeton gave an estimate of $1 million per missile to the NSC in September 1955. Secretary Humphrey commented that this was "relatively cheap."[42] A year later Eisenhower encouraged defense leaders in attendance at the 280th meeting of the NSC to cooperate to decrease defense costs, the president discussed the implications of deploying U.S. ground forces to Europe. Initially, he stated that the deployment of these troops was temporary. He continued by observing that U.S. security came from its ability to deploy aircraft armed with nuclear weapons, instead of ground troops. Eisenhower wanted the military services to work together to reduce the defense costs of securing the United States and its allies.[43]

In the same NSC meeting President Eisenhower referred to a conversation he had with General Taylor concerning the size of the Army. General Taylor said that the Army needed 28 divisions.[44] This represented an increase of 8 divisions from its 1953 strength of 20 divisions when Eisenhower entered office.[45] In 1956, the Army had 19 divisions; the president thought that the general's request was outlandish.[46] After General Taylor's suggestion, Eisenhower said, "he had nearly fainted." This was far too large an army for the type of war Eisenhower wanted to prepare for.[47]

Although Eisenhower advocated cutting defense manpower in his budgets during the mid–1950s, he did not believe this decreased the efficacy of U.S. security forces. Press Secretary James Hagerty noted in his diary that the decrease in manpower allowed for more concentrated focus on more sophisticated weapons such as guided missiles, atomic weapons, which were mainly Air Force assets.[48] Hagerty referenced a conversation with Eisenhower concerning World War II and the invasion of Europe. The president thought if Germany possessed the atomic bomb in World War II that it would have been impossible for the allies to invade Normandy. Eisenhower thought that an atomic strike would have easily destroyed both the concentrated invasion forces on the beachhead and the naval vessels supporting the invasion.[49] For President Eisenhower, nuclear weapons changed warfare completely. Since large land forces were lucrative targets for atomic strikes, Eisenhower saw them as very vulnerable on the battlefield. This was especially true when compared to the relative security of long-range missiles.

Hagerty discussed how the president should present this decision to the U.S. population. Hagerty, Robert Cutler, Eisenhower's National Security Adviser, and Colonel Andrew Goodpaster, staff secretary and defense liaison, suggested that Eisenhower justify his decision to cut the defense budget by referencing his military experience. They told the president that he should say that this decision was militarily sound and not done for purely fiscal concerns.[50]

In a conference with Eisenhower about a lack of unity between the Joint of Chiefs of Staff in March 1956, the president clarified his position on the possible use of atomic weapons in a conflict. He thought that the force structure of the United States military predetermined the use of nuclear weapons in a large-scale conflict. He also discussed his view of shorter-range missiles. He viewed the 1500- and 5000-mile range weapons as being in "the same class operationally." President Eisenhower understood that his defense decisions took several options off the table; one of them was a large ground force commitment to a limited war. He also understood that, although smaller in payload and range, a nuclear missile was a weapon that would change the character of any conflict that Eisenhower chose to use these new weapons to fight.[51]

President Eisenhower and General Taylor discussed Army missiles

3. Resistance to Massive Retaliation

again on April 2, 1956. General Taylor said that the Army had no specific plans for how to use these weapons. However, General Taylor said that one possible benefit was the stand-off provided by the IRBM. Such missiles could provide front-line coverage but from bases in North Africa, where it was more difficult for Soviet forces to target them. Of course, this required more robust communication and posed serious coordination issues to direct fire from such great distances. President Eisenhower admitted that he saw some promise in the plan but also expressed his skepticism about its viability.[52]

This exchange is evidence of the problem that Army leaders, such as General Taylor faced in arguing for the Army's need for an IRBM. Aside from having no specific plans for using these weapons, having such missiles deployed so far from the battlefield made sense in terms of security but it posed serious problems in making a coherent proposal. One of the reasons for the success of the Air Force's proposals for using these missiles was its similarity to the Air Force's strategic bomber plan. IRBMs and ICBMs, for the Air force, provided a way to hit strategic targets inside the Soviet Union. General Taylor's plan exposed U.S. and NATO forces to the possibility of friendly fire on an atomic scale.

One instance where this clash of conceptions of future war came to a head was the policy discussions concerning how the United States should deal with the uprising in Poland in 1956. The Joint Chiefs of Staff wanted to take an active role and support any revolution with unconventional forces and military aid. However, Eisenhower did not think that this was a viable strategy. The uprising in Hungary, in the same year, gave the administration the chance to discuss how to apply the New Look defense policy to a real-world situation.[53] One proposition by the Central Intelligence Agency, represented by Robert Armory in the Policy Planning Board, was to use tactical nuclear weapons in order to prevent the Soviets from using force to quell an uprising should it occur. However, during the Hungarian uprising, Eisenhower did not want to use tactical nuclear weapons because of the possibility of escalating the conflict into a general war.[54]

This caution concerning tactical nuclear weapons was another problem that the Army could not overcome in its efforts to show its capabilities on the atomic battlefield. If a tactical nuclear engagement escalated into a general atomic war, then the Air Force would have to become involved. Even though the Army continued to develop tactical nuclear weapons,

President Eisenhower was clearly skeptical of their ability to engage in a limited conflict without escalating it.

One Army leader who gave a good sense of the battlefield necessity of a mobile long-range missile was Lieutenant General James Gavin. General Gavin discussed his view of the atomic battlefield in his book *War and Peace in the Space Age,* which came out in 1958. General Gavin argued that ground units in an atomic war had to have access to long-range missiles in order to provide fire coverage for maneuvers. If Army units did not have access to these types of weapons organically to their formation, they lacked the capability to fight against the Soviets. Mobile launches, similar to those proposed by the Army for the Jupiter IRBM provided needed mobile firepower for Army division and corps commanders to ensure the survival and efficacy of their units in a future conflict.[55]

As the role of the Air Force in national security matters increased, the roles of the Army and Navy shrank. In a discussion during the 277th meeting of the NSC, the president said that U.S. ground forces main responsibility during an atomic was domestic security. In the aftermath of a nuclear strike, the Army's ability to provide security could ensure that society did not fall apart. Ground forces would also maintain the United States' ability to continue the fight. He said, "God only knew what the Navy would be doing in a nuclear attack."[56]

Although Eisenhower's conception of modern warfare centered on atomic weapons, he did not think that this new level of destruction created conditions for short wars in the future. His diary entry for January 11, 1956, discussed the need for the United States to prepare for a long-term war. He did not think that the "theory of the thirty to sixty day war had anything to back it up."[57] Eisenhower wrote that wars were a product of the will of the people and until the people would accept an end to the conflict, a war could not stop. He also thought that preparation for long conflicts allowed the U.S. a better chance to survive the devastation of a nuclear attack.[58]

Behind the discussion of general warfare and how to protect the United States in the Cold War was the knowledge that the Soviet Union was a quickly growing threat. NSC paper 5501, *Basic National Security Policy,* published in January 1955, outlined the advances of the Soviet Union relative to the United States. This document outlined that in five years the Soviet Union could deal a severe blow to the United States. Over the period discussed, the Soviet Union would be able to bring missiles with increasingly longer ranges into production, ending in 1963 with an

3. Resistance to Massive Retaliation

operational ICBM. NSC 5501 described the necessity that the United States missile to keep pace with that of the Soviet Union.[59]

Massive Retaliation required that the U.S. nuclear deterrent was equal to or greater than the Soviet Union's. Without the ability to counter a Soviet strike, the U.S. had little hope of deterring a general war. The NSC, in NSC 5501, explained that nuclear war was possible if the Soviet Union had a "technological break-through ... leading them to believe they could destroy the U.S. without effective retaliation."[60] This understanding of nuclear parity with the Soviet Union required the United States to maintain an atomic arsenal capable of delivering a comparable blow to the Soviet Union's. If the U.S. ability to retaliate to an atomic attack became too inferior, relative to the Soviet Union, then it invited a nuclear strike. This demanded constant improvement in the U.S. nuclear arsenal, since general nuclear warfare was the predominant conflict that President Eisenhower thought the nation faced.

Atomic weapons dramatically changed the scope of warfare. For the first time in history, the president of the United States had the ability to destroy an enemy without deploying massive ground forces. Also, the United States' main enemy now had the capacity to deliver the same destruction in return. This increase in the possible destructive capability of warring nations placed an artificial limit on warfare. President Eisenhower did not want to be responsible for starting World War III, so he used the policy of Massive Retaliation to prevent a direct conflict between the United States and the Soviet Union.

In conjunction with this new focus on atomic weapons and nuclear deterrence came a shift in defense spending priorities. The United States Army and Navy lost in relation to the Air Force in the fight for defense dollars. The Army lost manpower as well as funding to modernize its formations. Nuclear weapons were at the heart of this issue. Eisenhower's conception of future warfare focused on the atomic battlefield as a way to prevent American involvement in limited and conventional wars.

President Eisenhower focused on the most dangerous threat to the United States, a nuclear conflict with the Soviet Union. Developing missile technology was one of the important projects Eisenhower wanted to focus on during his administration. Long-range missiles allowed for the capability to deter a nuclear conflict with the Soviet Union without foreign military bases. IRBMs were a part of this emphasis on missile technology and fit the paradigm of Massive Retaliation and Eisenhower's understanding of the paradigm of warfare in the atomic era. They provided a way to limit the contribution of U.S. ground forces while still providing security for its allies in Western Europe.

Limited war in this context, while arguably a more likely threat, was not as dangerous. President Eisenhower did not seek to craft a defense policy that created a force that could handle anything from a limited conventional attack to a full-scale nuclear conflict. The New Look defense policy consciously focused on general nuclear warfare as the paradigm to guide budget allocation and force structure decisions. IRBMs fit this policy well and became a focus for the administration.

In order to understand why IRBMs came to Western Europe it is important to know how guided missile technology developed in the United States. This will reveal the history of cooperation between the United Kingdom and the United States in terms of nuclear research. It will also explain why that cooperation came to an end in the post–World War II period. Finally, it will demonstrate why the Army was unable to surmount the Air Force in the New Look era, although the Army initially had more success in its guided missile program.

4.

The Development of IRBMs

Throughout the 1950s, both the Army and the Air Force worked to garner a larger share of the public's attention, defense budgets, and congressional support. The Army focused its efforts on public information. It opened offices in Los Angeles and New York in order to ensure that it could effectively tell its story to the American people. The Air Force, however, did not have to rely on public opinion. The Air Force concentrated most of its efforts on courting and supporting its defense contractors and their efforts to lobby Congress on the Air Force's behalf. The fight for control over the IRBM programs was, in some sense, a proxy for the larger conflict over which service would control the direction of national security policy and defense budgets.[1]

One of the main points of contention between the two services was whether the Army or the Air Force would direct the development of America's long-range guided missile program. By the middle of the decade both the Army and the Air Force had long-range missile programs. In the early stages of these projects, President Eisenhower decided to let both branches continue to pursue their weapons. However, by the end of the decade the Air Force came out ahead and controlled both its Thor IRBM and the Army's Jupiter IRBM. There were obvious reasons for the Air Force to be the service that would direct long-range missiles but that did not stop Army leaders such as Generals Matthew Ridgway and Maxwell Taylor from arguing that their service should have input in the development and use of these weapons.

An important aspect of the Army's missile development program was the need to show that the Army was a sophisticated fighting force. One of the main points of emphasis that General Taylor wanted to showcase in his semiannual report to the president was the success of the Army in its research and development.[2] This was part of a broader effort in the

This is a test launch of a Thor missile in 1959 from Cape Canaveral, Florida. The Thor missile was the Air Force's Intermediate Range Ballistic Missile (IRBM). This missile was part of the Air Force's effort to create an Intercontinental Ballistic Missile (ICBM). The Air Force and the Army disagreed over whether or not the Army needed long-range missiles to support its missions. Although the Army's IRBM program, the Jupiter, had significant success, the Air Force eventually gained control over the program when the Eisenhower administration determined that the Air Force was the proper service to direct all the nation's long-range missile programs (U.S. Air Force).

4. The Development of IRBMs

Army to portray itself as a modern fighting force and not a force that resisted modern weapons and new methods.[3]

In many ways the Army was well suited for developing guided missiles. It had access to some of the best minds, such as the German scientist Werhner von Braun and it was able to capitalize on captured German missile designs, specifically the V-2. This rocket was the basis for the Army's Redstone missile. The Redstone became the foundation for the Jupiter program. Both of these missiles formed the Saturn rockets that were the first rockets that National Aeronautics and Space Administration (NASA) used for space exploration.[4]

Prior to the beginning of the Jupiter project, Army leaders worked to increase the range of the Redstone missile. General Gavin, the head of Army's Research and Development, discussed the need to improve the Army's Redstone missile with General Ridgway because of the obvious need for long-range missiles. Gavin expected that by the time the Redstone was capable

The Army Ballistic Missile Agency published this fact sheet in May 1960 to show the differences in size of some of the different missile systems that the Army developed, including (left to right) Redstone, Jupiter and Pershing. Note the human figure in the middle as a reference to indicate the size of the missiles (U.S. Government, Department of the Army).

of 500 mile range, the Eisenhower administration would support IRBMs and the Army would be able to capitalize on its Redstone experience.⁵

Although von Braun's presence gave the Army an initial lead in missile development, the structural design of the branch's development process hindered progress. The Army used a series of arsenals across the United States, like the Red Stone Arsenal in Huntsville Alabama, to conduct its research. While these facilities provided the Army with an in-house research and development team they cut out much of the defense contracting industry. The Army's decreased use of defense contractors meant that it did not have a solid foundation of corporate support to protect its interests in Congress.⁶

The Air Force, in contrast to the Army, did not have as well-developed of a system of internal research and development. It relied on civilian contractors to help generate new aircraft and missile designs. Although the Army's arsenals had support from their Congressional representatives, arsenals could not compete with the public relations teams and lobbying money that private contractors provided to the Air Force and its missile programs. Senator Barry Goldwater made this point when he said, "The aircraft industry had probably done more to promote the Air Force than the Air Force had done itself."⁷

Although the Air Force used more contractors, its contractors were energetic in their support. In a report to the Weapons Systems Evaluation Group (WSEG), the Thor program received the personal attention of Donald Douglas, the founder of Douglas Aviation. The Air Force provided a DC-6 plane to Douglas aviation to facilitate transportation for those working on the Thor program. Also, the Air force authorized as much overtime as they could for the Douglas company to reduce the time to develop the Thor. the Thor team planned to build nine prototype missiles before the Army Ballistic Agency (ABMA) had one. One problem that became evident through testing was the relative lack of preparation of the Thor compared to the Jupiter missile in test flights.⁸

The struggle over missile development between the two branches replaced the tensions over Universal Military Training (UMT) that occurred in the late 1940s. The Army's position was that it was important for national security to train every U.S. male when he came of fighting age. The Air Force, which did not support UMT, countered that a larger budget for its operations alleviated the need for such a large and expensive training operation. Secretary of Defense James Forrestal, who served

4. The Development of IRBMs

Both the Thor and Jupiter missiles used inertial guidance systems. These systems monitored the missile's velocity and orientation in order to make adjustments during the powered stage of the flight. This type of guidance system did not require any external signals to track its position as a satellite guided system does. However, its accuracy was not as good as later missiles. The Thor did have a radio back up guidance system, but this inertial guidance was the primary system (U.S. Air Force).

between 1947 and 1949, commented in his diary about the tensions between the two services. He wrote that the debate shifted from "UMT vs. no-UMT" to one of "UMT vs. a seventy-group Air Force." Forrestal continued that the Air Force convinced the nation that it could provide the same security without forcing all males into a period of service. As a result of its advocacy, Congress increased the Air Force's 1948 budget by $822 million and the UMT legislation never made it out of committee.[9]

This was one of the first examples of the Air Force's seductive argument concerning its position in national defense during the Cold War. More money provided a relatively painless increase in U.S. security. The Army's position of training every male for possible combat meant that

Eisenhower's Nuclear Calculus in Europe

the Air Force could promise better defense with only money, while the Army demanded both money and the lives of the nation's youth. Requiring both of these meant that Army leaders faced an uphill battle against the Air Force concerning their service's position in national defense, regardless of the viability of the Air Force's promises about wartime effectiveness or its deterrence capability. This debate continued as IRBMs and ICBMs became viable weapons systems.

Although both services argued that their approach to missiles was the right choice, one reason Eisenhower supported both projects was that he wanted to find a way to reduce the need for large ground forces. In pursuit of this, he spent 1.3 billion dollars in both 1957 and 1958 to research IRBMs and ICBMs. This was almost eight percent of the total defense budget in 1958 and is equivalent to $11 billion in 2017 dollars. Missiles were a significant part of Eisenhower's fiscal and strategic planning for national defense.

The Army made serious gains in its own missile development despite the less than clear strategic necessity of these weapons for ground combat. Ironically, by the mid–1950s, the Army's program, although not institutionally necessary, was more successful than the Air Force's. In 1955 von Braun's team solved the inertial guidance problems that plagued the Redstone's accuracy. Another improvement that the Army capitalized on was General John Medaris's success in building improved test stands at Cape Canaveral capable of withstanding a 500,000 pound-thrust blast-off, providing the ability to test larger missiles.[10]

Both of these improvements allowed the Army to continue its early lead. However, neither created a justification for the nation's ground force to maintain an expensive long-range guided missile program. This was the final nail in the coffin of the Army's sojourn into IRBMs. When President Eisenhower had to determine which service should control America's long-range missile development, the natural selection was the Air Force, regardless of any Army progress or arguments to the contrary.

One important distinction concerning guided missile development during the 1950s was the difference between long-range missiles and IRBMs, of which IRBMs were a sub-set. Long-range missiles included the Redstone, with a range of 200 miles, as well as ICBMs with ranges of several thousand miles. Under this large umbrella of long-range missiles were several classifications, such as ICBM, IRBM, and tactical guided missiles. Each long-range missile program had a role to play and at least one service sponsoring its development. However, not all were of equal strategic importance.

4. The Development of IRBMs

The competition between the Army and the Air Force made the U.S. IRBM program better. However, there was another element of missile development, allied participation, specifically that of Great Britain. U.S. missile development coincided with the U.K.'s efforts in the 1950s. Both spent a significant amount of money to develop larger atomic weapons and to create viable guided missile defense forces. The United States, led by President Eisenhower focused U.S. defense policy on atomic weapons. In the beginning of the decade, strategic bombers composed the nation's primary force projection capability. However, by the end of the decade, the U.S. had several squadrons of IRBMs deployed to Italy, Turkey and Great Britain. The struggle between the Army and Air Force about which service controlled long-range guided missiles provides insight into Eisenhower's understanding of the role of IRBMs in national defense. Also, the tensions between the U.S. and the U.K. over sharing atomic weapons information were indicative of how the president used these missiles to address domestic and allied security as well as redress problems in the Anglo-American alliance.

The development of IRBMs in the United States began as two projects, one under Air Force control and the other under Army control. Each of the services' points of view about their position in national defense illuminates how these two forces approached the problem of creating such weapons. The Army focused on improving ground operations and sought to create a mobile missile system capable of moving with its formations in a ground war against the Soviet Union. The Air Force built a missile that relied on permanent launch facilities that were obvious targets in the opening salvos of a war with the Soviet Union. The first generation IRBMs used liquid fuel and had a range of approximately 1500 miles. These missiles became operational in the United Kingdom, Italy, and Turkey in 1958 and 1959.[11]

The United States' missile program grew in capability as the nation's nuclear warhead development improved. In the early 1950s, there were no missiles capable of carrying a sufficiently large warhead to make long-range missiles a viable weapon. In March 1956, Eisenhower explained that he saw guided missiles as simply another way of delivering the destructive power that the U.S. already possessed. It was not until the late 1950s that warheads of small enough size with sufficiently large yields arrived to make long-range guided missiles cost effective. Advances in missile technology changed the perception of these weapons in warfare. No longer were they only auxiliary options, they took on a more prominent role in the defense of the United States and NATO. The problems facing the development of U.S. missile capacities were primarily technological. However, the initial successes in missile development led to a missile force that quickly faced obsolescence.[12]

Pushing the United States to develop its guided missile capability was the knowledge that the Soviet Union was becoming more successful with its program. By 1955, intelligence officials at the Pentagon understood that the Soviets had the capacity to reach European capitals with long-range missiles. In reaction to this information, President Eisenhower redoubled the research efforts of the Atlas and Titan ICBM projects. In addition, he also required that Air Force Brigadier General Shriever, head of the Western Development Division, the division responsible for the ICBM, and Defense Secretary Charles Wilson brief him monthly on missile progress.[13]

Soviet advances spurred Eisenhower to focus more on U.S. missile capability. The problem was that the ICBM was still years from completion. The Thor and Jupiter provided the short-term solution because of their shorter range and relatively less complicated technical problems. Development on these weapons continued while the ICBM was still in the formative stages. These weapons, Eisenhower hoped, could provide the U.S. and its allies enough protection against the increasingly dangerous Soviet missile threat.

Another nuclear weapons issue during the 1950s was the progress of America's closest ally. Britain's atomic program struggled in the post-war period. Although it benefited greatly from its wartime cooperation with the United States, this ended after the conflict. The British view of the importance of atomic weapons was very similar to that of the United States. Although the two nations continued to collaborate in other areas of defense, cooperation and information sharing concerning atomic weapons was difficult because of the legislative obstacles during most of the 1950s.[14]

The cooperation or the lack thereof, between the U.S. and Great Britain demonstrated the distance between these two nations in the post-war period concerning nuclear research. President Eisenhower did not have the political leverage necessary to alter the legislative restrictions concerning sharing of atomic information to allied nations early in his tenure in office. Many of these limitations came in response to the dis-

4. The Development of IRBMs

covery that the Soviet Union's intelligence stole much of the atomic research data used to build the Soviet atomic bomb. This reactionary fear of espionage took time to ebb and ease fears about sharing atomic information. The effort to research IRBMs, in the beginning, was a purely American project

One of the first bodies that undertook an investigation of guided missiles and their viability was the Technological Capability Panel (TCP), chaired by James Killian. He served as the president of the Massachusetts Institute of Technology and then as the scientific advisor to President Eisenhower.[15] Eisenhower's use of the TCP and the nation's top scientists in determining guided missile policy exhibited his emphasis on technical solutions as opposed to manpower intensive remedies. The TCP, which began in 1954, framed the problem of U.S. capability in terms of technological advances. Using these achievements as a metric made it imperative that the United States maintain its lead in sophisticated strategic weapons systems. This panel was fundamental in getting Eisenhower to support guided missiles as a way to protect the nation in the nuclear age.[16]

In addition to guided missiles there were other efforts aimed at defending the United States from Soviet attack. One of the most long-lasting was the creation of the North American Aerospace Defense Command (NORAD) in 1958. This was a joint operation between the United States and Canada and attempted to create a radar shield to warn of an impending Soviet attack. However, NORAD, unlike the IRBM program, did not center on weapons to provide protection. The TCP recommended the IRBM program as a short-term fix for the long-range solution of creating a viable ICBM program. This view of the IRBM as an interim option was similar to the Air Force's point of view that looked at the ICBM as the paramount weapon. The Army, by contrast, looked to the IRBM as an end for specific operational needs, not a means to a larger goal.[17]

The TCP began by defining the threat that the Soviet Union would pose during the next 10 years. They identified four different phases of danger during this time. The first period was one of American supremacy in atomic capability but vulnerability to surprise attack because of the lack of an early warning system, this would last until 1956. From 1956 through the end of the 1950s, the U.S. would continue to build upon its supremacy in the area of strategic bombers. It would also increase the destructive power of its atomic arsenal relative to the Soviet Union. This period, the panel reported, would see the largest disparity between the Soviets and the U.S., in terms of military power. The third period from the end of the 1950s until the middle of the 1960s the panel believed the Soviets would gain on America in striking capacity and atomic bomb yield. Although the panel argued that the U.S. would maintain its strategic superiority during this period it would continue to degrade until middle of the 1960s when the Soviet Union would possess similar striking power to the United States. The panel reported that when this happened it meant that each nation had the capability to destroy the other in a nuclear war.[18]

The TCP made technological statics and destructive capacity primary metrics for determining security. In order for the nation to maintain its position relative to the Soviet Union it required an advanced military. Such a definition of security benefited the IRBM projects, since these weapons represented a modern approach to warfare. Both the Army and the Air Force inculcated the spirit of the TCP and focused on defining security in terms of weapons payload, missile ranges, and accuracy.

By the end of 1956, the Army made significant progress in its missile program. The Army created the Army Ballistic Missile Agency headed by Major General John Medaris. This agency controlled the Jupiter missile development. In September 1956, von Braun's team launched a four-stage Jupiter missile. Although this missile had an inert fourth stage it still managed to reach a height of six hundred miles and a range of thirty-three hundred miles, equal to the altitude that the Soviet satellite *Sputnik* reached months later. General Medaris, worried that von Braun might try to launch the nose cone into space with an active fourth stage ordered him not to try it. He told von Braun to "personally inspect that fourth stage to make sure it [was] not live."[19]

Two months later Defense Secretary Wilson ordered the Huntsville team specifically and the Army in general to limit its missile programs to a range of two hundred miles. This was quite a blow to von Braun, who wanted to achieve orbit with his missiles and already showed that it was possible to do so. However, this decision was not about the success of the Army in developing a missile capable of launching a satellite, it was about which service had a reason for such weapons on the battlefield. Undoubtedly, this benefited the Air Force. Secretary Wilson's order, although it seemed definitive at the time, took another year to come into force. The Army did not accept this decision without a fight.[20]

Although President Eisenhower made the decision to support IRBM research and development early in his administration it was unknown

4. The Development of IRBMs

what the fiscal implications of this decision were. By 1957, the president realized that it made little budgetary sense to maintain two research and development programs aimed at creating the same capability. Eisenhower's understanding of how he wanted to fight future wars influenced his decision about which project to keep and whether the Air Force or the Army should control the research. This decision also projected how the administration envisioned these weapons working in NATO and U.S. defense systems.

The Air Force approached the development of its IRBM in a different way from the Army. It believed that the problems posed by the ICBM and IRBM were similar. By researching the IRBM, Air Force scientists and contractors planned to solve the problems associated with the ICBM along the way. The Army saw much success in researching its shorter range missiles. Its version of the IRBM actually came out of the Army's Redstone missile program.[21] The Redstone missile, with a range of 200 miles, was smaller and had a mobile launch capability to support ground operations.[22]

The Army and the Air Force both looked to guided missiles to provide improved force projection capability. These two projects approached the problem of guided missiles from two different points of view. The Army-Navy program, Jupiter, which the Navy soon left to research its own missile system, started from the beginning to design a missile with the range of 1500 nautical miles. The Air Force's missile program Thor had the same range as the Jupiter program. The hope was that two programs, although duplicative, provided a way to make quicker progress than just one program researching the problem.[23]

Although the Army and Navy began developing the Jupiter missile together it soon became apparent that the program did not meet the Navy's needs. Liquid fuel was too problematic for naval use, it caused too many problems with its demanding storage conditions. Liquid fuel required extremely cold conditions making storage on a submarine dangerous. If the propellant or the liquid oxygen spilled during fueling operations it posed great danger to the crew and the submarine. To mitigate this risk the Navy wanted to develop a solid fuel missile, Army leaders did not think that was possible in the short-term, so they did not try to stop the Navy from leaving the program.[24]

Lieutenant General James Gavin, head of the Army's research and development, did not worry about losing naval support. He did not think it was wise for the Army to lose the progress it made on the liquid fueled

The Jupiter missile was an outgrowth of the Army's Redstone missile program. Dr. Wernher von Braun's team at the Army Ballistic Missile Agency made significant progress on solving the problems that faced the IRBM program. The Army intended the missile to be support mobile operations and planned to have mobile launch systems. However, the Army lost control of the missile program to the Air Force, which is why this missile has the markings of the U.S. Air Force. Also, the mobile launch concept did not fit the Air Force's vision of the program so when the Jupiter IRBM deployed it went to fixed launch sites (U.S. Air Force).

Jupiter in order to accommodate the Navy's needs. Besides the Jupiter was a successful missile and was possibly the vehicle to carry an American satellite. Gavin did not want to lose this opportunity for the Army to shine.[25]

The Navy however, made good on its investment in research of solid-fuels. By going to corporations such as the Aerojet General Corporation and Lockheed's Missile and Space Division, the Navy found solutions to the barriers of solid-fuel missiles unforeseen by the Army research team. Capt. Levering Smith, commander of the Naval Ordinance Test Station, worked with the companies to develop a 50-foot solid propellant missile, "Big Stoop" in 1956. The two corporations, working with Capt. Smith,

4. The Development of IRBMs

developed a solid-fuel version of the Jupiter, called Jupiter-S. The problem with the Jupiter-S was its size; it was 44 feet long and 10 feet across. This meant that a submarine could only carry four missiles. This was not enough for sustained naval operations. So, the Navy abandoned the Jupiter but showed that the technical problems preventing the switch to solid-fuels were not insurmountable but required the proper help.[26]

The two-pronged approach to missile research between the Army and the Air Force, created as many problems as it solved. The two services did not agree with each other concerning how to use missiles on the battlefield. Eventually, Eisenhower had to decide which program best fit the nation's needs. This meant determining which branch would continue to receive funds to research and, eventually, field these weapons. It also meant that the losing service lost the ability to direct the progress of America's long-range missile program.

Losing missile research funding was only of part of the problem for the Army under the New Look defense policy; there was a larger bureaucratic struggle. Eisenhower's emphasis on cost cutting meant decreasing the manpower of the United States military, as well as its overseas contingent. Eisenhower was open to decreasing U.S. troop deployments in Europe by as much as 35,000 although he knew that he had to keep this information secret.[27]

Another aspect of the rationale for decreasing the United States' presence in Europe was that an improvement in its strategic weapons provided the same defense capability as ground forces deployed to defend Western Europe. This made guided missiles an important part of the deterrent program. They only required a small American force to operate them; reducing the need for large ground forces to deter the Soviet Union from attacking Western Europe.

By the middle of 1957, von Braun's team in Huntsville, Alabama achieved some measure of success on the Jupiter project. On May 31, the third test flight of the Jupiter was successful. The missile attained a range of 1,400 nautical miles and an altitude of 350 nautical miles. This was just over half the altitude of *Sputnik*, which reached just over 600 miles in altitude in October of that year. The Air Force's program, Thor, headed by Colonel Edward Hall, an expert in propulsion, had some difficulty.[28] In 1957, all three Thor test flights ended in failure. The one flight that came closest to success was the second flight, which launched effectively but because of safety problems the missile self-destructed.[29]

Eisenhower's Nuclear Calculus in Europe

There were two major variations of the Jupiter missile, the Jupiter A and the Jupiter C. The Jupiter A variation was the military version that carried a warhead. The C variation was the model used to test re-entry technologies; this was the missile that reached 600 miles in altitude in 1956. In order to perfect ballistic missiles, both U.S. programs had to determine how best to get the warheads back into the lower atmosphere. The Jupiter C nosecone had a fiberglass coating that dissipated heat in re-entry by burning off. It was also relatively blunt, compared to other designs. These innovations helped von Braun's team resolve many of the problems of ballistic missiles.[30]

By August of 1957, Secretary of Defense Charles Wilson wrote to Secretary of the Army Wilbur Brucker concerning the fate of the Army's IRBM program. Secretary Wilson told Secretary Brucker that the Army should not dedicate any more funds to the Jupiter program. Although, at this time, the IRBM panel had not officially come to a conclusion concerning which missile was the primary focus for the nation, Wilson's memo made clear that the Army lost control of the its IRBM program. The Air Force soon gained the responsibility to integrate the IRBM into its force and bring them into an operational use.[31]

President Eisenhower was sympathetic to Army leaders' arguments concerning the need for longer range missiles. In a conference on August 12, 1957, he stated that he did not want the services to feel too restricted by arbitrary distance regulations. This was in relation to the revamped Redstone missile. Eisenhower said that he understood there could be morale problems if a service felt underused. He also wanted Army commanders to have the support they needed for combat operations. The president said that the Air Force often undervalued the importance of close air support while championing strategic air operations. This left Army units without the necessary support and the president said that missiles could help in this capacity. President Eisenhower understood Army leaders did not like this new concept of warfare and the president was willing to compromise but not on the fundamentals of the New Look program.[32]

Both programs by 1957 achieved a modicum of success. However, by this time President Eisenhower grew frustrated with what he perceived as a lack progress and the increasing cost of the duplicate programs. He said, in a conference concerning security issues in general, that he would create only one program, similar to the Manhattan Project, if he could go

4. The Development of IRBMs

back in time and revisit the missile development decision. Consolidating the programs decreased overhead cost and contributed to a unified idea of how to use the weapon. Eisenhower understood that the decision about which service continued to develop its missiles meant more than just the budget allocations, this impacted the morale of both services.[33]

Another factor in the struggle between the Army and the Air Force was the loss of face. If the Air Force carried the day and took over both IRBM programs it would solidify its position in the national security structure. If the Army won, it would represent that the Army was still important in defending the nation and determining the future of the U.S. atomic arsenal. This was not just a technical discussion but also a disagreement at a fundamental level concerning which service was primarily responsible for national security, the Army or the Air Force.

The Army faced an uphill battle concerning its justification of its long-range missile program. Army leaders argued that guided missiles helped the Army face the new realities of the atomic battlefield. However, convincing President Eisenhower that the right place for long-range missile development was the ground service was not an easy task, especially considering the Air Force's natural need of such a capability. The Army, in 1957, wanted to modernize its Redstone missile in order to increase its range as well as switch from liquid fuel to solid propellant. This modernization would increase the range of the missile to 500 miles. The arguments that the Army leaders used to justify modernizing the Redstone missile indicated how long-range missiles fit into the ground service's strategic view.

Lieutenant General James Gavin argued that the German scientists understood that the German missile program failed in part because of the constant threat of allied bombing operations. Gavin asserted that U.S. designs should start from the ground up with the assumption that mobility was crucial to maintaining the security of a missile system. Mobility allowed the missiles to move out of contentious areas and precluded the military from having to defend an area just because it had missile bases present.[34]

Mobility was not the only problem that the Jupiter faced, the discussion to switch to a solid fuel system revealed the serious problems that the liquid fuel had. Liquid fuel was corrosive and so the missiles could not remain fueled for a prolonged period of time without destroying the fuel system. Liquid-fueled missiles required significant preparation time in order to fire since they had to be fueled shortly before launch. A solid propellant system did not have such issues. The solid propellant was stable and had the ability to withstand storage over a prolonged period. Missiles with solid propellant, such as the Army's proposed modernized Redstone and the Navy's Polaris were still years from realization. The first solid-fuel Polaris missile came into operation in 1960; its first successful test flight came in 1959. However, the Army did not design the first generation of Jupiter missiles with a solid fuel capability because General Gavin did not want to sacrifice the Army's substantial progress with the liquid fueled Jupiter. This decision inhibited the future of the Jupiter as a viable weapon system.[35]

Army leaders also saw Soviet advances in missile technology as creating a vulnerability not only for ground units but for the United States. The Soviets developed a 750-mile missile that could support ground maneuver. The U.S. was moving away from increasing the range of its ground missile, the Redstone and putting other long-range missiles in static launch facilities. To Army leaders, such as General Gavin, this meant that the U.S. was ignoring the requirement to counter Soviet capability and putting a large bet on static missiles that were vulnerable in the opening stages of an attack.[36]

On August 2, 1957, after much bureaucratic infighting, Defense Secretary Charles Wilson issued a memorandum concerning the Thor and Jupiter IRBM projects. He declared that the Air Force was the service responsible for determining how to the use these weapons. The Army could continue studies to determine how it could use missiles or use IRBMs to a limited extent. However, it could not plan for using any missile with a range greater than 200 miles. This meant that the Air Force took control of the Army's IRBM project. Although the Army continued to work on the project, it was under the direction of the Air Force.[37]

The Air Force continued to work on the Jupiter. In fact, this missile had the most success in terms of performance, irrespective of the guidance system or warhead. The Army clearly made significant progress with its missile program. The problem was that the Army could never overcome the basic fact that the Air Force's justification for IRBMs was superior to that of the Army's, no matter what arguments General Taylor or any other Army leader made.[38]

General Maxwell Taylor, Chief of Staff of the Army, wrote about his concern that the Army lacked a long-range missile in a memo to the

4. The Development of IRBMs

Secretary of Defense about the Army's Redstone modernization program. He wrote that the Army had a significant capability gap because its longest range missile was the 175-mile Redstone missile. The IRBM program planned to introduce a missile with a range of 1500 miles. Without an IRBM, there was a significant gap in what targets the Army could engage. General Taylor wrote that if the Army had to engage these targets it required the Air Force to execute these missions with "manned aircraft or air-supported missiles." He continued by writing that he thought both of these systems faced obsolescence soon, leaving only the IRBM to fill the operational gap. General Taylor characterized the IRBM as too expensive, too cumbersome, and not accurate enough to provide proper support for Army missions. He believed that this meant that the Army had to have its own long-range missile capability in order to directly support its own operations.[39]

General Taylor characterized many Army leaders' fears about the lack of capability in relation to the Air Force and the Soviet Union. The Army required a missile capable of supporting what Army leaders thought were their operational requirements. However, the original Redstone did not meet this criterion and the Jupiter, although capable of reaching such targets, was out of their control. Each branch developed missiles for their own purposes; however, in the case of IRBMs, the service that designed the weapon did not directly reap the benefits of its research program. General Taylor's vision of future wars that required missiles was incorrect. These missiles played no significant military role in any Cold War conflict and have yet to be used in any war.

The Air Force program, which fielded the Thor missile, operated parallel to the Army's IRBM project. Thor was similar to the Jupiter missile; however, it came as a result of the Air Force's research on the ICBM problem. The Thor was the first IRBM to become operational, although, as discussed previously, it was not the system with the best test record. The first deployment of these weapons was to Britain, 1959. Getting these weapons deployed was problematic. In October 1957, the administration had to deal with the launch of *Sputnik*. One concern was the lack of an effective ICBM capability to counter the Soviet missile threat. The Thor provided a way to create a relatively effective ICBM quickly. The problem, as outlined in a progress report concerning guided missiles written by Dr. Killian, the scientific advisor to the president, was that this solution was not without problems. If the administration chose to use the ICBM variant of the Thor, called the Thor-Able, it meant delayed operational readiness of the Thor squadron in Britain. Also, the Thor-Able missile was not a panacea. Its technical failings led to its quick obsolescence.[40]

The problems with both the Thor and Jupiter were readily apparent even in 1956. The Scientific Advisory Committee recommended that a solid propellant IRBM receive top priority. Neither the Jupiter nor Thor first generation missiles had the capability to burn solid fuel. The advisory committee also recommended in 1956 that the research of a solid fuel variant be independent of the Jupiter. This gave the Navy the ability to develop the Polaris missile, a solid fuel submarine launched IRBM.[41]

One reason that the United States focused on the development of IRBMs was the slow pace of progress on the ICBM program. Although the program planned to create an operational ICBM by the middle of the 1960s, there was not a feasible way to increase production or research quickly enough to meet the growing Soviet threat. The only option was to make the Thor variant the emphasis of the ICBM program. This provided the capability but at the cost of diverting resources from other programs. Killian characterized this option as something that would make sense as an "emergency measure only."[42]

Both the Army and Air Force's IRBM programs had their problems. However, each offered a reasonable solution to the problem that the nation faced; its lack of a long-range ballistic missile. By the end of the 1950s, it was clear that these weapons only served as temporary solutions until more effective weapons reached the battlefield. This lack of effectiveness did not eliminate the fact that the U.S. did not have an effective counter to the Soviet ICBM capability, at least in terms of its missile force. This was why both the IRBM programs were so important to President Eisenhower.

The Jupiter missile system completed 5 test flights from 1956 through 1957. Of these flights, three were successful and attained ranges over 1,000 nautical miles. Also, the Jupiter project managed to launch a missile with a working guidance system. During this time, the Jupiter team also launched and recovered a small-scale nose cone after a successful test flight of 1100 nautical miles. The Thor program did not have the same level of success. Although it was able to launch 8 test missiles during the same year-long period, only 2 were successful. One of these successful test flights attained a range of 2,300 nautical miles. By the end of the year, the Secretary of Defense limited the maximum production of

4. The Development of IRBMs

Thors to 2 missiles a month and Jupiters to one missile a month, until President Eisenhower chose one land-based system to move to full production.[43]

It was not surprising that the Army's missile project was so successful. German rocket scientist Wernher von Braun and his team worked for the Army in the immediate post war period. In 1956, von Braun was the lead scientist in the Army Ballistic Missile Agency, located in the Redstone Arsenal in Alabama. His work for the Army in weapons research continued until the creation of the Marshall Space Flight Center in Huntsville, Alabama, in July 1960, when he started his work at the center a part of the year-old NASA.[44]

Although the Army and the Air Force each had projects that completed successful test flights during 1957, both still had problems. The guidance systems were not tested in a majority of the flights. Also, the Jupiter missile was the only one to test a version of its operational nose cone. There were more problems with the Thor, which continued to see performance issues through most of 1957. By the end of 1957, these weapons still required much work to be viable. The following table illustrates the dates and results of the initial test flights of the Jupiter and Thor programs.

One reason for the emphasis on the IRBM program was the threat of a Soviet nuclear attack or an imbalance in Soviet capacity compared with that of the U.S. Secretary of Defense Neil McElroy in a conference with Secretary Dulles in November 1957, a month after the Soviet launch of *Sputnik*, which will be the subject of chapter 6, reminded him that the nation only had intelligence estimates concerning Soviet advances. This meant that the information could be erroneous, either underestimating or overestimating Soviet capabilities. McElroy suggested that the best path was to continue to emphasize IRBM production as a hedge against Soviet missiles. Since the U.S. lacked accurate knowledge of Soviet capability, outside of *Sputnik*, continuing IRBM research and production was a safe bet.[46]

In the same conversation, the Defense Secretary discussed how to pay for the increased production of IRBMs and what to do with them. He said that European states were not ready or willing to receive them. Their main concern was the ability of the U.S. to continue to provide an effective deterrent to Soviet incursion. It did not matter whether this was through strategic bomber coverage or through newly deployed missiles. What mattered was the technical proficiency and the quality of U.S. weapons protecting its European allies. The group wanting missile coverage were the

Eisenhower's Nuclear Calculus in Europe

Test Flight Information for Thor and Jupiter IRBM Programs from 1956 Through 1957[45]	
Date	Results of Test
February 11, 1956	Scientific Advisory Committee recommended continuing both the Thor and the Jupiter IRBM programs
October 18, 1956	Air Force received the first Thor IRBM for testing
January 25, 1957	First Thor test, contaminated fuel caused the missile to explode in the early stages.
March 1, 1957	Jupiter missile first full-scale test. Launch was successful but it lost control due to heat build-up in the control fins.
April 19, 1957	Second test flight of Thor, problems with safety instruments cause early explosion of missile.
April 26, 1957	Second test flight of Jupiter. After 93 seconds of successful flight the movement of liquid oxygen caused the missile to lose control.
May 21, 1957	Third test of Thor, problems in fueling operations led to the destruction of the missile on the launch pad.
May 31, 1957	Third test of Jupiter. Attained a range of 1400 nautical miles and height of 350 nautical miles. Test was 100 percent successful.
August 8, 1957	Jupiter nosecone tested on an 1100 nautical mile test flight. This was the first object recovered from space. The nosecone attained a height of 600 miles, equal to that of *Sputnik*.
August 28, 1957	Fourth flight of Jupiter was successful
August 30, 1957	Fourth test of Thor, launch was successful but a fire in mid-flight required the destruction of the missile.
September 20, 1957	Fifth test of Thor, this was the first successful test flight of the missile.
October 3, 1957	Sixth flight of Thor ended 30 seconds after launch due to engine malfunction.
October 11, 1957	Seventh flight of Thor was successful.
October 22, 1957	Fifth test of Jupiter, this was the first full-scale test of guidance system.
October 24, 1957	Eighth flight of Thor was successful, tested subsystems and fuel economy.

4. The Development of IRBMs

U.S. people. He said that U.S. citizens worried that they were under direct threat of an attack and missiles provided an effective counter to that threat. It is important to remember that until September 1959, with the acceptance of the first U.S. ICBM, there was only one type of guided missile system that could effectively reach Soviet territory with a sufficiently large nuclear warhead, the IRBM. Using the IRBM as a deterrent required the use of European bases since the missiles lacked the range to hit Soviet targets from North America.[47]

Secretary McElroy recommended producing both the Thor and Jupiter missile based on the political situation after *Sputnik* and to quiet domestic concerns. This allowed the U.S. to produce more weapons in a shorter time frame. This decision had the support of President Eisenhower although McElroy and Dr. Killian had the authority to work out the specific details of the program. This process was separate from the decision to allow the Air Force to lead IRBM development. When the Air Force gained control of both missile programs, it did not have the authority to stop the development of the Army's Jupiter missile. Only President Eisenhower could order the elimination of the Jupiter missile program.[48]

Dulles's comments revealed that there were two different sets of priorities for security. One set dealt with how to secure European allies and the second on how to secure the United States directly. Missiles mainly catered to the concerns of U.S. citizens. *Sputnik*, at least in Dulles's estimation, did not affect European citizens as much as it worried U.S. citizens. The Eisenhower administration had to contend with the reality and perception of security. This required the president to act to create the conditions for the right perception of security in the minds of U.S. citizens. In order to do this, Eisenhower had to expend resources to produce weapons that, in reality, the United States did not need. So, the push to produce a guided missile force answered domestic security concerns, although it directly impacted European nations. This was Dulles's problem with missiles; he had to find nations willing to allow these weapons within their boundaries. This problem was not easy to solve and caused significant disruption within Europe and NATO.

Expediting missile research and production required about $200 million dispersed over the two to three years of increased production.[49] This was in addition to the baseline costs of missile production. Secretary McElroy discussed his perception of the production program; he did not think it was necessary to make a large number of weapons. Instead, he wanted eight squadrons ready by the beginning of 1960. His main motive was "psychological" in order to "stiffen the confidence and allay the concern particularly of our own people."[50]

The specifics of the reaction to the launch of *Sputnik* are outside the scope of this chapter, they will follow in a subsequent chapter. However, it is clear that with the launch of the Soviet man-made satellite, the U.S. missile program was important to national pride and national defense. The problem was that the missile program was still years away from an operational ICBM and lacked a clearly viable IRBM. *Sputnik* threw into relief the problems of American guided missile development.

The United States was not the only nation researching sophisticated weapons during the 1950s. The United Kingdom also had a nuclear weapons program. The United States and the United Kingdom worked together on the Manhattan Project, which was the name of the project for the development of the atomic bomb in World War II. In the immediate post war period, the United States ended this cooperation and carefully guarded its atomic secrets from all its allies. Although no allied nation got complete disclosure of U.S. atomic secrets, the U.K. and Canadian governments did receive special exemptions from certain American security classifications. Officials could disclose information classified through TOP SECRET to U.K. and Canadian officials with a need to know. This exemption included information concerning weapons systems and technical research information but not of an atomic nature.[51]

This openness demonstrated the special position of the United Kingdom and Canada. Both English speaking nations had clearance not afforded to any other NATO or Commonwealth nation. Although the U.S. did not work directly with the U.K. to develop its guided missiles, it ensured that the U.K. was up to date concerning U.S. progress of its missile program. This information did not include specific technical data or warhead development.

The cooperation between the United States and the United Kingdom on nuclear issues had a troubled history. Prior to World War II, Great Britain, Germany, and the United States each had scientists aware of the possibility of nuclear fission. Much of this research took place at universities and did not primarily focus on the military applications of this new energy source. In the late 1930s, Great Britain's nuclear research program was ahead of the United States' research. The U.S. reached out to the U.K. and offered to cooperate on nuclear research. However, the U.K. rejected this offer because of the lack of progress from the U.S. program. Another

4. The Development of IRBMs

reason for the British hesitancy was the perceived inability of the United States to safeguard its nuclear information or British nuclear information exchanged in any cooperative agreement.[52]

One of the reasons for the disparity between the United States and the United Kingdom in atomic weapons research was the difference in the focus of the nations' research programs. In the late 1930s, British scientists spent much of their time researching the military applications of this new atomic field. In contrast, U.S. scientists mainly focused on the industrial or energy generating possibilities of atomic power. Britain faced a direct threat from the growing power of Germany and this influenced its atomic research. British scientists understood that they needed weapons much more than they needed plentiful energy. The U.S. did not face such a threat and concentrated on using this technology mainly for economic purposes.[53]

The situation changed dramatically after World War II. During the war, the British and the Americans did cooperate on researching nuclear weapons. The framework between the two nations was the Quebec Agreement. This agreement, signed in 1943, included Canada in the cooperative research program. When the United States dedicated significant national resources toward the problem of making nuclear weapons it ensured that the U.S. soon eclipsed the United Kingdom in terms of its research efforts.[54]

The Quebec Agreement also outlined how the three nations would and could use nuclear weapons. Specifically, no signatory state could use a nuclear weapon against any other signatory state. The research effort was completely cooperative and involved a free exchange of certain information between the nations in the accord. No nation in the pact could disclose any of the information from the research to any other nation. The use of atomic weapons required the consent of other states in the agreement. Any industrial or commercial information that came out of the research would only go to the United Kingdom after the consent of the president of the United States due to the large amount of money and resources that the United States contributed to the project.[55]

The United States quickly stopped cooperating with the United Kingdom and Canada in weapons research after World War II. The Atomic Energy Act of 1946, known as the McMahon Act, ended the British and U.S. cooperation established under the Quebec Agreement of 1943. This act prevented United States agencies from disseminating atomic information to any other nation. The act specified that Congress could not pass any agreement authorizing the exchange of atomic information until there was a viable set of "international safeguards." This restriction only related to research that led to "destructive" ends. The act specifically allowed and encouraged the exchange of nuclear information that aided atomic energy endeavors.[56]

The United States was now in the position of worrying about the ability of its allies, specifically the United Kingdom, to protect sensitive nuclear weapons information. This expressed not only the change in U.S. technological growth during wartime; it also demonstrated Britain's decreased influence in the world. No longer was the U.K. dictating terms in its relationship with the United States as it did prior to World War II; now it was in the position of having to accept the termination of its nuclear cooperative agreement with the U.S.

The end of Anglo-American atomic cooperation made it more difficult for the United Kingdom to continue researching nuclear weapons. However, the fruits of the collaboration between the two nations continued to influence and aid the development of Britain's nuclear weapons program. After the war, the U.K. did not have to start from scratch in its quest for nuclear weapons. It had significant leads in the theory and the technical knowledge necessary for building an atomic weapon. Creating a functioning weapon still required significant amounts of money and research. The British were far ahead of what was possible, had the United Kingdom pursued such an endeavor alone.[57]

President Truman's decision to stop cooperation between the U.K. and the U.S. on atomic weapons shaped Britain's atomic program because it set the nation back to its 1943 position in terms of its progress. Another influence on its atomic program was the decision to keep most of the research under the auspices of the government and not allow private industry to conduct contract work on atomic research. This was a different approach from the U.S. strategy, which allowed significant contributions from the private sector in atomic exploration. The decision to maintain most research in the public sphere arose from economic concerns of the United Kingdom. It did not have the economic resources to pay for several different research contracts to investigate similar problems. The British government had to come to terms with the economic reality of its situation; it could not afford to build a large nuclear arsenal without U.S. support. One benefit of the beginning of an independent British nuclear program was the concentration of British scientists working in their home-

4. The Development of IRBMs

land. During the war, most of the prominent British researchers worked in labs in the United States. After the end of wartime cooperation, they returned home and worked for the United Kingdom directly.[58]

Britain's atomic program produced its first atomic weapon in 1952. Although it was an atomic power, its economic situation was not as powerful as its weapons arsenal. In a letter to Richard Austen Butler, Chancellor of the Exchequer, Harold Macmillan, Minister of Defense from 1954 through 1955, discussed the economic implications of securing the United Kingdom. Although this letter did not specifically address the issues of atomic weapons, it does reveal the problems that the United Kingdom faced in the postwar world in terms of economic and defense predicaments. Macmillan did not see any way to decrease defense spending in the short-term. In fact, he thought that defense spending would increase as the Royal Air Force's mission continued to increase. The British government worried as much about defense expenditures as President Eisenhower did. However, both Eisenhower and Macmillan believed that spending money on atomic weapons was important. These similarities in thinking between Eisenhower and Macmillan allowed them to work well together when Macmillan became prime minister in 1957. Both thought that these weapons provided a solid foundation for national security in the Cold War.[59]

Early in the atomic age there was a breakthrough in the power of atomic weapons. This was the hydrogen bomb. It increased the yield from the kiloton range into the megaton range, a thousand-fold increase in power. These weapons used nuclear fusion and not nuclear fission for their power. The creation of fusion atomic weapons changed the paradigm of atomic warfare. Using technological sophistication and bomb yield as a measure of effectiveness in the absence of an actual nuclear war meant that hydrogen weapons called into question an arsenal based only on fission weapons. The dramatic increase in destruction raised the risk of one Soviet missile or bomber getting through America's defenses. If one hydrogen bomb hit a U.S. city it meant the complete destruction of that city and, possibly, its surrounding areas as well. This was different than the previous generation of atomic weapons with yields in the kiloton range. Failure to stop or deter one attack, in the hydrogen bomb age, meant the death of possibly millions of Americans.[60]

In 1955, the British Ministry of Defense commissioned a study to discern the implications of a hydrogen bomb attack on the United Kingdom.

This report, chaired by William Strath, described the horror of such an attack in great detail. It also disclosed the planning assumptions of the British military staff during the mid–1950s. Strath wrote that hydrogen bombs would be a part of any future war that the United Kingdom fought. He advocated that preparing for an atomic or conventional attack was not effective. He believed that the government should focus on planning for defense against hydrogen bomb attacks and in order to save the money necessary for planning on conventional and atomic attacks.[61]

This report expressed the British government's belief that atomic weapons, and later hydrogen weapons, defined the postwar security paradigm. In a 1954 cabinet meeting, Prime Minister Winston Churchill made his position clear concerning the importance of atomic weapons in protecting Great Britain. He said that Britain's atomic capability allowed it to prevent war. This made it vitally important that the nation continued to research and develop the best atomic and hydrogen weapons. In this meeting, Churchill announced that the nation had to begin work on the hydrogen bomb and to continue to improve its atomic capability.[62]

Churchill's decision to make the hydrogen bomb came about two years after the United States detonated its first fusion, or hydrogen bomb, in 1952 and one year after the Soviet Union detonated its first fusion weapon in 1953. The quick progress of the United States and the Soviet Union spurred the United Kingdom into action. It demonstrated the difference between the U.S. and the U.K. atomic research programs. During this period, there was limited cooperation between the U.S. and the U.K. concerning atomic weapons research. The American program produced significant results in short period of time. The British program took until 1957 to reach the thermonuclear or hydrogen bomb stage.

The British nuclear program was effective. However, the United Kingdom struggled to balance fiscal and defense issues during the 1950s. The United States faced similar concerns but did not face the problems of rebuilding an economy and society damaged by World War II. The United Kingdom wanted to cooperate with the United States in its atomic weapons program. Churchill expressed optimism that this would happen soon in 1954. However, this cooperation did not move beyond the surface level until three years and several international crises later. The United States and Britain only shared physical data concerning atomic weapons and destruction estimates of their weapons. They did not cooperate on a technical level or on a research level.[63]

4. The Development of IRBMs

Although there was not cooperation on atomic weapons research, there was collaboration in other defense areas. In 1955, the United Kingdom Ministry of Defense asked to purchase Corporal missiles in conjunction with a bulk purchase of the United States Army. Harold Macmillan, then the defense minister wrote the request along with the Secretary of State for War, Anthony Head. They argued that the missile provided the British Army a much needed short-range atomic capability. The Corporal missile had a maximum range of 75 miles. This cooperation was only for the missile and not for the warhead. The British government had to develop their own warhead to arm this missile.[64]

There was a significant amount of cooperation between the two nations throughout the 1950s in non-nuclear areas of defense. This collaboration expressed Eisenhower's desire to work with the British on nuclear issues. The Anglo-American alliance in the post war period did go through some strain. The United Kingdom and the United States each needed each other, although the balance changed through the decade. The United States continued to need access to the United Kingdom because of its proximity to the Soviet Union. The United Kingdom continued to need the U.S. to provide economic and military aid and support as it dealt with the implications of its decline on the international stage.

The progress of the U.S. IRBM program through the 1950s allowed the U.S. military to begin to change from using only strategic bombers to a combined force that relied on guided missiles as well as bombers to project force into Soviet territory. President Eisenhower's decision to delegate the control of the IRBM program to the Air Force did not come from an assessment of the technical progress of each program. If this were the case, then the clear leader was the Army's Jupiter program. However, the Army faced an uphill battle because its national security mission did not require a long-range missile. Although General Taylor argued that ground operations required such a long-range missile, this did not sway President Eisenhower. The Air Force carried the day because it was the force that had a missile program aligned with its operational needs. The Air Force's missile program also meshed well with what the administration wanted from the weapon system, a way to de-emphasize ground operations and focus more on strategic nuclear war as a way to deter future conflicts with the Soviet Union.

The relationship between the U.S. and the U.K. concerning atomic research also revealed the problems that Eisenhower faced in building an effective relationship between the U.S. and Great Britain. Although the two nations did not cooperate in atomic weapons research in the early Cold War period, it was obvious that both looked to nuclear weapons to secure their respective nations. However, in order for the U.S. to take full advantage of its IRBM force it needed European bases. This required the consent of individual nations to have U.S. nuclear weapons deployed within their boundaries. Great Britain, the closest U.S. ally in Western Europe, was a key part of this strategy.

With the launch of *Sputnik* there was great concern in the United States about the ability of the Soviets to strike America with a long-range missile. Europeans did not share this concern. President Eisenhower needed some political leverage to convince European nations to agree to IRBM deployment to meet U.S. concerns. This leverage, in the case of the United Kingdom, came from the disruption of the political relationship with the U.S. because of the Suez Crisis and the Bermuda Conference of 1957, which saw both nations seeking to repair the special relationship between America and Great Britain.

5

The Suez Crisis and Bermuda Conference Reconciliation

No one expected July 26, 1956, to be a watershed day. Gamal Abdel Nasser was due to give a speech celebrating the revolution in Egypt that deposed King Farouk. This coup, led by the Free Officers in 1952, was part of the growing Arab Nationalism movement that started in North Africa and the Middle East in the 1950s. The officers led by Muhammad Naguib and Nasser not only wanted to change the political structure in Egypt, they wanted to end British occupation. However, ending the British presence in Egypt took several years.

When Nasser came to Alexandria to give his commemorative speech, many expected him to discuss the importance of the revolution and to reveal a major policy proposal, as was customary at these events. He began his discussion by talking about Egypt's history of oppression and exploitation. Nasser explained to the attentive crowd that they suffered under both domestic and foreign oppressors. He wanted to give them something else.[1]

The crowd consisted of a quarter of a million people packed densely to hear their leader's address. They were there to celebrate the freedom of Egypt but Nasser had greater plans. As he continued to discuss Egypt's oppressors he started to talk about the building of the Suez Canal. He reminded the crowd how Ferdinand de Lesseps imposed conditions upon Khedive Said, then the leader of Egypt. When Nasser said de Lesseps' name, he signaled to his associates to start the takeover of the Suez Canal Company offices.[2]

As Nasser's conspirators seized the offices, the president of Egypt continued to tell the people of his plans. He told them that he had previously signed a decree nationalizing the canal. This move ended the foreign ownership of the waterway and allowed Egypt to claim all of the canal's revenue, instead of only getting a royalty. The implications of this decision would lead to war with Great Britain, France, and Israel. This conflict forced President Eisenhower into an uncomfortable position. He could support U.S. allies and by implication help re-establish colonialism in North Africa. Or, he could choose to alienate his closest allies in order to salvage the U.S. position in the Middle East. These decisions caused Eisenhower much frustration and he did not appreciate his allies forcing the U.S. into such a situation. Eisenhower's adept handling of the crisis helped him defuse the conflict and prevent it becoming a wider war. Just as important was the rapprochement process between the U.S. and the U.K., although Eisenhower was not very sympathetic to British objectives in Egypt, he still needed British cooperation to build a Western European defense coalition.

Nasser's nationalization of the canal called into question the ability of the United Kingdom and France to use the canal to supply and support their colonial holdings as well as both of these states positions as first-rate powers. This was a direct threat to the national security and prestige of both the U.K. and France. This slight could not go unchallenged because if it did, it would quicken the dissolution of both empires.

President Eisenhower focused his defense policy on deterring war with the Soviet Union; this was a globally focused end state. Eden, in response to Nasser's nationalization, made efforts to restore British influence in the Middle East, a regional objective, with strategic implications for Britain. The different areas of focus added to the tensions between the U.S. and the U.K. Eisenhower did not want to sacrifice his global goal of avoiding a direct conflict with the Soviet Union in order to support the regional aspirations of the United Kingdom, even if it meant an uncontrolled slide into decolonization for Britain.

The diminishing role of Great Britain in world affairs was another complicating factor in the Suez Crisis. Although the United Kingdom was part of the successful coalition in World War II, after the conflict, the U. K. faced significant challenges in rebuilding its economy and maintaining its empire. This tension between remaining economically solvent and keeping the vestiges of empire in a postcolonial world forced the U.K., and Anthony Eden specifically, to face hard truths about the British role in international affairs and its position relative to the United States. The British and French Empires were dissolving, as nationalism influenced more peoples.[3]

5. The Suez Crisis and Bermuda Conference Reconciliation

Eisenhower was not sympathetic to the problems of decolonization. This lack of consonance contributed to the disagreement between the president and Anthony Eden about the threat that Nasser posed. Although Eisenhower understood the security risks that Britain and France faced if they lost prestige in the region; he did not support their duplicitous actions to reaffirm their control over their shrinking realms.

The Suez Crisis represented a turning point for Great Britain. After the conflict, British leaders had to ensure their foreign policy closely aligned with the United Kingdom's most powerful ally, the United States. The British invasion of Egypt represented Eden's last attempt to act unilaterally to protect the British Empire from collapse. This last act failed. The reasons for its failure are beyond the scope of this chapter but the influence of the crisis and the need for an Anglo-American rapprochement are important understanding how and why Eisenhower deployed IRBMs to Great Britain.

After World War II, alliances were a fundamental part of U.S. foreign and military policy. Secretary of Defense Charles Wilson reported to President Eisenhower the state of America's national defense structure and its relative advantage compared with the Soviet Union in a memo in early 1956. This memo laid out the recent progress each of the branches made in terms of atomic capability. It also described how they were integrating these new weapons into their organizational structures. He further discussed how the U.S. should approach its allies in order to make it clear that the interests of the U.S. aligned with their own interests. He wrote that U.S. allies had to understand that U.S. forces provided security for both the U.S. and its allies. However, Wilson stated, that U.S. policy aimed at preventing warfare, which benefited everyone. This was in line with Eisenhower's strategic design.[4]

Eisenhower did not want to fight the Soviet Union or any other nation. His national defense policies specifically tried to calm tensions and deter direct conflict. In order to be effective, U.S. allies had hue to a similar line and not involve themselves in conflicts that required U.S. support. The Suez Crisis of 1956 uncovered the problems inherent in this strategy. The United States was subject to the actions of its allies in the Middle East and did not have complete control of the situation. One reason for the lack of influence in the region was that parts of the Middle East were in the peripheral zones, not clearly in the U.S. or Soviet sphere of influence. Although the Suez Canal was in a peripheral zone, the Suez

Crisis strained the special relationship between the United States and Great Britain.

Another point covered by Secretary Wilson in his memo to Eisenhower was the key to making this cooperative strategy successful was ensuring that U.S. allies understood the mutually beneficial aspects of a U.S. alliance. This, according to Wilson, ensured that U.S. allies knew that their needs mattered to U.S. leaders and that they were not simply helping the U.S. fights its own conflicts, at the expense of their own security. Of course, when the interests of allies conflicted with those of the U.S. it did cause significant disruptions in relations between the U.S. and its associates. The Suez Crisis was one episode that showcased the problems that occur when nations' interests diverged.[5]

Admiral Radford, Chairman of the Joint Chiefs of Staff, provided an indication of the tense security situation that the U.S. faced in the middle of the 1950s. In a memorandum to the Secretary of Defense written in March 1956, he aired the defense concerns of the Joint Chiefs of Staff. Although the Chiefs all understood the importance of reducing security spending because of its deleterious effect on the economy, they could not recommend any defense reductions at that time. The primary reason the Chiefs could not countenance any decrease in defense spending was because of the persistent threat of conflict with the Soviet Union.[6]

Throughout the Cold War, the threat of a future conflict with the Soviet Union pervaded any discussion of America's national defense strategy. Any action that precipitated a potential conflict with the Soviet Union was antithetical to U.S. policy. The Suez Crisis put this aspect of Cold War doctrine under considerable strain. If the British, French, and Israelis pushed the issue too far and made Egypt seek support from the Soviet Union it possibly created a situation where U.S. allies faced a Soviet sponsored enemy. This set the stage for either the U.S. or the Soviets entering the conflict and risked greatly expanding the scope of the war.

As discussed earlier, U.S. defense planners expected any conflict with the Soviet Union to be nuclear in nature. Although the Suez Canal Crisis began as a limited conflict, if the Soviet Union intervened it had the possibility to destroy any artificial limitations on the use of military power. Eisenhower was hesitant to act too forcefully to change Nasser's position because of the threat of Soviet involvement combined with the express purpose of U.S. policy of deterring war. For the president the main threat was always the Soviet Union, he did not want to take any undue risks in

5. The Suez Crisis and Bermuda Conference Reconciliation

provoking a war over anything that was not an existential threat to the U.S. Nasser's nationalization of the canal represented a significant threat to British and French national interests. Both Eden and French Prime Minister Guy Mollet saw this threat as one that approached that of the Soviet Union because of what it communicated about the crumbling power of each of their empires. The canal crisis forced these two interpretations of security issues into stark relief. Eisenhower faced the decision of supporting American allies at the cost of potentially engaging the Soviet Union.

Nasser's takeover of the Suez Canal was part of his effort to regain Egyptian sovereignty over its territory, sovereignty the British and French held since the 19th century. His decision to nationalize the canal came after U.S. efforts to improve its image in Egypt. Prior to the nationalization decision, the United States offered to support Abdel Nasser in his desire to improve the infrastructure of Egypt as a way to keep Egypt out of the communist orbit. The highest profile project of this effort was the promise aid to build the Aswan Dam. However, President Eisenhower decided to withdraw aid for the project due to Nasser's addition of several conditions on the Aswan Dam project. Nasser also began to receive weapons from the Soviet Union, through Czechoslovakia, furthering alienating his Eisenhower. This, in the president's estimation, made the deal more trouble than it was worth.[7]

Allen Dulles, director of the Central Intelligence Agency, told the NSC in June 1956 that the Soviet Union agreed to help Nasser build the dam. This aid offer consisted of a no interest loan of $400 million with a 60-year term. In addition to this loan, the Soviets agreed to forgive all of Egypt's debt for the Soviet arms purchased prior to the agreement. The Soviet Union also promised to buy the nation's entire cotton crop and build a steel mill. The discussion then turned to the impact that Soviet aid had on U.S. influence in the region. Secretary of the Treasury Humphrey did not think that it was problematic that the Soviet Union wanted to help Egypt. He did not see it as a loss for the U.S. but he believed "it was the best possible thing" for the United States because of the second and third order effects of the agreement.[8]

Secretary of State John Dulles agreed, he added that while the near-term impact was negative, for the long-term the United States actually dodged a bullet for its image in the region. He told the council that any nation that decided to help Egypt build this dam risked becoming the object of scorn by the Egyptians. The construction project, even though it came with significant financial aid, eventually required the Egyptian people to sacrifice to pay for it. Once the people experienced the fiscal impacts of this project through reduced government spending on public programs and other hardships they would first blame their own government. However, they would also look to the foreign power that loaned the money to Egypt and now wanted repayment. Dulles believed that it was a good thing that the Soviet Union had to be the one to call the Egyptian government to task if it didn't pay its obligations; this allowed the U.S. to sidestep the problem in the future as well as remove itself from any further economic entanglements with Egypt.[9]

Eisenhower elaborated on this issue in his diary on August 8, 1956. In this entry, he discussed Nasser's nationalization decision as well as U.S. efforts to help him build the Aswan Dam. Eisenhower wrote that Nasser decided to nationalize the canal as a result of the U.S. decision to withdraw funding for the dam project. Eisenhower continued that Nasser said he expected to receive approximately $100 million in profit in the first year of nationalization. This required a steep increase in the tolls charged by the canal company. The Suez Canal Company, according to Eisenhower, only netted $35 million and that was after the rental of $17 million paid to Egypt. As a consequence of nationalization, the company would not pay rent on the canal to Egypt. Under the rate structure prior to nationalization, the company only profited approximately $52 million a year. In order for Nasser to reach his goal of $100 million he had to double the tolls charged by the canal. This estimation assumed no drop in traffic because of Nasser's actions. Another problem the Egyptian president faced was the need to improve the canal in order to accept larger ships. This required about $750 million in the short-term, according to Eisenhower.[10]

In addition to laying out the problems of nationalization, Eisenhower also articulated what Nasser had to do in order to see the profits he hoped for. In his entry, Eisenhower did not reveal any animosity concerning the Nasser's decision. Rather, the tone was calm and the president simply provided an accounting of the problems of this decision in financial terms. Nasser's actions, while Eisenhower did not think them prudent, were not a cause for panic for the United States.

Eisenhower's diary entry also contained his version of the Aswan Dam decision. The project was going to involve the British and the U.S. in a combined effort. After the initial investment of these two nations, the World Bank would provide the aid required for Nasser to finish the dam.

5. The Suez Crisis and Bermuda Conference Reconciliation

Eisenhower wrote that he thought the project was feasible but very expensive for Egypt and could consume almost all of its domestic spending. According to Eisenhower, Nasser then sent a list of conditions that the U.S. and British had to meet in order for him to agree to the project. Next, Eisenhower wrote, that Nasser began a military improvement program that detracted from the funds required to build the dam. Eisenhower did not think that Egypt had the necessary resources to complete its military improvement program and pay its share for the dam so he withdrew U.S. support from the project.[11]

Once again, Eisenhower's tone was not angry. He related these events in a matter of fact manner. He simply wrote that he had "lost interest and said nothing more about the matter." It was not a dramatic decision for Eisenhower; it was simply a potential investment where the costs became too onerous for American support. When Nasser replied in July 1956 that he withdrew any conditions for Egyptian participation, Eisenhower wrote that the United States considered the project dead and did not have any interests in reviving it. Although Eisenhower did not convey any significant security concerns about Nasser's actions, this was not the case for the British Prime Minister Anthony Eden.[12]

In a letter to Prime Minister Anthony Eden, written on September 2, 1956, Eisenhower advised him that the best option for the United Kingdom was to ensure a successful outcome of the discussion with Nasser concerning the future access to the canal. Eisenhower brought up the possibility of taking the issue to the United Nations. He wrote that the problem should not go to the United Nations until the talks that the British government was participating in fell through. Eisenhower cautioned Eden that the most important thing was maintaining a united diplomatic front. If the British, the Americans, and the other nations in the Suez Committee of Five user nations of the canal stayed together, there was a greater chance of Nasser backing away from his nationalization policy. Eisenhower did not think that there was any need to resort to force at that time and he wanted the diplomatic process to have the full participation of all those concerned.[13]

Eisenhower treated this problem as a diplomatic conflict. It was not something that required the use of military force. He believed that the nations involved should be able to bring it to a close without any violence. He saw certain British actions, such as evacuating its civilian personnel, as provocative and thought it precipitated a military response that only served to strengthen Nasser's appeal. Eisenhower told Eden that this crisis was improving Nasser's position in several areas where previously he was unpopular. The president felt that this was where the British and U.S. positions started to diverge from each other. The British thought that force was the proper tool, given that Nasser was not bowing to their desire. However, Eisenhower wrote to Eden that neither he nor the U.S. people thought that resorting to force was the proper way to resolve this problem.[14]

The letter to the prime minister continued by stating that Eisenhower did not see a possibility that using force was a viable option. If the dispute spurred military action, Eisenhower told Eden that Europe would not survive long without access to Middle Eastern oil imports. Any military conflict, according to Eisenhower, risked uniting many of the neutral nations in Africa and Asia in opposition to the Free World. It made Nasser a potential rallying point for anti–Western sentiment, which Eisenhower thought could last for decades. He ended this section of the letter by writing that before he could support a resort to military action there had to be a consensus among nations that nationalization risked their key interests.[15]

The differences between the United Kingdom and the United States concerning the Suez Canal Crisis were stark. Eden believed that the United Kingdom had to act in order to protect its interests in the region. However, these were not just issues of a financial nature. Egypt, for Eden and Britain, represented empire. If Nasser's ploy succeeded it showed Britain's weakness in projecting power to its imperial interests and threatened to quicken other nascent independence movements. Eden, and Great Britain, wanted to manage the decolonization process. If he were unable to stop Nasser, then it might become impossible to create the commonwealth of former colonies to secure Britain's post-colonial legacy.[16]

The post war British Empire was a shell of its Victorian apogee. Following World War II, many British colonies sought independence, chief among them was India. In the late 1940s and 1950s maintaining its colonial presence was expensive. Although giving colonies independence allowed the British government to recoup some costs of maintaining large colonial police forces it also eroded Britain's position as a world power. The immediate post war period for Britain was one of compromise. The first task was to rebuild after years of conflict; the second task was to find a way to keep its relevance and position as a world power. Both proved very difficult.

France also struggled in the post war period. The spread of nation-

5. The Suez Crisis and Bermuda Conference Reconciliation

alism through North Africa undermined French rule in the region. In Indochina, present day Vietnam, a communist movement led by Ho Chi Minh fought to separate that colony from Paris. Similar to Britain, France had to rebuild from the destruction imposed on it from Nazi Germany. French leaders also wanted to maintain France's prewar position as a world power. Overcoming the malaise of defeat in World War II and decolonization pushed French leaders, particularly de Gaulle, to demand recognition of France as a senior member of NATO.

Anthony Eden replied to Eisenhower's letter about the Suez Crisis on September 6, 1956. In it, Eden restated his support for a diplomatic solution. He stressed that the United Kingdom did see the diplomatic approach as the primary avenue to settle this dispute. Eden told Eisenhower that any preparations taken came from his experience in the anti–British riots in 1952 that killed a little more than a dozen British citizens. He replied to Eisenhower that he found any concern that the president had about the evacuation of civilians from the region unsettling. However, the letter changed in character when Eden discussed his view of the threat that Nasser posed in Egypt.[17]

In discussing Nasser's threat to the United Kingdom, Eden recounted the concessions that the European community gave to Hitler in the 1930s. He compared Nasser's goals with those of Hitler, by claiming that Nasser's move was analogous to the gradual expansion of Germany in the 1930s. Eden reminded Eisenhower that no European power resisted these moves in the interwar period because no one thought it proper to question what Hitler did inside his own territory or in those territories that acquiesced to his control.[18]

Comparing Nasser to Hitler was evidence of the dramatic difference in opinion of the threat posed by the nationalization of the Suez Canal. For Eden this was an issue that went far beyond access to the canal. It threatened the British ability to control the transformation of its empire into a commonwealth. If Eden failed, British colonial holdings could revolt and drag the United Kingdom further away from being a world power. Eden saw this as a test case for decolonization. If Eden and the United Kingdom were unable to stop Nasser it proved that the British Empire was hollow. If the U.K. was successful, it improved the chances for a successful commonwealth. A strong commonwealth of nations could form a foundation for Britain's global strength. If it failed and the Empire fractured into disassociated states, Britain only had its own strength to leverage for international prestige. In the 1950s, with Britain still hurting from the social and economic costs of World War II as well as the psychological damages from the war, the crisis represented a way for the British imperialism to stem the tide of waning power. For Eisenhower, the crisis risked possible confrontation with the Soviet Union. From Eisenhower's perspective, the potential for trouble far outweighed any potential benefit for a controlled British imperial transformation.

Although Eisenhower hoped that the talks with Nasser would provide an acceptable solution for the British, this was not the case. In October 1956, the British and French governments supported a draft resolution in the United Nations Security Council that backed their positions and authorized international control over the canal. If enacted, it put an end to Nasser's hopes to nationalize the waterway. The British and French submitted this draft resolution for consideration to the United Nations Security Council. The hope was that if the Security Council authorized international control of the Suez it made it more difficult for Nasser to get international support.[19]

John Foster Dulles met with the British and French foreign ministers about this proposed resolution on October 5, 1956. Dulles said that he wanted to make sure that he understood their position and that they understood the U.S. position. He told the ministers that the U.S. people did not know what to make of French and British actions. He continued that he found it surprising that the two nations submitted a draft to the United Nations in such a short time. Dulles told the ministers that when he left London only a few days before, he felt sure that neither Britain nor France planned go to the U.N. Now there was a draft resolution prepared for the Security Council.[20]

The change in British and French diplomatic stances caught Dulles by surprise. The primary reason for this was the lack of communication between the British, French, and U.S. governments concerning the Suez Crisis. As discussed earlier, Prime Minister Eden believed that Nasser posed a significant threat to the future of the United Kingdom regarding its ability to transition its colonies into commonwealth member states. Eden's regionally focused approach to the problem clashed with the global scope that Eisenhower used to interpret the crisis. This divergence made miscommunication and misunderstanding almost inevitable. Eisenhower made it clear in his correspondence to the prime minister that the preferable, and primary, solution was the multilateral conference of Suez Canal

5. The Suez Crisis and Bermuda Conference Reconciliation

user nations. Only after that avenue failed would the United States support going to the United Nations.

The meeting between Dulles and the foreign ministers then turned to the motivation behind the potential Security Council resolution. The Secretary of State suggested that the intent behind the resolution was to offer cover for a future military strike that would force the issue of who controlled the Suez Canal. Dulles wanted to know why the French and British wanted to go to the Security Council so that the U.S. government, specifically President Eisenhower, would at least understand why they submitted the resolution. He cautioned the two ministers that the U.S. and any other nation would not follow without knowing where the British and French intended to lead them. The stakes were too high in this situation to allow for any unintended consequences.[21]

On October 29, 1956, Israel invaded the Suez Canal Zone. The Israelis invaded the Sinai in order to open the Straits of Tiran and stop Egypt's blockade of Israeli shipping in the region. This military maneuver advanced to within 25 miles of the Suez Canal in the first day. Eisenhower's initial reaction was to honor the U.S. commitment to prevent aggression in the region. He thought that "the United States was pledged to support the victim of an aggression in the Middle East. The only honorable course was to carry out that pledge."[22] Anthony Eden sent a letter to President Eisenhower on October 30, 1956, discussing the Suez conflict. Eden explained to Eisenhower that the Israeli invasion was in response to the Nasser's actions concerning the Suez and his belligerent attitude towards Israel. He told Eisenhower that when the British government received word of the movement of Israeli troops, Eden cautioned Israel to ensure it did not move against Jordan. The prime minister wrote that this infringed upon the British treaty with Jordan and Britain to support its treaty obligations. Eden implied that he did not know that Israel planned a military incursion into Egypt. However, he opened his letter saying that he did not hide his feelings that Britain had every right to defend its "vital interests" against Nasser's encroachment.[23]

Eisenhower responded to Eden on the same day. He related to Eden that the U.S. sent its ambassador to the U.N. to meet with the British representative in order hammer out a policy to mitigate Israel's military action. However, the U.S. ambassador did not receive a warm reception to this invitation of cooperation. Instead the British ambassador said his government saw no need restrain Israel. Eisenhower told Eden that he did not know why the British government took such a stance and that this was quite a departure from what he expected from such a close ally.[24]

The letter to Anthony Eden continued with Eisenhower telling the British prime minister about the possible implications of the British support for Israeli military activities. If the French and British involved themselves in a regional war and the Egyptian government asked for help from the Soviet Union, it put the United States in a very awkward position. If the United Nations determined Israel to be the aggressor and the Soviet Union intervened, the U.S. then faced the stark choice of abandoning its European and Israeli allies to a Soviet proxy war. Otherwise, Eisenhower had to aid them in a likely long conflict. If the Soviets became directly involved, Eisenhower wrote that the United States would be "confronted with a de facto situation that would make all our present troubles look puny indeed."[25]

None of these scenarios boded well for the U.S. Engaging in a proxy war or a protracted limited war required the repudiation of the doctrine of Massive Retaliation and fighting a war similar to the Korean conflict. Fighting the Soviet Union directly would put Massive Retaliation to the ultimate test and would disclose whether or not America's nuclear arsenal could stop a Soviet attack. Choosing any of these alternatives eliminated any chance Eisenhower had of providing national security at an affordable price. Abandoning the British and French to a Soviet sponsored conflict, if that happened, risked creating a rift in the Western European alliance making it difficult for the U.S. to use NATO to defend against Soviet European incursion.

In a conversation on October 30 with Secretary Dulles, President Eisenhower voiced his frustrations with British actions. The Secretary of State told Eisenhower that he believed that Eden was trying to force the United States to support them by "confront[ing] us with a de facto situation." Dulles continued that although the British may recognize that their actions were "rash" they "would say that the U.S. could not sit by and let them go under economically." Eisenhower replied that, "he did not see much value in an unworthy and unreliable ally and that the necessity to support them might not be as great as they believed."[26]

In the conference, colonialism was also a topic of discussion. The president said that he thought that neither the French nor the British had proper grounds to go to war. For Eisenhower, this was not a conflict about the Suez Canal. For the French, as Eisenhower interpreted the situation,

5. The Suez Crisis and Bermuda Conference Reconciliation

it was about Algeria and for the British it was about their prestige in the Middle East. Dulles told Eisenhower that he worried about the implications of allies advancing their colonial policies at the expense of U.S. interests. The Secretary said that he recently told British and French officials as much and they did not respond well to his comments. Dulles cautioned the president about the possible expansion of the conflict. He reminded Eisenhower that the United States got involved in the previous World Wars, in some sense, in order to support its allies. The Secretary did not want this to happen with this conflict because the international community could judge U.S. allies as the aggressors. Eisenhower's main focus during the crisis was how to maintain the balance of power between the Soviet Union and the United States. Backing the U.K. and France, in a bid to secure their imperial holdings in the Middle East, did not further that goal.[27]

The military phase of the Suez Canal Crisis revealed the depth of the divergence between the U.S. and the U.K. concerning the need to take action against Nasser. Britain supported, and secretly helped plan, the Israeli military operation. On October 31, British and French airplanes launched air raids against Egyptian targets in the Sinai Peninsula and the Suez Canal Zone. Eisenhower did not know that the British and French worked with Israel to plan and conduct a military campaign.[28]

Although the president was unsure of exactly what his allies were doing, he was suspicious. Secretary Dulles, in a telegram to the U.S. Ambassador in Paris on October 29, related what Eisenhower's reaction would be if the crisis became violent. He told Douglas Dillon, the U.S. ambassador, that any possible military action was a tremendous setback for European relations with the Middle East. As it allowed the Soviet Union to increase its influence in the region. He also reminded the ambassador that the United States would not come to the aid of its allies in this situation, because they were the instigators. Secretary Dulles' remarks revealed Eisenhower's laser-like focus on the global implications of the crisis. Britain's regional or imperial concerns were not part of Eisenhower's strategic calculus. This difference of perception made it very difficult for the two allies to share any common ground.

On October 30, 1956, the British and French governments issued a 12-hour ultimatum to Nasser and David Ben-Gurion. Both nations, according to the ultimatum, had to withdraw their forces from the Canal Zone and cease military actions. Of course, this required the Egyptians to forfeit control of the Canal Zone to European occupation. This was unacceptable to Nasser and the ultimatum was only a pretense for the British and French to involve their forces in the war.[29]

In a phone conversation with John Foster Dulles on October 30, Eisenhower vented his frustrations about the British and French actions in the crisis. He said he could not believe that the America's allies expected the U.S. to offer some form of assistance. He continued, "They are our friends and allies, and suddenly they put us in a hole & expect us to rescue them." Eisenhower told Dulles that he had no intention of considering military action to aid the military maneuvers against Egypt and was also cool to the idea of financial support for the operation.[30]

In a subsequent phone conversation on the same day between the Secretary of State and the president, Eisenhower and Dulles discussed the text of a public message about the invasion. The president said he wanted to express his distaste for the ultimatum that the French and British issued. Although Eisenhower felt that the U.S. had to issue the declaration to communicate that the nation did not support the ultimatum, he understood that neither the British nor the French would change their actions as a result. The declaration, Eisenhower knew, would also influence the perception of the Arab states. It made clear that the United States was not a part of the invasion.[31]

Eisenhower worried that if he did not communicate his lack of support for Britain and France then the U.S. image in the Middle East would suffer. If this damage occurred it meant that the U.S. surrendered ground to the Soviet Union in the region. The president, although he didn't believe Nasser's tactics were productive, saw no reason to forcefully impose the will of nations that were, until recently, imperial masters over the canal.

The Suez Crisis was not the only international conundrum Eisenhower faced in October 1956. Adding to the international tensions, on October 19 the Central Committee of the Polish United Workers' Party ousted the Soviet supported Deputy Chairman of the Council of Ministers Konstantin Rokossovsky. Rokossovky, a Marshal of the Soviet Union and a Marshal of Poland, was also the Polish defense minister. Although he was Polish by birth, many Poles considered him a Russian and looked at his leadership as proof of Soviet oppression. Nikita Khrushchev flew to Warsaw on October 20 to force Rokossovsky on the Polish people; they refused and maintained their support for Wladyslaw Gomulka, a Polish Communist leader. This unrest soon spread to other Eastern European satellites, notably Hungary.[32]

5. *The Suez Crisis and Bermuda Conference Reconciliation*

When news reached Hungary about the Polish uprising, many Hungarians took to the streets. They called for the removal of Soviet forces and demanded the right to elect their own communist leaders. With the unrest continuing to grow, the Hungarian government invited Soviet forces into the nation in order provide security. However, this supposed security came with a heavy price. Days after the Soviet intervention there were reportedly over 5,000 dead. Eisenhower issued a statement on October 25 decrying the Soviet action. He also said that the Hungarian people desired freedom and that Soviet actions only demonstrated the oppressive nature of the Soviet alliance.[33]

The Hungarian problem gave Eisenhower a quiver full of arrows to target Soviet imperialism and draw attention to the dangers of nations becoming too close to the socialist alliance. Making the most of this situation opened an opportunity for the president to sway neutral nations away from Soviet influence and U.S. American prestige at the same time. However, the Suez Canal Crisis, especially the military action of Israel, France, and Britain, made it difficult to demonize Soviet actions too much when U.S. allies were committing similar, although not as deadly, acts in the Middle East. Secretary Dulles relayed the president's frustration in a phone call with the Canadian Secretary of State for External Affairs, Lester Pearson on October 30. Dulles told Pearson that the Hungarian situation was forcing the Soviet Union into "losing all credit"; however, due to the actions of U.S. allies the Secretary said "we [came] along with action as bad or worse."[34] Not only did the Suez Crisis clash with the global focus of Eisenhower's strategic framework, it also detracted from his ability to make gains at the expense of the Soviet Union.

As the conflict continued, Eisenhower again tried to influence the British and French prime ministers. On October 30, in response to the ultimatum issued by both nations, President Eisenhower wrote to Eden and French Prime Minister Guy Mollet stating, "I feel I must urgently express to you my deep concern at the prospect of this drastic action even at the very time when the matter is under consideration as it is today by the United Nations Security Council. It is my sincere belief that peaceful processes can and should prevail to secure a solution which will restore the armistice condition as between Israel and Egypt and also justly settle the controversy with Egypt about the Suez Canal."[35]

Eisenhower's main concern was in keeping the conflict from expanding in scope. He also saw U.S. credibility in the region at stake. Eisenhower intended to keep his commitment to protect any Middle Eastern nation from aggression. However, with U.S. allies now the aggressors in the region; maintaining fidelity to this promise stressed the ties between Eisenhower, Eden, and Mollet.

Neither the Egyptian nor Israeli forces abided by the ultimatum; as a result, the British and French moved to reoccupy the canal. On November 1, the British and French forces began bombing Egyptian targets in order to prepare for an invasion. By November 3, the bombing campaign destroyed the Egyptian air force. The destruction of the air assets allowed the ground phase of the operation to start sooner than planned. By November 5, elements of the invasion force were on the ground in Egypt and secured El Gamil airfield.

Eisenhower, though frustrated with the British action, still understood that eventually the Anglo-American alliance had return to good relations. In a letter written on November 3 to Lew Douglas, a personal friend, he discussed his understanding of the British actions. He told Mr. Douglas that he had "no intention of using the British Government as a whipping boy." The president believed that their actions were "stupid" and that Eden and the British allowed their "distrust and hatred of Nasser to blind their judgment." Eisenhower claimed that the British chose an inappropriate method to handle their problem. Eisenhower's understanding of the long-term value of the Anglo-American relationship was clear even in the middle of the military phase of the crisis. The president's high regard for the U.S.-U.K. alliance, though strained through the crisis, helped repair the relationship after the conflict died down.[36]

Two days later, in a letter to Dr. Eli Ginzberg, a professor Eisenhower became acquainted with while president of Columbia University, the president connected the Suez Canal Crisis and the Hungarian rebellion. He told Dr. Ginzberg that he recently received a telegram from a Hungarian national who claimed that the uprising was going well until the Suez Crisis. Eisenhower's Hungarian contact argued that the British, French, and Israeli actions "encouraged the Russians to come in and batter down the insurgents." Eisenhower told Dr. Ginzberg that significant events, like the uprising in Hungary or the Suez Crisis, reverberated throughout the world.[37]

The situation deteriorated further when the Soviet Union unsurprisingly chose to support Nasser. On November 5, Soviet Premier Nikolai Bulganin issued a statement that said that the Soviet Union would return

5. The Suez Crisis and Bermuda Conference Reconciliation

peace to the region even if it required Soviet military intervention. This increased the morale of the Egyptian military and gave them renewed enthusiasm for the conflict. Bulganin also contacted President Eisenhower and recommended that the Soviet Union and the United States join forces to bring peace back to the region.[38]

The military action ended quickly after the Soviet offer to join with U.S. forces or, failing that, to intervene unilaterally. Eisenhower, on November 5, worried that the Soviets were desperate and could possibly act as recklessly as Hitler did in the closing stages of World War II.[39] The following day, November 6, Admiral Radford commented that Soviet intervention would likely come in form of air strikes, as the Soviet Union did not have much capability to deploy its forces so far away from its bases. Radford thought that this made any serious intervention by the Soviets improbable. However, the geographic proximity of the USSR to the theater of operations indicates that it was possible for the Soviets to intervene with ground forces.[40]

On November 6, the date of the 1956 presidential election, the belligerents in the Suez Crisis agreed to a cease-fire. One of the first problems Eisenhower faced after the crisis was repairing the relations between the U.S. and its allies. Eisenhower told James Hagerty, his Press Secretary, and Admiral Radford that it was critical to repair the U.S.-U.K. relationship. Herbert Hoover, Jr., Under Secretary of State, asked if the president wanted to contact the French Prime Minister Guy Mollet as well. Eisenhower declined to call the French premier instead he decided to send a cable. The president only decided to contact Mollet after Hoover suggested that Eisenhower contact him because Mollet was certain to hear of the president's phone call to Eden.[41]

In the immediate aftermath of the crisis, Eisenhower first wanted to repair relation with Britain, France came as an afterthought. This was the likely path for events to take because of the close ties between the United Kingdom and the United States. Although Eisenhower did not agree with the Eden's actions, the president understood that he could not sacrifice the closest alliance that the U.S. had over the Suez Crisis. The fact that France did not receive the same focus on repairing its relations with America had second and third order effects as Eisenhower brought the Anglo-American alliance back to its pre–Suez state.

While French and British actions were problematic in the Middle East, their participation in the defense of Western Europe was extremely important. Repairing the Anglo-American alliance came much easier than those with France. Part of the process to repair U.S.-U.K. relationship was the Bermuda Conference held in March 1957. This summit meeting gave President Eisenhower and the new Prime Minister Harold Macmillan a chance to ease the tensions between their two nations. One significant outcome of the discussion was the formation of an agreement between the U.S. and the U.K. concerning the transfer of IRBMs to Britain. Eisenhower believed the IRBMs to be vitally important to the defense of the U.S. and its allies. He also described the conference as "by far the most successful international conference" since the meetings at the end of World War II."[42]

This process did not start at the Bermuda Conference; there was discussion about the implications of this decision prior to the meeting. The talks concerning the transfer of IRBMs began in early of 1957 and stirred up misgivings in the State Department. In a meeting between Defense Secretary Wilson and British Minister of Defense Duncan Sandys on January 28, 1957, the pair discussed guided missiles and decreased military expenditures. Both of these topics paralleled President Eisenhower's plans for the American military forces deployed to protect West Germany. According to Sandys, Britain needed to relieve the fiscal pressures of keeping large forces in Germany. In order to achieve this reduction, it needed to remove approximately 80,000 men from the British contingent. In addition to this, the British government proposed cutting its Second Tactical Air Force by over 200 aircraft, from 466 to 220. Sandys finished the discussion by turning to the subject of guided missile cooperation between the U.S. and the U.K. He said that this area was an example of effective collaboration. He wanted to continue this beneficial relationship between the two governments and improve upon them.[43]

The following day, January 29, Dulles and Sandys discussed the IRBM transfer agreement in more detail. Sandys told Dulles that the outlines of the potential agreement gave the British control over 4 squadrons of IRBMs with the nuclear warheads to remain in U.S. custody. He continued by saying that the structure of the agreement was like the one concerning V bombers and nuclear warheads. The British owned and operated the delivery vehicle but did not have possession of the atomic weapons. However, if the British developed their own nuclear warheads they retained ownership of the IRBMs, giving them a fully functioning nuclear ballistic missile weapon system.[44]

5. The Suez Crisis and Bermuda Conference Reconciliation

In reaction to the potential IRBM agreement between Britain and the U.S., Edwin Martin, the Alternate Permanent Representative on the North Atlantic Council (the primary political body in NATO), wrote a memorandum raising important questions about the implications of such an agreement. Martin wrote that the Defense Department representative, Acting Assistant Secretary of the Air Force for Research and Development Richard Horner, did not wait for State Department approval before agreeing with the British memorandum outlining the potential agreement. Martin's concern centered on the possible complications with giving the British such a powerful weapon system in the immediate aftermath of the Suez Canal Crisis. He cautioned that the agreement put forward gave them a free hand with the missiles.[45]

Martin also saw the early finalization of an IRBM agreement as giving up too much too soon in the rapprochement with the British. He advocated, in his memo, that agreeing prior to the Bermuda Conference prevented the U.S. from having the ability to communicate its policies at the highest levels and use these weapons for leverage with the British. He called the agreement to transfer the IRBMs to Britain key to the repairing of relations between the two nations. However, this meant that the U.S. should make the most of this opportunity and not squander it by agreeing to any proposal before it could garner the most successful terms.[46]

It was in the interests of both nations to improve their relationship. The question was how best to achieve this objective. The transfer of IRBMs allowed the British to have a sophisticated, although still not proven, guided missile capability. This was something that they currently lacked and did not want to commit financial resources to achieve.

President Eisenhower resolved the question of how to use the IRBMs in the Anglo-American relationship when he declined to approve the British proposal concerning the agreement. Eisenhower did not think it appropriate to make a decision with U.S. policy still at an early stage of development. Giving IRBMs to Britain was not an approved policy; it was only a National Security Council proposal. Eisenhower did not want his deputies making commitments before he made the decision to endorse such a program. He wanted to be ready to discuss the matter at the Bermuda Conference in March and until then, he would not agree to any position concerning the transfer of IRBMs to Britain.[47]

The transfer proposal and the discussions between Macmillan and Eisenhower during the Bermuda Conference provides insight into how these weapons worked to improve the nature of the U.S.-U.K. alliance. The president formally introduced the agreement in the early stages of the conference to the prime minister and by the end of the summit meeting both leaders announced the acceptance of the framework. In the coming months, U.S. and British diplomats worked together to hammer out the specifics of the agreement and start to put it into action.

One of the reservations President Eisenhower had about the agreement was the possibility that the accord committed the U.S. to missile production before it was ready. In a conversation in the opening stages of the Bermuda Conference the president spoke with his advisors about the state of American IRBM technology. Secretary of the Air Force Donald Quarles told Eisenhower that the agreement only required the U.S. to produce missiles when both the U.S. and U.K. agreed that they had a viable weapon. After that decision, the U.S. controlled the scale and timeline of production, not Britain.[48]

On March 22, 1957, in Bermuda, Eisenhower made the official offer of guided missiles, IRBMs, to Prime Minister Harold Macmillan. The president told the prime minister that much of the specifics of the agreement were still to come but he wanted to make the offer formally. Eisenhower continued by stating that the weapons were still in development and perhaps the missiles given would not be IRBMs but something of the same capability but different name.[49]

Eisenhower told Macmillan that the four squadrons of missiles would be deployed under this agreement. Two of the squadrons would be under U.S. control, while the other two would be under British control. As part of the agreement, the United States could change the missiles in the future for improved versions; if it became necessary. Eisenhower did not want anything specifically said about the IRBMs at the time, he only allowed a general reference to guided missiles in the communiqué issued after the Conference. Eisenhower did not intend this program to become widespread when discussed at the Bermuda Conference. The agreement also made clear that the British only owned two squadrons of missiles, although not the warheads.[50]

Harold Macmillan asked the president when the missiles would be ready. Eisenhower replied that he could only give estimates. His best information, he told Macmillan, was that the first missiles would arrive in July 1958, the first squadron in June 1958, and by July 1960, four squadrons. Macmillan stated that this information helped the U.K. determine whether

5. The Suez Crisis and Bermuda Conference Reconciliation

or not to continue its own research program for a long-range guided missile. If the missiles provided by the U.S. fit British defense needs then the U.K. could put more emphasis on other defense assets. Macmillan would not have made such comments if he were not confident about his ability to control the use of these weapons for British needs. If the prime minister thought that the weapons deployed by the U.S. only served American interests, there was no incentive to give up on researching a British missile. However, the promise of ownership of half of the planned IRBMs provided a strong guarantee that these weapons helped British ends.[51]

The discussion of IRBMs shifted to limiting nuclear testing as a method of preventing nuclear proliferation. Macmillan told Eisenhower that he thought that the test ban was important to prevent other nations from getting nuclear weapons. Eisenhower agreed and said that the expansion of atomic weapons was problematic. Stopping the proliferation of these assets was something that both the prime minister and the president supported as an effort to ensure the nuclear club did not expand its membership. Of course, this meant excluding another important European ally, France.[52]

In the afternoon session on March 22, the prime minister brought up the issue of the Western European Union (WEU) and the research and development of advanced weapons. The WEU was a group of seven European nations, including Britain and France that were also members of NATO. The WEU was a defense union, similar to NATO, but much more regionally focused. British Foreign Minister Selwyn Lloyd assured Eisenhower that the WEU weapons development program did not involve nuclear matters. President Eisenhower agreed and said he wanted to keep the existing U.S., Canada, and British cooperation concerning nuclear technology.[53]

On the next day, March 23, 1957, the British Foreign Minister Lloyd and U.S. Secretary of State Dulles had a conversation about nuclear proliferation. The two diplomats discussed the French effort to manufacture nuclear weapons. If successful, it would make France the fourth nation to have an atomic capability. Both ministers agreed that neither the British nor U.S. governments should openly or discreetly support the French effort. However, they also could not openly condemn such an effort, since France was an ally.[54]

The U.S. accepted and supported improving an independent British nuclear capability, as displayed by the offer of IRBMs. The possibility of

Eisenhower's Nuclear Calculus in Europe

France joining the nuclear group of nations presented an opportunity to deploy guided missiles even closer to the Soviet Union. This benefit did not seem to outweigh the potential problems associated with an independent French nuclear deterrent.

The exclusion of France from the group of nuclear nations soon caused problems in the European alliance. France didn't detonate its own nuclear weapon until 1960. Its weapons program was independent of the United States and the United Kingdom. The agreement to limit the expansion of nuclear weapons excluded France from gaining a very important national security asset and a prestige weapon, an independent nuclear deterrent.

Much of the problems between the United Kingdom and the United States concerning the Suez Crisis stemmed from the different strategic frameworks used by Eisenhower and Eden. The president measured the events, as well as the potential expansion, in terms of the global Cold War. Since his primary policy goal was avoiding a direct confrontation with the Soviet Union, the nationalization of the Suez Canal was hardly worth fighting a nuclear war to reverse. This focus on the global context made it difficult for Eisenhower to support Eden and the British position concerning the canal.

Similarly, Prime Minister Anthony Eden did not approach the nationalization crisis from the same point of view as Eisenhower. Eden wanted to maintain control of the British decolonization process; this required stopping Nasser from thumbing his nose in the face of British authority. Either, Eden stopped Nasser or he believed that the British Empire faced a rapid and uncontrolled collapse. While Eden did not want war, in the initial stages of the conflict, he did not feel that there were many other options to affirm British prestige and power in the region as much as a show of force. The regionally focused concentration of his assessment meant that Eisenhower and Eden had little common ground when discussing the threat posed by Nasser because each focused on different sets of ramifications of the Egyptian leader's actions. However, the British understood well the potential threat of the Soviet Union and Soviet power. Eden's actions were proof that he was willing to risk Soviet intervention because he judged the risk lower than Eisenhower and the costs of nonaction greater.

Although Eisenhower's global concentration on the Cold War was part of the reason for the tensions between the two nations concerning

5. The Suez Crisis and Bermuda Conference Reconciliation

the Suez Crisis, they were also a large part of the rapprochement in the Anglo-American alliance. Even during the crisis, Eisenhower knew that he had to work to reaffirm the U.S.-U.K. relationship because of its importance to defending Western Europe. His understanding of the Cold War was a doubled-edged sword for the United Kingdom; it could be detrimental in the short-term if the two nations approached an issue with divergent policies but in the long-term it ensured that the relationship with the U.S. endured. This was not the case with France, especially with the rise of Charles de Gaulle and his nationalistic aspirations for returning France to prominence both in the alliance and the world.

At the conclusion of the Bermuda Conference there was still much left to do to make the IRBM agreement a reality. The accord made clear that the alliance between the U.S. and the U.K. was improving. Eisenhower's hesitation to support an independent French nuclear weapons program expressed his concerns about the Franco-American alliance, especially when compared with the Anglo-American reaffirmed friendship. The work between U.S. and British diplomats to make the IRBM deployment a reality manifested the improved relationship between the two nations. Similarly, the actions of President Eisenhower and his advisors concerning France, combined with the resistance of Charles de Gaulle, revealed that the relationship between France and the U.S. still had serious complications.

6

A European Solution to an American Problem
Eisenhower's Initial Reaction to the Soviet Launch of Sputnik

On October 4, 1957, the Soviet Union launched the first artificial satellite into orbit. While the United States had a space program at the time, it was not yet capable of launching a satellite. This was a technological as well as a propaganda victory for the Soviet Union. The long-term impact of the *Sputnik* launch provided the impetus for the creation of NASA as well as other federal programs to advance science and technology; however, the short-term impact was less dramatic. In the months after *Sputnik*, President Eisenhower evaluated the military and political impact of the Soviet accomplishment. He initially showed some concern about the military implications, but the political ramifications soon became paramount. The Soviet satellite launch further reinforced the importance of the decision made early in 1957 to deploy IRBMs to Great Britain. This was a solution that answered domestic, not European, security concerns.

The United States satellite program at the time, Project Vanguard, did not plan for a payload as large as that of the Soviet *Sputnik*. Dr. Joseph Kaplan, head of the United States program for the International Geophysical Year, described the weight of the Soviet launch as incredible. Its weight of 184 pounds was over seven times as heavy as the projected 21 ½ pound American satellite. The U.S. program lagged behind the Soviet program in terms of capability and results.[1] Project Vanguard was not the only missile program capable of launching a satellite. The Army's Jupiter program already showed that it was possible to use that launch vehicle and put a

6. A European Solution to an American Problem

satellite into orbit but von Braun could not continue his research because of the bureaucratic restrictions placed upon him by President Eisenhower's decision to put control of the IRBM program in the hands of the Air Force.[2]

Another hurdle von Braun encountered was the resistance of the Vanguard project lead, John Hagen, to understand the urgency of the situation. Von Braun told astronomer John O'Keefe, who worked for the Army Engineer Corps, that he was willing to "paint 'Vanguard' right up the side of my rocket." O'Keefe replied that the he did not think that Hagen worried much about getting into space first and this led to the lack urgency in the Vanguard program. Von Braun responded, "If that's what he really thinks, will he for Christ's sake get out of the way of the people who think it makes a hell of a lot of difference!"[3]

Wernher von Braun served as the director of the Development Operations Division of the Army Ballistic Missile Agency and then later at the National Aeronautics and Space Agency (NASA). Von Braun's early experience with rockets came from his youth in Germany. During World War II, he was instrumental in building Germany's rocket program (National Aeronautics and Space Administration).

Von Braun did not speak out of hubris; his missile was indeed ready for launching a satellite. By the end of 1956, he had already achieved a height of six hundred miles; this was comparable to *Sputnik's* orbit of five-hundred and fifty-nine miles above the earth.[4] Von Braun again succeeded in achieving this altitude on August 8, 1957, when his team used a Jupiter C missile to test a redesigned nose cone. Von Braun had the ability to beat the Soviets but he did not have the blessing of the Air Force, which now controlled his missile program.

Dr. Wernher von Brown (left) and President Dwight D. Eisenhower discuss the Saturn V model. Von Brown was adamant that his team could produce a rocket capable of putting a satellite into orbit but he was unable to do so because of strict orders from his military bosses. His work was fundamental in creating the missile foundation for the Army with the Redstone and Jupiter missiles (National Aeronautics and Space Administration).

6. A European Solution to an American Problem

Eisenhower's understanding of the importance of getting to space first initially resembled Hagen's. Although he became frustrated when he realized that the United States had the capability to launch a satellite much earlier if it concentrated its resources on other rockets, prior to *Sputnik*, he did not want to risk involving military technology in order to assure a quick launch. Eisenhower changed his mind in the wake of *Sputnik*, but it required the realization that U.S. citizens worried about *Sputnik* much more than Eisenhower did.

The irony of the *Sputnik* situation was that it showed how advanced the Jupiter program was. After the Vanguard rocket failed to successfully launch a satellite, President Eisenhower gave his permission to use the Army's Jupiter C to launch America's first satellite, Juno I. The only change was the addition of a fourth active stage. Although von Braun and his Jupiter team clearly produced a superior missile, Eisenhower's decision to give authority over IRBM production to the Air Force meant that the Jupiter was a first-rate program with second-class status. Another influence was Eisenhower's resolution that the U.S. satellite program be free of military technology. This restriction was short-lived after the drama of the Soviet launch of *Sputnik*.

U.S. scientists expected the Soviets to launch a satellite; however, they were unsure of when the U.S.S.R. would do so. One reason for the lack of urgency was the different point of view of those in charge of the Vanguard program. Rear Admiral Rawson Bennet, who worked for the Office of Naval Research, the organization in charge of the U.S. satellite program, said he did not think that his program was in competition with the Soviet Union. He believed that the Vanguard Project did not need to change its schedule to have an earlier launch date.[5]

President Eisenhower's reaction to the launch at first was unimpressive. He and his senior administration officials did not understand the importance of the Soviet accomplishment. Eisenhower did not see it as a security risk. Of course, he had the benefit of U2 photo reconnaissance to prove to himself that the launch of the satellite and a Soviet ICBM were unrelated. The problem was that he could not communicate this intelligence to the people without divulging how he attained it.[6]

Although Eisenhower did not put much stock in the Soviet achievement, his people did. In a Gallup poll taken in in the week following *Sputnik*, the majority of respondents said that they believed that the Soviet Union was ahead of the U.S. in the development of missiles and long

(Left to right) Nina Kukharchuk Khrushchev, Mamie Eisenhower, Nikita Khrushchev, and President Dwight D. Eisenhower at a state in 1959 dinner celebrating the Soviet premier's visit to the United States. During Khrushchev's visit, he and President Eisenhower discussed the U2 overflights that, while frustrating for the Soviets, provided vital intelligence for the United States to discern the nature of the Soviet atomic threat. The IRBMs were part of the U.S. response to this threat (National Archives and Records Administration).

distance rockets.[7] Also, in November 1957, fifty-three percent of the respondents said that they believed that defense policies should change.[8] The majority U.S. residents did not agree with the initial interpretation of Eisenhower and his administration, they wanted action to address what they saw as a security issue. Many did not agree with Eisenhower when he said that there was nothing "significant in that development [*Sputnik*] as far as security is concerned."[9]

6. A European Solution to an American Problem

Eisenhower changed his initial reaction to the Soviet launch and by the end of the year he called for the expansion of the deployment of IRBMs to Western Europe. He intended this deployment to both answer the domestic security concerns as a result of *Sputnik* and as an attempt to change the nature of the U.S. security commitment to its NATO allies. This plan had significant ramifications with U.S. allies particularly Britain and France.

President Eisenhower understood that the U.S. government had to react to the Soviet's success. Eisenhower asked, in one of the first discussions of the launch on October 8, 1957, what the capabilities of the satellite were. He wondered if it had the ability to communicate any information in its signal. Deputy Secretary of Defense Donald Quarles said that the satellite could transmit its location according to what the Soviets said publicly about the satellite. However, Dr. Alan Waterman, director of the National Science Foundation, said that the *Sputnik* signal did have some modulation. However, he could not say whether this was by accident or was some attempt to code the communication from the satellite.[10]

Eisenhower did not want to make any drastic changes in reaction to the Soviet success for fear of giving the Soviets too much credit. In the conference about the launch on October 8, the talk turned to whether or not the United States should reorganize or speed up its launch program in order to get some surveillance vehicle quickly into orbit. Sherman Adams, Eisenhower's Chief of Staff, said that, in his opinion, the administration should not approach this project in a rushed manner. He said that the Soviets approached their program with a focus on speed, the U.S. did not. Adams characterized it as a project intended to enhance scientific understanding. Adams stated that the Soviets conducted their program in a hurried way with the goal of beating the United States. Eisenhower asked those present to think ahead five years and tell him what the U.S. would have in terms of surveillance capacity. Secretary Donald Quarles said that that Air Force had a research program with satellites as the end state.[11]

Sherman Adams' statements about the desire to altruistically transmit knowledge did not tell the entire story. Of course, there were issues of prestige involved, even if President Eisenhower did not see this as a serious problem, for the U.S. population the Soviets proved their superiority in guided missiles. This continued to affect Eisenhower's handling of the fallout of the launch through the rest of the 1957.

Eisenhower's questions, in his conversation with his Chief of Staff and other administration officials on October 8, relayed his concerns about the Soviet capacity to make some military use of their space program. However, he did not want to take dramatic action. Any quick changes in policies or programs from the United States suggested that there was a need to panic. Eisenhower did not want to give this impression and so chose not to discuss any radical alterations in the direction of U.S. research programs at that time.

The *Sputnik* launch was not all bad news. President Eisenhower believed that the Soviets had in fact contributed to the freedom of orbital space with their satellite. He called this launch a "good turn" because the satellite was in "orbital space ... which the missile is making an inoffensive passage." Eisenhower felt that *Sputnik* orbited in international space and so no nation could take action against it. He continued that this was an unintentional benefit of the *Sputnik* launch.[12]

The conversation then turned to what the United States had at that time that could launch a satellite into orbit. Secretary Quarles said that the Army's Redstone missile, which was undergoing a modernization program, was capable of launching a satellite. The Secretary made it clear that for over a year, the Redstone had the capability to launch a satellite. The Redstone missile, which was a tactical missile, had a range of 200 miles. The Jupiter missile was part of the Redstone family. However, it was capable of space flight, with some modifications. As an example, NASA used a Jupiter missile for the first stage of its booster rockets. The first sub-orbital flights, which took place in 1961, used Mercury-Redstone boosters.[13]

However, the U.S. did not take advantage of its military missile programs because the Scientific Advisory Council, chaired by Dr. James Killian, recommended that the U.S. not mix military and civilian research programs. Secretary Quarles continued that the council thought that this made the peaceful intentions of the American program clear to the international community. Also, since the project involved international scientists, any military technology used posed greater security risks and inhibited the cooperative spirit of the program. President Eisenhower cautioned that members of Congress would wonder why the U.S. did not try to launch a satellite sooner, since it clearly had the capability. He then stated that he did not think that the date of launching a satellite was as important as ensuring that international scientists had the opportunity to gain from the U.S. program.[14]

6. A European Solution to an American Problem

The Soviet launch did not interrupt Eisenhower's efforts to rein in spending. In a Cabinet meeting on October 11, 1957, the Cabinet talked about how to cut the defense budget from the fiscal year 1957 high of $43 billion. Secretary Quarles presented information about the personnel reductions planned for the fiscal year 1958, which began in October 1957. He said that the first quarter reductions accomplished 20 percent of the yearly goal.[15]

Eisenhower, in the immediate aftermath of the *Sputnik* launch, did not radically change his perception of the security situation. It did not invalidate the U.S. strategic manned bomber force nor did it require a quick change of emphasis to replace manned aircraft with guided missiles. Following the discussion of personnel cuts the Cabinet then discussed Congressional cuts in defense spending. The president said that the legislative appropriations were below what the administration asked for. Eisenhower stated that the Defense department had to continue to pursue missiles as well as maintain manned aircraft. He still thought that the goals he entered office with in 1952, decreasing defense spending with new technology, were still viable and worth striving for.[16]

Eisenhower pushed the Cabinet to focus on the long-term economic viability of the nation. He did not want to sacrifice the strength of the U.S. economy to the U.S.S.R., although there were significant defense issues that the nation had to face. Ideally, Eisenhower said, he wanted to have a surplus in the budget in order to reduce taxes in the event of an economic slump in the coming year. If he were able to do this, he thought it had a beneficial "psychological value."[17]

President Eisenhower actually planned to resist pressure from Congress to increase defense spending in the coming year. He told his Cabinet that the administration had to ensure that it defused new legislative initiatives to increase defense spending in light of *Sputnik*. Eisenhower recommended to his Cabinet officers that the administration submit a budget that contained "the costs of those programs which the Administration wished to carry and excluded those it was forced by Congress to carry." Eisenhower wanted to clearly communicate where he intended to focus his fiscal resources and demonstrate to Congress how the administration planned to proceed. If legislators increased defense spending it made it difficult for the president to maintain the defense spending ceiling of $38 billion he wanted.[18]

Another reason for Eisenhower's relative calm after the launch was the U-2 spy plane. This aircraft had the ability to fly over Soviet territory and take photos of missile sites. The program became operational in 1956. Eisenhower understood more about Soviet capabilities than he could publicly disclose. If he let the U.S. people know what the U-2 program uncovered then the Soviets would know what U.S. intelligence capabilities were.[19]

Eisenhower had access to information about the Soviet missile capability. He understood, although not with perfect clarity, that the Soviet capability was not far superior to that of the United States and in many cases was equal or inferior to U.S. capabilities. This information, however, was still classified. This was one of the reasons why Eisenhower's reaction to the *Sputnik* launch seemed so out of touch with the general public's reaction. He did not see it as much of a security concern because he had a more accurate assessment of what the Soviets were capable of, most citizens did not. This disconnect soon forced Eisenhower's hand into expediting the deployment of IRBMs to Western Europe.[20]

In a meeting outside of the Cabinet meeting on the same day, October 11, the president discussed missile research with Secretary of Defense McElroy. Eisenhower wanted to make sure that the first priority of the IRBM program was to have a successful missile test. He wanted a missile that hit its intended target and reached the prescribed range. Concerns such as how to deploy the missile or which service owned it were of lesser importance to him. The president also suggested that there should be a fourth service, apart from the Army, Air Force, or Navy to control missile functions. He thought that this would prevent many of the service rivalries that he said detracted from the important work being done on guided missiles.[21]

Eisenhower's suggestion about creating a fourth service never materialized. However, it did make clear how serious he was about maintaining a focus on guided missiles. He thought that having individual services control such important weapons programs divided both the branches of the military and their resources. In the aftermath of *Sputnik*, guided missiles were still important and the IRBM program represented one of the more successful programs. Although the IRBM project, both the Jupiter and Thor variants, had successful test launches they had yet to have full-scale test flights that checked their guidance systems and the ability of the missile to transport a payload to the proper range.

Sputnik caused several discussions immediately following the launch; however, there were other issues that Eisenhower faced. One problem was the relationship between the United Kingdom and the United States. In preparation for a visit from the British Prime Minister Harold Macmillan,

6. A European Solution to an American Problem

the president and the Secretary of State talked about what to bring up during the visit. Although *Sputnik* was not part of the conversation, which focused on nuclear issues, the influence of the *Sputnik* impacted the discussion about the close relationship between the U.S. and the U.K. Specifically, the IRBM issue, which was a central part of the planned meeting.

Secretary of State Dulles discussed the diplomatic problems that faced the United States in its policies in Western Europe and NATO. He said that the changing character of warfare in the nuclear age made America's allies want atomic weapons. Dulles told Eisenhower that since the U.S. was clearly telling its allies that these types of weapons were increasingly becoming part of the conventional spectrum of available military weapons, it was more difficult to prevent or discourage U.S. allies from attaining them. Dulles wanted to close the agreement concerning the deployment of IRBMs to the U.K. and then work on extending it to other nations. He thought that the U.S. presented its allies with an unacceptable situation, that nuclear weapons, specifically IRBMs, were going to be a major part of the defense plan for Western Europe yet they could not have these weapons for their own defense.[22]

During the discussion, Eisenhower voiced his hopes that the U.S. and U.K. could work more closely together on defense issues. He also stressed the fact that the U.S. and the British were the only nations in the alliance with nuclear weapons. Eisenhower said that this was one reason why the two nations should collaborate in order to help the whole alliance. Dulles cautioned the president about making close cooperation between the two nations too prominent at the risk of alienating other NATO allies. This tension between the Anglo-American relationship and its effect on the NATO alliance as a whole continued to be a problem as the deployment of IRBMs came to fruition.[23]

Secretary Dulles proceeded to discuss what he felt were the British intentions for this visit. He said that the prime minister hoped to solidify the relationship between the United Kingdom and the United States. Dulles thought that this was potentially problematic; since such an affirmation could upset relations with other European allies, if Eisenhower made it obvious how unique the relationship between the two nations were. The president, in contrast, hoped to communicate to the U.S. people the importance of IRBMs in the nation's security as well as in the security of its allies. He also wanted to make it clear to the U.S. public that the it was not possible to continue to deny these weapons to its NATO allies.[24]

Eisenhower's Nuclear Calculus in Europe

Eisenhower wanted to use the British deployment and subsequent European deployments of IRBMs to reassure the U.S. public of its safety in the missile age. The Soviets demonstrated with *Sputnik* that they had the ability to launch a missile that could reach the U.S. Eisenhower knew that the U.S. did not have such a capability but IRBMs offered the same capacity with bases in Western Europe. This fit with the emphasis of the New Look defense policy's focus on decreasing defense spending by concentrating resources on technologically sophisticated but less manpower intensive solutions to defense issues. It also fit with President Eisenhower's understanding of warfare in the atomic age; these weapons provided the strategic deterrent that would prevent Soviet military incursions into Western Europe.

The next day, October 23, Eisenhower received a memo from Bernard Baruch, a close personal friend and advisor to the president, concerning the domestic impact of the *Sputnik* launch. Baruch wrote that the American people worried about the security implications of the Soviet satellite. However, he also thought that this put the U.S. population in a position to support defense measures intended to restore the balance between U.S. and Soviet military capabilities. Baruch told Eisenhower that he must make sure that Secretary of Defense McElroy drove the missile program ferociously. He compared the need for dedication in missile research to the need for rubber in World War II. He wrote that if it were necessary the "impossible" had to become possible with this program.[25]

At the close of the Bermuda Conference earlier that year, the two parties released a statement declaring the intent to deploy U.S. missile to the U.K. Although the press release did not specify the IRBM as the missiles a story printed in March 1957 made it clear that these were the missiles from the Bermuda Agreement.[26] However, making this a reality was difficult. When discussing the deployment with General Goodpaster, Eisenhower stated his frustration with the legal niceties involved in the transfer. He said that one of the important aspects of an alliance was the confidence each nation had in the other. If the U.S. did not engage in a "liberal exchange" of information then he did not think they were living up to the spirit of the alliance. He hoped that the new agreement would resemble the Quebec Agreement that defined the Anglo-American cooperation in nuclear matters during World War II. Specifically, he said that each side "should be able to expect to receive whatever the other has."[27]

This meeting did not set any specific policy. However, Eisenhower made his views on the matter clear. If the U.S. worried too much about

6. A European Solution to an American Problem

the legal minutia of such an agreement it destroyed the very thing that such an agreement was supposed to create, a healthy spirit of cooperation between the two nations. The relationship with the British was clearly important to Eisenhower. Although Secretary Dulles previously counseled against becoming too close to the British because of the risk of alienation of the other NATO allies, Eisenhower still felt that there was much benefit in renewing a special relationship with the United Kingdom. This close alliance included significant sharing of atomic information, if Eisenhower got his way.

The British alliance was not the only important issue discussed in the wake of *Sputnik*. In a conference concerning NATO, on October 26, the former U.S. representative to the organization Ambassador George Perkins conveyed the member nations' concerns about the security of Western Europe. Perkins said that many European nations worried about the decreasing presence of U.S. soldiers. They believed that this was a sign of America's lack of commitment to the alliance. They feared that as the U.S. and the Soviet Union approached an atomic stalemate the U.S. would be less willing to engage the Soviets in combat. Eisenhower countered that the U.S. forces in Europe at the time were more powerful than before. He said that he entered office with the idea of using smaller but more powerful military formations. This increased firepower came from innovations like the IRBM and tactical nuclear weapons. The president referenced the new pentomic divisions deployed to Europe that, while smaller, had more striking power than a traditional division. Eisenhower then vented his frustrations with the U.S. budgetary process. He said it was troubling that military forces manifested themselves only in terms of manpower and not in actual strength. U.S. divisions did not decrease but the new formations had less men assigned.[28]

This consternation about how to measure military power frustrated Eisenhower throughout his implementation of the New Look defense policy. He believed that military formations under his administration were more effective because of their reliance on atomic weapons. However, Eisenhower worried, as shown above, that many focused on the total number of soldiers in a military unit and then used that to calculate the fighting power on the battlefield. The president preferred to relate military power "on the basis of units and their combat power."[29] A missile unit was much more powerful than the sum of its individual soldiers. The president did not see his policy as weakening any military formation. Rather, his New

Eisenhower's Nuclear Calculus in Europe

Look program provided these formations the ability to defeat Soviet forces for less cost. This proved a hard sell to the New Look's critics both at home and abroad.

The discussion then turned to atomic weapons and their role in future conflicts between the Soviets and the NATO alliance. Ambassador Perkins said that the European nations worried about the staying power of U.S. forces in Europe. Eisenhower stated that the presence of U.S. troops in Europe was not a permanent policy. However, he also understood that the U.S. had a commitment to act to protect NATO from Soviet advances, which he would honor as long he was in office. He continued by saying that the atomic capability of U.S. forces was part of that guarantee. Eisenhower wanted "no doubt as long as he [held] his present responsibilities. Atomic weapons would be used in case of attack." U.S. forces represented the U.S. guarantee to protect Europe, no matter how small the actual number of troops present.[30]

NATO integration also came up in the discussion as well. Eisenhower did not think it was profitable for each nation to work toward a self-contained force. Instead, NATO should operate as a consolidated whole. This approach allowed for greater efficiency in using resources and eliminated the waste of each nation duplicating efforts in fielding similar forces.[31]

The problem with this idea was that it asked NATO nations to do something that the U.S. and British governments were unwilling to do, stop pursuing advanced weapons, particularly atomic weapons. The view that NATO nations should accept the U.S. and British atomic monopoly as beneficial was problematic. It also demonstrated that the special relationship between the U.S. and the U.K. interfered with NATO relations as a whole. The U.S. wanted to offer an atomic umbrella to protect NATO. However, the intent of this protection was to frustrate any effort for an independent atomic program, unless that nation was the United Kingdom. There were clearly two levels of membership in NATO, atomic members and those nations not part of the atomic club.

Sputnik, while not directly discussed in this conversation, was still important. The U.S. public worried about the security implications of the Soviet launch. However, for European nations the main concern was the presence of U.S. troops and the promise that they represented. Western European nations lived under the threat of Soviet missile, bomber, and ground forces assault, so *Sputnik* did not radically alter their perception

6. A European Solution to an American Problem

of security. Getting more nuclear weapons to Western Europe was part of Eisenhower's response to NATO member states' worries but it did not directly address their primary concern, the continued presence of U.S. ground forces. Deploying nuclear capable guided missiles targeted the domestic security concerns of U.S. citizens. *Sputnik* sent two different messages one to the U.S. people and another to the Western European public.

The subject of force cuts came up again two days later, October 28, 1957, in a discussion concerning NATO. Eisenhower understood that the U.S. could not drastically reduce its manpower in Western Europe. It had to slowly and cautiously reduce troop strength and ensure that its allies agreed, or at least didn't object to, these cuts. The president said that the cuts would not decrease the 5 divisions and 4 regiments currently stationed in theater. However, the cuts would reduce headquarters units. Also, with the addition of missiles, much of the U.S. tactical air units could redeploy to the United States. These cuts would not decrease the fighting power of its forces in NATO, according to Eisenhower. He also understood the importance of allowing General Norstad, the Supreme Allied Commander in Europe, to determine how best to make these cuts. The Defense Department provided guidance but it was up to General Norstad to make them a reality.[32]

On October 29, the president discussed the possibility of a Soviet ICBM with Dr. Isidor Rabi, a Noble Laureate and professor of physics at Columbia University, where President Eisenhower previously served as president. Dr. Rabi said that the Soviets would have an ICBM soon, as well as a warhead for such a weapon. The conversation also covered whether or not the U.S. should push to halt nuclear testing. Dr. Rabi said that the time to stop testing was prior to the Soviet Union's detonation of its thermonuclear device; however, this already occurred in 1953. He said that if the U.S. continued to test new weapons and allowed the Soviet Union to do so also it meant that both nations were now in competition to improve their respective nuclear arsenals.[33]

Although European security was important, it was one of many competing interests that the president dealt with in the immediate aftermath of *Sputnik*. The subject of the U.S. launching a satellite came up again on October 30, 1957. Eisenhower expressed frustration at the suggestion of adding the Jupiter rocket to the Vanguard program in order to launch a satellite sooner. Although the president agreed with the recommendation, he reminded the Secretary of Defense that he had suggested the same thing 18 months prior. However, at that time, the Department of Defense, then under Charles Wilson, counseled against such a combination of civilian and military programs. The current Secretary, Neil McElroy, agreed that combining the programs meant that it transformed the nature of Vanguard; it would no longer be a purely civilian program.[34]

This represented a change not only in schedule of a U.S. satellite launch but also a change in the necessity to keep such a program purely civilian and open. The Soviet advance, although not publicly admitted, did have an influence on the decision to accelerate the U.S. satellite program. Secretary McElroy saw a way to prevent such a jarring change in the public sphere by announcing the addition of Jupiter as a secondary option for launching a satellite. However, this secondary option became the launch vehicle for the first U.S. satellite on January 31, 1958.[35]

The U.S. military response to *Sputnik* relied on IRBMs, principally the Army's Jupiter program. This weapon system was capable of carrying a satellite into orbit before the civilian booster was ready. This proved the success of the Army's rocket development, which was largely a result of its service's capitalization of German scientists such as Wernher von Braun. Although the launch of a U.S. satellite did not directly influence the Western European security situation, it did announce to the U.S. public that the Soviet Union's lead in the space race was not insurmountable.

One issue that the Soviet success brought closer to home was the damage of a nuclear attack. President Eisenhower and his administration already started planning for such an event prior to October 1957 but *Sputnik* gave such efforts more relevance. In a conference on November 4, 1957, the members of the Gaither Committee presented their findings to the president. Formed in April 1957, this committee had the task of assessing the destruction of a Soviet atomic strike in terms of nuclear fallout and blast damage. Several members of the advisory panel came to the conference to discuss their findings with the president; these members were retired military officers, elite businessmen, and university faculty.

The conversation also included the committee's estimates of the future Soviet threat and what they thought the nation should do to stop it. The group told the president that the nature of the Soviet threat came from the growing military might of the Soviet Union, in terms of their technology. They advocated that proper metric was megatons. This view meshed well with Eisenhower's perception of modern warfare. It also

6. A European Solution to an American Problem

downplayed the ability of the Soviet Union to call up much larger number of soldiers than the United States. While putting the threat purely in terms of atomic yield made it more dramatic, it also framed the problem in terms of a conflict that the United States could win, at least in the mid–1950s.[36]

Unstated in this discussion was what the U.S. would actually win if it were victorious in a general atomic war with the Soviet Union. After a large nuclear barrage, especially one that contained hydrogen bombs, there would be massive destruction in both human lives and social infrastructure. Depending on the number of missiles and bombers unleashed there would be catastrophic damage to major population centers on both sides and those who did not die in the initial attack would have to struggle with the radioactive fallout and reconstruction. Such a victory could well be pyrrhic.

Sputnik, in Eisenhower's view, did not immediately upset the strategic balance of power between the U.S. and the Soviet Union. He said, in the conference with the Gaither Committee members, that strategic bombers would still be the key to U.S. nuclear superiority over the Soviets. However, the U.S. risked falling behind the Soviets, in the near future, even though he was more confident over the long term. The president saw his main duty in the next five years as convincing the U.S. population of the importance of making the required effort to stay ahead of the Soviets. This education had to focus on the specific technological and scientific necessities to defeat or, at least, be more effective than the Soviet Union.[37]

Throughout his time as president, Eisenhower continued to focus on the long-term security problems of the United States. His understanding of how to fight war in the atomic age required establishing a far reaching program of innovation and advances in order to reform the U.S. military into a force ready to fight on the nuclear battlefield. The launch of *Sputnik* did not alter his thinking concerning the importance of advanced weapons and strategic force projection in U.S. defenses. If anything, it actually made these elements more important since many in the U.S. saw this as a direct threat to the continental United States.

The committee told Eisenhower that they expected casualties of close to 50 percent in a Soviet ICBM strike on the U.S. They did not think that the U.S. deterrent force was adequate to prevent a Soviet ICBM attack. The committee recommended deploying IRBMs in 1959 in order to have some type of deterrent to the expected Soviet ICBM threat expected to come online that year.[38]

Eisenhower's Nuclear Calculus in Europe

The president replied that he thought that group overstated the U.S. vulnerabilities in some areas. He felt that the Soviet Union was at a disadvantage because of its central position, in relation to the United States and the free world. The free world, Eisenhower said, held the peripheral positions and this allowed it to disperse its strategic weapons yet concentrate them on the Soviet Union. The Soviet Union did not have the same advantage. Eisenhower said he still thought that the policy of Massive Retaliation should be the basis of U.S. and NATO defense strategy.[39]

Although *Sputnik* exposed the Soviet Union's recent advances in its ability to project power strategically. This new capability did not cause the president to question his policy of Massive Retaliation to deter Soviet aggression. Although the Gaither Committee reported that the U.S. could fall behind the Soviet Union and was still vulnerable in many aspects, Eisenhower maintained his conviction that U.S. defense forces continued to pose a significant threat, at least for the time being, to the Soviet Union. *Sputnik* demonstrated the U.S. deficiencies in its missile program. From the beginning of his administration, Eisenhower wanted to focus on missile development. *Sputnik* did put more focus on the IRBM program in two ways. First, by developing a viable weapons system the U.S. decreased the necessity for large ground units. This improved Eisenhower's effort to reduce defense costs, in theory. Secondly, a successful IRBM program, Eisenhower hoped, could boost the confidence of the U.S. population about the ability of their military to prevent or counter an attack by Soviet missiles. This second issue was a concern that Eisenhower's advisers told him existed but they did not have much real evidence to back up the claim that the U.S. public cared much about the progress of their nation's guided missile program.

The successes and failures of the U.S. missile program were not secret. Several days after *Sputnik*, *The New York Times* ran an article discussing recent advances that the U.S. missile projects made. It also discussed the reason why the Secretary of Defense still wanted two different missiles fielded and researched. Although the specifics of each program remained classified, successful test firing and range estimation did not receive the same secrecy.[40]

In a meeting on November 6, the president met with members of the Joint Chiefs of Staff and the Secretary of Defense. Eisenhower said that his three previous conferences that day convinced him that the U.S. citizens had great concern about their security because of the rivalry between

6. A European Solution to an American Problem

the services. Eisenhower said he thought "that our people now believe the services are more interested in the struggle with each other than against an outside foe. He said the people in Defense must give their heart to national interests and welfare." The president thought that the security problems facing the U.S. were also part of the problem not only the inter service rivalry. He cautioned that the correct response to *Sputnik* was a measured one, neither too strong nor too weak. Eisenhower reminded the chiefs that their main consideration should be on a joint national defense against the Soviet Union, not in ensuring the best conditions for their particular service.[41]

Although Eisenhower said that he worried about the concerns that the U.S. public had about inter-service rivalry the only evidence he had of such a problem was from those within the administration. There is little evidence that the public worried about the struggles between the military services. However, Eisenhower's overall concern was that this inter-service rivalry prevented the services from effectively cooperating to provide the national defense. The doubts he had about the unity of the U.S. military affected his relationship with service Chiefs of Staff, especially those who were not sufficiently supportive of the president's agenda such as the Army Chief of Staff General Taylor.

The nature of U.S. retaliatory forces, and by implication, the ability of the U.S. military to protect it was the subject of a conference following a National Security Council meeting on November 7, 1957. This conference dealt with the ability of the U.S. Air Force's Strategic Air Command (SAC) to adequately scramble its planes in response to an early warning of an impending Soviet attack. Robert Sprague, advisor to the NSC on continental defense issues, gave the findings of the report to the president and select members of the NSC as well as the leadership from the Air Force. Sprague said he calculated that the Soviet Union needed approximately 240 aircraft to hit all of America's 60 counter-attack positions. He said that the Soviets had more than enough aircraft available for this type of operation. The problem with the U.S. response forces was the concentration of Soviet air-defense assets at the proposed Soviet targets. He said that the U.S. could launch up to 150 counter strike weapons. However, due to the integrated and effective nature of Soviet air-defenses this meant that the Air Force could not guarantee the effectiveness of a U.S. counter strike.[42]

Sprague continued that SAC's other major problem was the inability to quickly get its aircraft in the air. He said that during a surprise inspection he found that SAC could not get any of its planes in the air within 6 hours, excluding those already in the air for testing purposes. Of course, any aircraft in flight at the time of an attack might not necessarily have the required weapons loaded or fuel capacity to be part of an effective counterattack.[43]

Another concern Sprague had was the lack of overseas deployment of strategic assets, specifically bombers. He said that his information revealed that there was no significant presence of U.S. strategic bombers outside the continental U.S. Any overseas base was only a post-strike base, meaning that after the planes launched their initial counterattack, they would use these bases to land, refit and refuel. However, while on the ground at these bases, these planes were vulnerable due to a lack of effective radar facilities to detect a Soviet attack on overseas bases.[44]

As Sprague made clear, there were significant problems with the U.S. ability to launch a counter-attack from American soil. The IRBM program, with its focus on European deployment, would alleviate some of these issues. IRBMs deployed to Europe would provide a relatively quick and ready response force to a Soviet attack. Such a deployment would answer both the domestic and international security concerns raised as a result of the *Sputnik* launch. IRBMs would provide a remedy for the inability of the U.S. military to adequately deter a Soviet attack on the continental United States as well as address the significant amount of money that the nation spent defending its Western European allies.

Eisenhower, in a letter to his close friend Swede Hazlett, written on November 18, 1957, commented on the fears he felt the U.S. people held concerning *Sputnik* and the Soviet Union. He wrote that many worried about the supposed superiority of the Soviet Union. One problem Eisenhower identified in the letter was his inability to publicly speak about many of the things that could reduce these concerns.[45]

Eisenhower did not want to publicly discuss many of the coming advances in U.S. military technology. Although this would give him some political relief from charges of his inaction in the wake of *Sputnik*, he did not think it was prudent to tip his hand to the Soviets. That was the burden of the Commander-in-Chief, he knew many secrets but if he used them for his short-term political gain he could endanger the future security of the United States. Eisenhower, of course, had the benefit of this crisis coming during his second term, so he did not have to face the problem of running on his record. However, this does not discount the fact that he showed

6. A European Solution to an American Problem

great restraint in keeping intelligence secrets instead of divulging information to counter his critics who claimed he did not act forcefully enough to defend the United States.

This concern for public perception came up again during a phone call with Secretary of Defense Secretary McElroy concerning funding for guided missiles and the anti-missile weapon system. Eisenhower thought the new figures were too high. He thought that the people might infer that previous efforts were not enough, if the programs required such a dramatic increase in funding in the wake Soviet advances. The president also said that his science advisors related to him that the problem was not merely money and that significantly more money was not a panacea for the technical problems facing these programs. The Defense Secretary countered that if the U.S. intended to deploy these weapons to its European allies, including the British, the budgets for missiles had to increase dramatically.[46] This increased pressure for missiles in Europe came again the next day during a conversation with the Secretary of State. The president said that he had several people telling him that both the State and Defense Departments wanted to put missiles in Europe more quickly. Dulles agreed with the president that there was a need to speed up the planned deployment of guided missiles to Europe.[47]

IRBMs and ICBMs, at their inception, represented a way to reduce expenditures on costly ground forces. However, as the Secretary McElroy's concerns revealed, this was not true by the end of the decade. These weapons required significant outlays in defense spending and the administration was unable to fully realize its reductions in ground forces because of the political reasons discussed earlier. By 1957, the United States spent $11.8 billion on military missile research and production, at a time when the entire defense budget was $45 billion. This was the equivalent of 102 billion in 2017 inflation adjusted dollars.[48] However, Eisenhower could not change the paradigm of the New Look national security strategy because he spent too much political effort defining the U.S. position in terms of technological advances relative to the Soviet Union. It also went against his understanding of what the U.S. needed to do in order to succeed in preventing war and, if necessary, fighting a successful war in the atomic age.

The president presented more formal plans for advancing the deployment of IRBMs to Europe in a bi-partisan Congressional meeting on December 3, 1957, held at the White House. Secretary Dulles outlined 4 important points that the administration planned to present at the next NATO meeting. The first was an atomic stockpile under the control of Supreme Allied Commander Europe (SACEUR), a U.S. four-star general. No nuclear warheads would change hands but it required the transfer of some nuclear capable weapons for training NATO forces. Dulles did not think that this needed a change in the McMahon Act and he referenced a JCS report that outlined their justification for the program and why it fell in line with the current legislation.[49]

The second issue that Dulles spoke about was the expanded program to offer IRBMs to all NATO nations that wanted them. This program, Dulles explained, was in accord with what the administration agreed to with the British at the Bermuda Conference earlier in the summer. It required that the nations that wanted IRBMs to make the preparations, mainly to build the infrastructure to support the missiles, in order for the U.S. to agree to deploy them. The third issue brought up was the scientific research program, which was a cooperative research initiative in order to make the most of the physical and intellectual resources in Europe for atomic research. This research potentially benefited every NATO member state and was to be open to all of them. However, this nuclear research did not include the transfer of any nuclear weapons technology; its intent was peaceful research and not to expand the number of nations with atomic weapons.[50]

The final program discussed intended to improve the NATO nation's ability to manufacture "advanced weapons." This excluded the nuclear warheads of the weapons it only included the actual delivery system or other conventional component of the weapon system. Under this proposal, NATO nations still had to rely on the U.S. for providing and authorizing the use of nuclear warheads, since by law the U.S. could not allow other nations to control its nuclear weapons.[51]

These programs focused on NATO as a whole. However, the superior position of Britain became clear later in the discussion concerning nuclear weapons cooperation. Director of the Atomic Energy Commission, Lewis Strauss, told the Congressional delegation that the U.S. would not give away its most secret atomic designs. However, he did say that the administration may seek to change the legislation to allow this in some specific issues. One issue he wanted dealt with under an amendment was the acquisition of plutonium for France. This opened the opportunity for President Eisenhower to offer some assistance to René Coty, the president of

6. A European Solution to an American Problem

France, without giving the French concrete support in building a nuclear weapon. More importantly, Strauss said that the administration sought an amendment to allow for more collaboration between the U.S., U.K., and Canada. This requested change did not apply to any other nations. This demonstrated that the Bermuda Conference improved the strained relationship between the United States and the United Kingdom. The special alliance continued and it influenced atomic cooperation between the two nations.[52]

Strauss explained why Eisenhower wanted to improve the atomic cooperation between the British and the U.S. He told the legislators that the combined atomic stockpile of the two nations greatly exceeded that of the Soviet Union. However, the lack of formal cooperation meant that both nations duplicated certain efforts. In order to make this relationship more effective and make the combined stockpile more efficient, the administration needed some legislative changes.[53]

One of the final issues discussed was the influence of *Sputnik* on the defense budget. Secretary McElroy said that the launch did cause the administration to reassess the nature of its budget allocations. He continued that the actual expenditures increased, in order to accommodate increased research and production of missiles. However, these increases set the conditions for an eventual reduction in ground forces. He reminded the delegation that they should not think of the power of the U.S. military only in terms of the number of soldiers. Rather, increased sophistication and striking power provided by new weapons had the same defense capability as older force structures.[54]

At the end of the 1957, in the wake of *Sputnik*, Eisenhower still favored atomic weapons and that the paradigm of nuclear warfare as the dominant form of future wars was still foremost in the president's security plans. In light of *Sputnik*, defense spending increased but, as Secretary McElroy explained, Eisenhower continued to believe that this would allow future decreases in defense spending. In the wake of the Soviet launch U.S. allies became more important. The IRBM program expanded to include any willing NATO nation and not just the U.K. However, the program extended to NATO nations placed the missiles inside European nations without the concessions concerning the control of the missiles that the British government received. This answered the domestic security concerns that *Sputnik* raised as well as provide an opportunity for the president to restructure U.S. defense commitment to Western Europe.

Eisenhower's Nuclear Calculus in Europe

President Eisenhower, in the aftermath of *Sputnik*, did not take dramatic action. He realized that many in the U.S. perceived the Soviet advances as proof in the inadequacy of the U.S. in the technology and military power. However, he did not act rashly. Rather, Eisenhower chose to advance the only viable atomic weapons program that fit his understanding of what modern warfare required, the IRBM. It was the only missile system the U.S. had available that had some hope of being ready relatively soon. It also had the range to attack targets deep inside the Soviet Union, if deployed in Europe. The problem was getting these weapons ready for deployment and in getting NATO nations, other than the U.K. to accept them.

7

U.S.-U.K. IRBM Agreement

After the Suez Crisis, the relationship between the United States and the United Kingdom suffered strains. The Franco-American alliance was also put under stress during the crisis. The Bermuda Conference in 1957 did much to restore the relationship between the U.S. and the U.K. However, notably absent from the conference was France.

During the conference, President Eisenhower made an offer to deploy IRBMs to Britain. Under this agreement the British owned the missiles but the U.S. maintained control of the warheads. Also offered was an expansion of Anglo-American cooperation in field of nuclear weapons research.

In response to the Soviet launch of *Sputnik*, President Eisenhower offered IRBMs to NATO as a whole. However, the character of the bilateral agreement between the U.S. and the U.K. was fundamentally different from the subsequent NATO agreement offered to the alliance. The U.S.-U.K. agreement was outside of the NATO framework, it was purely a joint agreement between two nations each with independent nuclear arsenals. The other NATO agreements proposed by the U.S. were bilateral but still fell under NATO authority.

Two reasons for Eisenhower's offer of IRBMs to Britain showed the differences between nations in the NATO alliance. One was that Britain already had its own nuclear weapons program. The other was the affinity that Eisenhower had for the British and the special relationship between the two allies. These two issues allowed Britain to become first among equals in the NATO alliance, relative to the other European nations.

Britain, as the only other nation in NATO to have its own nuclear capability, saw the New Look defense policy framework as a viable path forward for balancing its security and fiscal needs. As Britain continued to define security in terms of nuclear power it sought to separate itself and the U.S. into the top tier of the NATO alliance. The unique bilateral agreement concerning IRBMs that the British and the U.S. agreed to support this perception. British white papers and discussions between President Eisenhower and Prime Minister Macmillan displayed the influence of the president's conception of modern war and the New Look defense policy on British security policy.

The Anglo-American IRBM agreement did cement a rapprochement between the U.S. and U.K. after the Suez Crisis, but it also solidified a two-tier alliance inside of NATO. The two nations with independent nuclear weapons occupied the first tier of member states. Those nations without an independent nuclear capacity found themselves relegated to the bottom tier of the alliance. They had to accept the offer of IRBMs under NATO or not receive any IRBMs in their nation at all.

In order to understand why Britain agreed to accept Eisenhower's offer of IRBMs in 1958 it is important to know how nuclear weapons fit in the British national defense plan. In April 1957, the British government published a white paper titled "Defence: Outline of Future Policy" discussing how it intended to use these weapons. One of the key concerns in the white paper was limiting the British contribution to European defense. British leaders understood that the security of the United Kingdom and Western Europe required cooperation.[1]

The white paper laid out the close association of Britain and its allies; it also discussed how Britain intended to fulfill its commitments to defending Western Europe. According to the plan proposed in the paper, the British planned to reduce their troop commitments by approximately 10,000 soldiers. Nuclear artillery provided to the remaining units made up for this reduced combat power. The British paper implied that though there were reductions in some fighting units this did not reduce any real combat power. Nuclear weapons balanced any reductions in manpower levels. This argument was similar to one that President Eisenhower made concerning his New Look security policy.[2]

According to the British policy paper the United States protected Western Europe and other U.S. allies through its nuclear deterrent. Britain, at the time, was unable to match the U.S. in quantity or quality of nuclear weapons. However, the white paper was evidence of the importance of an independent nuclear deterrent for the British government. In the near future, according

7. U.S.-U.K. IRBM Agreement

to the paper, the British planned to test their first thermonuclear weapon and so join the U.S. and the Soviet Union as the only nations in the world with that capability. Britain successfully tested its first thermonuclear weapon in May 1956, showing it was a first-rate atomic power.[3]

This focus on nuclear weapons was also similar to that of the New Look defense policy. President Eisenhower's defense policy laid the main burden of national defense on nuclear weapons. So, when Eisenhower offered IRBMs to Prime Minister Macmillan it meshed easily with the British need for a robust nuclear deterrent. The independence of Britain's nuclear force was unique in Western Europe. This caused problems with expanding the IRBM program to the rest of NATO.

One of the final sections of the white paper discussed cooperation with the United States on weapons programs, specifically guided missiles. It referenced an agreement signed in 1953 as the framework for this cooperation. However, this agreement was not as generous as the agreement codified in 1959 between the U.S. and the U.K.[4] This later agreement showed that there were two tiers to NATO membership, nations with nuclear weapons and those without them. The deployment of IRBMs to Britain, initially, and to Western Europe, later, brought tension between the Anglo-American part of the alliance and France.[5]

In December 1957, in conjunction with the NATO heads of government meeting, the U.S. created a working paper to determine its position on a joint decision making process for using nuclear weapons. The working group stated that the U.S. position concerning the use of nuclear weapons was that they were a vital part of NATO's defense plans. In their paper, the working group wrote that reacting to a nuclear attack might not allow for a timely discussion of how to respond. If there were time to discuss how to respond to such an event, the U.S., according to the group, would coordinate with other NATO nations prior to any action. If this were not possible, the U.S. committed to discussing its actions at the soonest possible time after the retaliation occurred. Member nations in NATO, especially those without their own nuclear deterrent had little ability to deny the protection of America's atomic umbrella, so they had to accept the terms that the U.S. offered.[6]

One aspect of having joint possession of nuclear weapons, as the IRBM agreement created, was having a joint decision making process in their use. One issue that the paper brought up was the bilateral relationship between the U.S. and the U.K. This relationship was not a secret in

NATO. However, the U.S. did not have a similarly close relationship with any other nation in NATO at the time.[7]

Expanding the relationship between the British and the U.S. to include NATO nations would made using nuclear weapons problematic. A nuclear attack launched from a joint base or using a jointly owned weapon required the approval of both member nations. If this type of agreement expanded to include all NATO nations, the working group stated that it was impossible to launch an atomic attack in a timely fashion. Under such an arrangement, one veto could derail a quick response. The working group advocated that the U.S. adopt a position that cemented individual agreements between nations in NATO. This avoided the problem of having one nation using a veto to prevent a retaliatory response. Each of these individual agreements still fell under NATO and SACEUR.[8]

A proposal discussed at the heads of government meeting that December was the concept of a NATO atomic stockpile. The purpose of the stockpile was to put atomic weapons in Western Europe under NATO control. However, the decision to release warheads for military action would come solely from the United States, since it gave the atomic weapons to the stockpile. This meant that General Lauris Norstad, the NATO Supreme Commander and a U.S. general, was in control of the entire NATO nuclear arsenal. Under this plan President Eisenhower, as Commander-in-Chief of the U.S. military, had the authority to withhold such weapons, even if the other member nations disagreed. The working group stated that the Eisenhower should clearly communicate U.S. willingness to use atomic weapons and its trustworthiness to be the sole provider of NATO's atomic retaliatory capability.[9]

The exception to this was the United Kingdom. Since the British maintained their own nuclear arsenal, the U.S. had no ability to stop them from using it as they saw fit. This did not include any joint weapons systems, such as the proposed IRBMs. However, the U.K. had a fleet of strategic bombers and a newly tested thermonuclear warhead; it was a first rate atomic power in quality, although not quantity.

Nuclear testing was another area of tension. The deployment of IRBMs was one way that President Eisenhower sought to reduce the Soviet threat to the United States. The suspension of nuclear testing provided another avenue to stop the arms race and at least maintain a manageable status quo in the Cold War. Prime Minister Macmillan expressed his doubts about the efficacy of such a course of action in January 1958.

7. U.S.-U.K. IRBM Agreement

He wrote to Eisenhower and explained that such a ban did not serve British interests. Only if the United States were willing to alter its legislation to allow for the transfer of knowledge to the United Kingdom, then the British could support such a position. Macmillan's concern for supporting a test ban was to limit the proliferation of nuclear weapons to other nations. Only if the U.S. offered its knowledge would the sacrifice of improving British weapons be worth knowing that other nations were unable to attain such devices. Proliferation continued to be a major concern for the prime minister and his government concerning U.S. nuclear policy.[10]

Another problem that Macmillan had with the test ban treaty was that it could possibly lead to a ban on nuclear weapons entirely. He did not think that this was a viable solution. Macmillan reminded Eisenhower that the Soviet Union had a large surplus of manpower compared to the nations of Western Europe and America. If the alliance did not use nuclear weapons, it had no possibility of winning in a conflict with the Soviet Union. If it were only a conventional conflict the balance of power tilted too far in favor of the Soviets. Again, the British perspective recalled that of President Eisenhower's New Look defense policy.[11]

As a report to President Eisenhower and Prime Minister Macmillan later that year explained, the decision to launch jointly held atomic weapons was between the two nations exclusively. In this report there was no mention of any NATO control. The president and prime minister had to personally speak to each other in order to authorize a nuclear attack. This report did not include any weapons held by the U.S. outside the United Kingdom. It only included Royal Air Force medium bombers capable of carrying nuclear weapons, R.A.F. IRBMs under the bilateral agreement, and any U.S. Strategic Air Command forces in the U.K.[12]

Although the plan to deploy IRBMs originated in 1957, the missiles were not actually operational until 1959. During this time there was discussion to expand the deployment to other NATO nations, in order to increase the force projection of the United States and deter Soviet attacks into Western Europe. One problem with the expansion of the program was the relatively primitive nature of the Thor and Jupiter missiles offered. In a telegram from Armory Houghton, the American ambassador to France, he expressed doubts that General Norstad had concerning the current state of IRBM development. Houghton wrote that new developments in the missile field made the current IRBM systems obsolete.

Norstad did not recommend expanding the deployment of first generation IRBMs too much because of the technological advances planned in the near future.[13]

First generation IRBMs suffered from accuracy problems and took approximately fifteen minutes to be ready for launch due to the liquid fueling system. However, this did not stop the British from accepting the offer of these weapons. The offer of IRBMs to Britain also came with the offer of technical cooperation in the field of guided missiles as well as atomic weapons research. This took longer to cement because of the legislative hurdles but it made the capabilities of the IRBMs less of an issue. Other NATO nations did not receive assurances of future cooperation in weapons research, primarily because of nonproliferation concerns. The two-tier NATO alliance determined which nations benefited the most from the expansion of the American nuclear umbrella in Western Europe. It would make Britain more powerful, in relation to other non-nuclear member states.

The United Kingdom's Permanent Representative to the North Atlantic Council (NAC), Frank Roberts, discussed the agreement between the U.S. and the U.K. concerning IRBMs in his statement about an upcoming British defense white paper in 1958. The NAC was the senior political body inside of NATO. He told the council that the agreement between the two nations would be complete soon. He then alluded to the possibility that Britain would develop its own IRBM system. The cooperation between the U.S. and the U.K. was helpful in advancing the British missile program.[14]

The promise of IRBMs, although they were liquid fueled, provided some breathing room for the British government. Having the missiles under British control also provided their scientists the ability to research and learn from them. Ambassador Roberts communicated to the council the British desire to maintain proficiency in the nuclear field. Eisenhower's New Look defense policy influenced British planning for national defense, as the white paper of April 1957, "Defence: An Outline for Future Policy," implied by putting more emphasis on atomic weapons and deemphasizing the importance of ground troops.

Roberts attempted to defuse some criticism about Britain's withdrawal of soldiers from NATO defense forces by stating that the majority of the United Kingdom's defense allocations still supported conventional forces. However, Roberts told the council that strategic deterrent forces

7. U.S.-U.K. IRBM Agreement

were the "decisive factor" in stopping a war with the Soviet Union. Although the British still supported conventional forces, if strategic weapons were the decisive force in preventing a global war, it detracted from the assurances of the importance of the conventional forces.[15]

One reason Roberts gave for the necessity of nuclear weapons was the overwhelming superiority of Soviet manpower in relation to that of NATO. Conventional forces, according to Roberts, held the line until a nuclear retaliatory strike stopped the Soviet advance. Without a large nuclear arsenal, there was little hope for the U.K. and its allies to defeat the Soviet Union in force on force conflict.[16]

Again, this undercut Roberts' assertion of the importance of ground forces in the defense of Western Europe. If the role of ground forces was simply to hold the line until nuclear weapons stopped the Soviet horde in its tracks, then it was increasingly distasteful for the British to commit their ground forces to such a mission. If Britain had the ability to substitute nuclear armed units, with fewer soldiers, in lieu of large conventional ground forces, there was little reason not to. Indeed, that was the rationale for the substitutions and withdrawals outlined in the previous white paper of April 1957.

Although Roberts tried to dampen concerns about the British withdrawals, the white paper he referenced did little to allay such fears. The white paper discussed the British view of the proper alignment of responsibility in manning the defenses of Western Europe. According to the United Kingdom each nation should contribute its most effective assets to the consolidated defense of NATO. Instead of trying to have each member nation contribute similar forces and then create a unified force out of the disparate units. The U.K., in the white paper, proposed assigning specific areas of contribution to each nation according to its capability. This provided a more efficient way to create a defense force for Western Europe, according to the British.[17]

The effect of the Soviet satellite launch, *Sputnik*, received mention in the white paper of February 1958 titled, "Report on Defence: Britain's Contribution to Peace and Security." Specifically, *Sputnik* did not upset the status quo. The white paper cited the guided missile capability of the United States as well as its strategic bomber force in deterring a Soviet attack. The benefit of missile attacks, according to the white paper, was that no effective counter existed. The white paper implied that the most important part of the defense of NATO came from nuclear weapons, supplied mainly from the United States.[18]

In fact, the white paper endorsed the use of nuclear weapons for preventative purposes. It stated that such a nuclear deterrent could continue for the foreseeable future. Since nuclear deterrent was such an effective way to control war. No political end was worth going to war when a nuclear conflict was a certainty.[19]

Soviet power was also part of the discussion, not just the development of *Sputnik*. The Soviet Union had 200 active divisions, in the estimation of the British government. This was an astounding sum when the British recently had to make the case to NATO to reduce its troop commitment by 10,000 because of financial constraints. The Soviet Union's superiority in soldiers, as interpreted by the Western allies, put the alliance in dire straits and made any conventional battle out of the question.[20]

Since the defense of NATO, at least in the perception of the United Kingdom, relied on the United States and its nuclear arsenal, it was important to organize the other member nations efficiently to balance with conventional assets the U.S. nuclear contribution. The paper stated that the alliance had to form a closer network of individual states. One problem with this was that the British government was a member of other alliances and had its own international security concerns, associated with its imperial possessions.[21]

While seeming to make the case for increased cooperation in security matters, the white paper also laid the foundation for a move away from intense coordination as well. Several pages later the white paper stated that Britain needed to work with the United States closely to use its independent nuclear force most effectively. This was a departure from the need to work together with NATO nations. The prime minister and his government, as shown in the white paper, wanted to move the U.K. from a dependent nation that relied on the U.S. to a partner nuclear power that coordinated with the United States.[22]

In relation to the growing nuclear capability of the United Kingdom, the white paper continued by stating recent advances in British atomic weapons. It cited the increasingly large number of kiloton warheads that Britain owned. The Royal Air Force also started making megaton, or thermonuclear, bombs the after successful testing at Christmas Island. The United Kingdom, as described in the white paper, was a nuclear power similar in type to the United States.

Frank Roberts, in explaining the recently released white paper, told the North Atlantic Council that Britain continued to reassess its defense

7. U.S.-U.K. IRBM Agreement

contributions. He referred generally to new technological developments and said that this allowed the British government to take a "fresh appreciation and a new approach" to its defense policy. Roberts emphasized that these changes were not new. He reminded the council that the white paper released the previous year set the stage for these changes.[23]

This again showed the influence of Eisenhower's interpretation of modern war and the New Look defense policy on the British defense strategy. The white paper released in April 1957 communicated the ground forces cuts but promised to reinforce smaller units with larger atomic weapons. This, planners hoped, mitigated or eliminated any supposed weakness of the smaller units. Arming smaller units with more powerful weapons was similar to U.S. Army experiments with the Pentomic division in the late 1950s.[24]

Prime Minister Macmillan sent a letter to the president on February 16, concerning the IRBM agreement between the two nations. He said he thought that the agreement would become final in the next week. However, Macmillan did have some reservations about the agreement. He worried about the possibility that U.S. personnel operating the missiles instead of Royal Air Force personnel. He cautioned Eisenhower that if that were the case the British people might not be enthusiastic about the deployment of the weapons.[25]

In order to clear up any confusion about who would crew the missiles, the prime minister proposed the following text for the agreement, "The missiles would be manned and operated by the United Kingdom personnel, which will be trained by the United States Government for the purposes of this project at the earliest feasible date." This proposed change, Macmillan thought, made it unmistakable that the United Kingdom personnel were in charge of the missiles.[26]

Another concern Macmillan had was that of launch of the missiles in the event of an attack on a NATO ally. He worried that the current wording could mean that the weapons would be part of a retaliatory attack with no input by the British government. Macmillan's proposed wording specifically stated that the United States and the United Kingdom alone determined when and how to use the IRBMs covered under the agreement. He included references to Article V of the NATO treaty. This article covered any attack on a member nation. It stated that any member nation considered an attack on an alliance state as an attack on itself.[27] However, Macmillan's proposed text stated that the U.S. and U.K. would interpret their joint decision in light of the requirements of Article V and did not say that the IRBMs would automatically be a part of any retaliatory attack.[28]

Until there was an operational squadron deployed, much of the concern about additional nuclear forces in NATO, and the IRBMs specifically, was speculative. In February 1958, Secretary of State Dulles sent a proposed response to President Eisenhower answering questions that Prime Minister Macmillan raised about the IRBM agreement. Macmillan had concerns about the political ramifications if U.S. Air Force personnel manned the missiles initially. Although the agreement fleshed out at the Bermuda Conference stated that Royal Air Force personnel would man the missiles, they did not have the proper training and resolving their deficiencies pushed back any operational date. Dulles proposed telling the prime minister that the U.S. would tamp down any speculation that this was the case.[29]

Dulles continued his proposed response to the prime minister by stressing the need to get the missiles ready as soon as possible. He stressed to Macmillan that both of their governments shared the desire to speed up the operational employment as much as possible. He continued that if this meant having U.S. personnel crew them temporarily it did not change the terms of the agreement concerning their use. Dulles referenced previous agreements between the U.S. and the U.K. concerning Strategic Air Command bases. He reminded the prime minister that the U.S. could not unilaterally launch the missiles even if U.S. personnel, not R.A.F., personnel manned them.[30]

The following day the president sent a reply to Macmillan. He agreed to the prime minister's proposed changes to the IRBM agreement. He reminded Macmillan that the U.S. and the U.K. maintained joint control over the weapons, as they did over Strategic Air Command bombers in the United Kingdom.[31]

The prime minister's worries about the knowledge of temporary manning of IRBMs by U.S. personnel indicated that he wanted no question in Britain about who controlled the weapons. If U.S. personnel manned the missiles it called into question the authority that the British exercised over the use of the missiles. However, if British personnel operated the missiles from the beginning, even if the U.S. controlled the warheads, no launch could occur without British agreement.

Prime Minister Macmillan came to the United States for a meeting with President Eisenhower in June of 1958. Eisenhower expressed to Macmillan the importance of the Anglo-American relationship. He said

7. U.S.-U.K. IRBM Agreement

that the two nations should work as closely together as possible. Eisenhower told Macmillan that it was not possible that this cooperation always be public. In fact, Eisenhower told him that in some cases the U.S. might have to take an opposing tact publicly but that this did not indicate any real separation between the two nations.[32]

President Eisenhower's affinity for the Anglo-American relationship was obvious. His proposal of IRBMs to Britain was one example of how important it was to him. The character of the agreement differed greatly from that offered to other NATO nations. Part of the reason for this was Britain's independent nuclear program. However, another aspect was the affection Eisenhower had for the British relationship with the United States. This intimate relationship did not extend to the entire NATO alliance. This caused tensions with other nations, particularly France.

Eisenhower, Dulles, and Macmillan discussed how the U.S. and U.K. should deal with France and General de Gaulle later that day. Secretary Dulles summarized the position of the president and prime minister by saying that the two nations deal with France in a three-party form where there was precedent for this. In other areas, where there was no precedent, the U.S. and U.K. should deal with France through NATO with bilateral accords.[33]

This had significant implications as France pursued nuclear weapons and the U.S. expanded the IRBM offer to other NATO nations. It meant that France had to agree to NATO authority over any nuclear weapons agreement. Unlike agreements with the British that fell outside of NATO authority. This set France in the second-tier of the alliance, mainly because France did not have an independent nuclear capability and neither the U.S. nor the British were keen that de Gaulle should realize his atomic aspirations.

The McMahon Act came up later in the afternoon. Secretary Dulles gave a report to the president and the prime minister concerning amendments to the legislation to allow sharing of nuclear weapons research information. Dulles communicated that such joint action in atomic weapons research was critical to the United States. He said that the Joint Congressional Committee was able to secure adequate changes to the legislation, although not everything that the administration hoped for. Dulles encouraged the president and prime minister that the two nations should not wait for legislation to officially become law before linking British and U.S. scientists so they could start work as soon as possible.[34]

Eisenhower's Nuclear Calculus in Europe

In August of 1958, prior to the deployment of IRBMs to Britain but after Eisenhower's offer of them to the U.K., Macmillan proposed the purchase of Thor missiles. These missiles were to have British warheads and provided a completely independent IRBM asset to the United Kingdom. Ray Thurston, the political advisor to General Norstad, wrote to Robert McBride, the State Department European Affairs Specialist, concerning the sale of Thor missiles to Britain. Thurston communicated to McBride that Norstad was uneasy about the purchase because it violated the spirit of the NATO IRBM program his command tried to begin in December 1957.[35]

Although Eisenhower's offer of IRBMs to Britain meant that the U.K. did in fact own the missiles themselves, the warheads used on these particular missiles would be from the U.S. This meant that the U.S. would had a veto over whether or not the British fired the missiles and vice versa. However, the new proposal for the United Kingdom to buy Thor missiles was dramatically different. It gave the British an independent guided missile with no U.S. control over their use. These weapons would not fall under any bilateral agreement concerning the use of nuclear weapons. The British would notify the U.S., in some cases, about the potential use of such weapons but only as a courtesy.

General Norstad's hesitation concerning the sale of these weapons showed his doubts about giving the United Kingdom such a capability with no U.S. ability to check its use. The addition of guided missiles under independent British control was contradictory to Norstad's proposal to bring IRBMs deployed in Europe under NATO control. This was one of the differences between the Anglo-American agreement covering IRBMs and other bilateral agreements that Eisenhower offered to other NATO nations for IRBMs. The bilateral agreement between the U.S. and U.K. did not include NATO controls over the missiles. Other NATO agreements, although still in formative stages, had some connection to NATO as a whole, even if this connection were only through their association with SHAPE headquarters.

General Norstad not only objected to the sale of Thor missiles to Britain he also objected to the sale of Corporal missile warheads to the British. B.E.L. Timmons, the Director of the Office of European Regional Affairs, discussed this sale in a memo to Major General John Guthrie, Director of the European Regional section of the International Security Affairs in the Department of Defense. According to Timmons, Norstad's

7. U.S.-U.K. IRBM Agreement

concern about the sale was that it was bilateral and did not involve NATO. General Norstad wanted to freeze the correspondence between the two nations about this issue until the U.S. had a final position on the sale. Timmons did not think that sale fit Norstad's vision of a NATO atomic stockpile.[36]

The U.S. delegation to NATO sent its assessment of the proposal to the U.S. State Department. Joseph Wolf, U.S. representative to NATO, wrote the communiqué. He first described U.S. policy concerning atomic weapons in Europe. He wrote that the position of the United States was to increase nuclear capability under Supreme Allied Commander Europe (SACEUR), who was General Norstad. This, according to Wolf, prevented any uncoordinated use of these weapons.[37]

Wolf continued to criticize the British proposal by discussing the problematic strategic implications. He wrote that if the U.K. attained these missiles it created an independent thermonuclear capability. The fact that the British did not yet support the broader NATO program of researching a solid fueled IRBM was an indication of its lack of commitment to the NATO atomic stockpile.[38]

The idea of Britain separating itself from the rest of the European NATO nations came through in this memorandum. Other European nations, in Wolf's words, could feel that they were "second class citizens" if the U.S. supported the sale of missiles to Britain. The NATO IRBM project needed to be the top priority, selling Britain its own fleet of IRBMs implied that this was not the case.[39]

The IRBM agreement between the U.S. and the U.K. received specific mention in the memo. Wolf said that this agreement did not represent a viable model for other NATO agreements. Citing the Anglo-American agreement about IRBMs showed that the two-tier character of the organization, although informal, was already causing tensions in the alliance. The British possession of nuclear weapons was a large part of its status in the alliance. No other NATO nation received the unique type of bilateral agreement offered to Britain. It is important to understand that the agreement only offered the missiles, the warheads remained in U.S. custody until firing. This was similar in structure to other NATO agreements offered later. However, these subsequent agreements were under NATO control.[40]

The communication also referenced the decrease in British contributions to NATO shield forces. The British white paper of April 1957 explained the need to withdraw some troops from the shield forces for financial reasons. However, the British continued to increase the amount of money dedicated to strategic weapons, more than in accordance of their requirements under SHAPE agreements. Wolf argued that Britain's reluctance to contribute to the shield forces in favor of the strategic forces inhibited other nations from meeting their requirements.[41]

Britain's focus on strategic weapons did have an impact on the larger questions of European security. However, from the British perspective, focusing on strategic weapons was what nuclear powers did. President Eisenhower made clear through his New Look defense policy and his reliance on Massive Retaliation that nuclear weapons provided a more efficient way to defend the interests of a nation. Britain was the only other independent nuclear power; it was only reasonable that it followed the lead of the most powerful atomic nation in the alliance and not other non-nuclear states. Continuing down this path would increase tension in the alliance as it became clear that nuclear weapons offered a nation admission to the upper-tier of the NATO alliance.

There were other problems with the sale of Thor missiles to Britain. Wolf worried about the precedent that such a purchase set. He called to attention other agreements in early stages with the governments of France, Greece, and Italy. Each of these agreements did not include bilateral controls over the IRBMs; these offers fell under NATO authority. If the British bought IRBMs it exacerbated any complications with other nations agreeing to the deployment of these missiles. Wolf brought up the French case specifically. He wrote that the French government sought an independent nuclear capability. Allowing Britain more freedom by selling it missiles encouraged the French to demand some similar concessions in its agreement concerning IRBMs.[42]

Wolf ended his memo with a warning about the overall effect on the entire NATO stockpile. He advocated that selling the British IRBMs for their independent use inspired more emphasis on independence of atomic weapons in Europe. This removed much of the enthusiasm for the stockpile idea. If this happened tensions in the alliance would increase.[43]

The NATO stockpile intended to give European nations some control over the use of atomic weapons on the continent. Building an atomic arsenal was an expensive proposition, which only a few nations could hope to afford. If the situation in Europe devolved to an assembly of independent nuclear arsenals it removed much of the resources that went to funding

7. U.S.-U.K. IRBM Agreement

NATO shield forces. This devolution could fracture Eisenhower's attempts to build a unified European defense alliance.

In December 1958, General Norstad alerted the Standing Group of NATO that Thor and Jupiter missiles would soon be available to Allied Command Europe. In light of the arrival of these weapons, Norstad encouraged NATO nations to start the production of advanced missiles. Norstad's call for a combined research program demonstrated the U.S. dedication to limiting the proliferation of nuclear weapons in Europe.[44]

In addition to the introduction of IRBMs to NATO, in April 1959 General Norstad said that other atomic weapons programs were also coming that improved the defense system of Western Europe. He told the North Atlantic Council that the Heads of Government meeting in 1957 approved multiple systems including Honest John rockets, aircraft, as well as the IRBMs. Each of these required separate agreements with each nation that agreed to accept them. However, each of these new agreements still fell under the broader NATO defense system. He told the NAC that Allied Command Europe would have a stock of warheads for use irrespective of nationality.[45]

Although the U.S. planned to provide the warheads for different NATO nations to use in their defense, only the approval of President Eisenhower could release these warheads for use. This was an important distinction between the Anglo-American agreement and other agreements offered to the rest of NATO. The British, with their own nuclear stockpile, had their own independent retaliatory capability outside of the IRBMs offered by the U.S. Also, the British, at this time, sought to develop their own IRBM system, either through purchase or research and development. Britain was in a league of its own concerning atomic capability in Western Europe.

General Norstad explained to the NAC how these weapons would come to the individual member states and what agreements covered concerning their use and deployment. He said that each nation would enter into two different bilateral agreements. The first agreement concerned the stockpile placement or weapons deployment in the territory of the nation. The second allowed for the release of some atomic data from the U.S. to the nation. This data was technical in nature and more for planning purposes and not research information.[46]

The release of this type of data helped the nation plan to use the atomic weapons. It did not require a change in the McMahon act as the research and development agreement with the U.K. required. Norstad told the NAC that the second agreement allowed for the nation to have "full atomic capability."[47]

The problem with Norstad's characterization of the second agreement lay in its intention. Since the release of the technical data did not require changes in the McMahon act, it did not fall under the restriction placed on scientific development information concerning nuclear weapons. This meant that this data, although helpful in planning purposes, was not very helpful in developing future nuclear weapons. In this light, Norstad's offer of nuclear weapons, to include IRBMs to Allied Command Europe, was a move to limit nuclear weapons proliferation. General Norstad as the senior American commander still held primary authority for releasing the weapons to individual nations, although officially it came from President Eisenhower.[48]

Again, this was different in character than the British agreement. President Eisenhower had to communicate personally with the prime minister in order to give approval. Since the weapons discussed by General Norstad fell under NATO control, the president could authorize General Norstad to give approval for their use. This was not just a technicality. It represented Britain's level of importance in the alliance. The president had to explain his case directly to the prime minister in the event of a nuclear attack. This was not the case in the other agreements presented to NATO. Of course, if the individual nations disagreed with the decision to launch an atomic strike there was little doubt that President Eisenhower would then have to discuss with the head of state the urgency of the situation, but only if required.

Another important difference Norstad discussed was that of financing the infrastructure and development of nuclear weapons for NATO. In his address, he commended the NAC for their respective nations taking the responsible path of sharing the burden of paying for building nuclear storage sites. He hoped to see this continue as NATO started to develop its own IRBM program. Norstad said that he believed such weapons should provide protection for all of Western Europe and not just individual nations in the region.[49]

This raised another issue concerning the European IRBM program. Paying for something implied a certain amount of ownership or at least an interest in the use of a weapon system. Only Britain and the United States paid for the IRBMs stationed in the United Kingdom. This meant

7. U.S.-U.K. IRBM Agreement

that there was little leverage any other European nation could use in controlling such weapons. On the other hand, with the NATO IRBM program if every Western European nation in the alliance paid for a portion of the weapon it was impossible to exclude any paying nation completely from discussions about their use.

Norstad did reference the Anglo-American IRBM agreement. He implied that the agreement was similar in terms to what he was offering the other NATO nations. He explained that the U.S. was now negotiating agreements of the same kind with member states in the alliance. As shown above, this was not the case. There were striking differences between the type of agreement offered to Britain and those offered to the rest of the NATO alliance.[50]

Much of the difference between the two types of agreements stemmed from the British possession of an independent nuclear capability. This allowed them certain exemptions in the political agreements that covered the deployment of IRBMs and subsequent cooperative nuclear weapons research between the U.S. and the U.K. Nuclear weapons provided not only military benefits but also political benefits when it came to control of nuclear weapons deployed in Western Europe.

The introduction of IRBMs to NATO caused concern in Britain. Walworth Barbour, Deputy Chief of Mission in London, sent a telegraph to the State Department on August 14, 1959, outlining some of these issues. Richard Powell, the Permanent Secretary in the Ministry Defense, brought up the main concern of Prime Minister Macmillan, which was the expansion of nuclear weapons on the European continent. Powell reminded Barbour that the U.S. and U.K. agreed to postpone or delay the proliferation of nuclear weapons in Europe, specifically in the case of France. He wanted to know if that was still the U.S. policy. Macmillan worried that the NATO IRBM program would erode the proliferation policy agreed to in Bermuda.[51]

Powell cautioned Barbour that the possession of missiles could possibly lead to clamoring for ownership of warheads as well. The prime minister, according to Powell, did not want to have to explain the independent possession of nuclear weapons by France or Germany to his people. Powell wrote that, in the British estimation, the NATO IRBM program exacerbated the proliferation problem in Western Europe, which increased tensions with the Soviet Union, especially if the program expanded to West Germany.[52]

The British understood the problem of possessing the missiles but not the warheads. In the prime minister's estimation, as communicated by Richard Powell, missiles eventually opened the door to warheads, which then created independent nuclear nations in Western Europe. Any expansion of the nuclear weapons, especially outside of the NATO framework offered by General Norstad, stood to undercut the British position of being the only other independent nuclear nation in the alliance, except the U.S. Although France had a nuclear weapons program, it did not have a successful test yet. As seen by the British Permanent Secretary's position concerning the NATO IRBM agreement, the prime minister wanted to delay such success as long as possible.

Powell told Barbour that the prime minister would support the U.S. and its position. However, Macmillan thought that the best course of action was to choose either to delay the expansion of nuclear weapons, including the NATO IRMB program, or to put as much emphasis behind the program as possible to ensure its success. The prime minister preferred to push back the expansion of IRBMs to Western Europe but in the end would fall in line with the U.S. decision.[53]

Macmillan communicated to Powell his reservations concerning France and nuclear weapons. The prime minister did not think that the French would be amenable to the NATO program but would demand a joint decision making process between the senior alliance members, including the U.S. Any joint process for nuclear retaliation placed France in the same league as the British in the alliance; however, as General Norstad explained the NATO IRBM program it did not require a decision making process that operated outside of the alliance.[54]

The British concerns about France was evidence that the NATO IRBM program was different in character to that of the bilateral agreement with the United Kingdom. Macmillan did not want de Gaulle to pressure Eisenhower into agreeing to a joint decision making agreement concerning nuclear weapons. This would remove any future French-American IRBMs from NATO control and put them in the same category as the Anglo-American IRBMs. Again, the possession of nuclear weapons had political ramifications. The prime minister did not want to expand the joint decision making process concerning atomic weapons to include any other nation.

Nuclear weapons provided political leverage. Possession of an independent atomic arsenal, as well as Eisenhower's affinity for the United

7. U.S.-U.K. IRBM Agreement

Kingdom, allowed Britain to be in the top-tier of NATO. The two-tier system in NATO raised tensions in the alliance. It made clear the importance of a state having its own nuclear arsenal. Britain and the United States created policies to limit the proliferation of nuclear weapons and cement the split nature of NATO in the late 1950s. By 1959, there was some sense in NATO, from General Norstad's staff, that the special relationship between the U.S. and the U.K. was problematic. The IRBM agreement between the two nations, which the British tried to expand to include the purchase of an independent Thor force for the R.A.F., potentially carried a heavy political price.

8

Unintended Consequences

After World War II, French leaders faced similar problems as British leaders. Post war French premiers, Vincent Auriol, René Coty, and Charles de Gaulle, had to contend with a crumbling empire and a diminishing role on the global stage. Almost immediately after the cessation of hostilities in World War II, French soldiers deployed to Indochina to restore French hegemony in the region. They fought the communist Viet Minh in one of the first armed conflicts of the Cold War.

As the Cold War continued and Arab nationalism began to expand through North Africa, the conflicts moved closer to France. By 1954, Algeria rose up in rebellion. Putting down this conflict required substantial effort in manpower and material, it also cost France much in the public eye. However, this was not the only problem that Coty and de Gaulle struggled with through the 1950s.

Gamal Abdel Nasser accelerated the spread of decolonization with his nationalization of the Suez Crisis. As shown previously, France desperately wanted to stop Nasser from succeeding in his attempts to dictate terms to the European powers. Coty, the French president during the crisis, learned how the lack of nuclear weapons deprived him of the ability to deal with the United States on equal terms. Due to the Algerian war and popular unrest about French actions in quelling the uprising, Coty did not have the opportunity to remedy the problem.[1]

General Charles de Gaulle took control of France after René Coty and led France in the wake of the political turbulence that unseated the Fourth Republic. De Gaulle took the pursuit of independent French nuclear weapons to a new level. These weapons were not just for national defense, they were part of the French national identity. A powerful nuclear arsenal made it clear that France was worthy of great nation status. France detonated its first nuclear weapon in 1960 on a test range in Algeria.

8. Unintended Consequences

Although the test was successful it was obvious that time was running out on France's desert testing facilities. General Ailleret, commander of the Special Weapons Section, reported two years earlier that the Algerian site was too problematic for long-term use.[2]

President de Gaulle also saw nuclear weapons as a fundamental issue that directly related to a nation's sovereignty. He did not think that it was wise for France to seek to share weapons that were so powerful and greatly increased the risk of attack for France. If de Gaulle allowed U.S. controlled atomic warheads on French soil, even if under a dual-key arrangement, he viewed this as giving away vital parts of French control over its own security. No amount of protocols could reduce the risk of this type of cooperation and it proved to be a hurdle as President Eisenhower and his administration explored the possibility of deploying IRBMs to France.[3]

Domestic and colonial concerns were not the only thing that hamstrung de Gaulle in his rush to develop an independent French nuclear force. His allies, Eisenhower and Macmillan, worked to passively frustrate French nuclear efforts. At the Bermuda Conference in 1958, the U.S. and British leaders agreed to delay French efforts to gain nuclear weapons in order to stem the proliferation of atomic arsenals in Europe.

During the planning of the deployment of IRBMs to Britain, Eisenhower made the decision to expand the program to other NATO nations. His intent was to ensure that all U.S. allies had access to the security of America's nuclear umbrella. The problem with the expansion of this program was that the framework of the Anglo-American agreement offered little guidance. The U.S.-U.K. IRBM agreement provided for concessions that were not possible for other NATO nations. This was particularly frustrating to de Gaulle who did not think that his nation deserved second-class status.

President Eisenhower made the offer of IRBMs to Britain in the wake of the Suez Crisis. This was a bilateral agreement that put the missiles under British control but the U.S. maintained control of the warheads. It required the approval of both the British prime minister and the president of the United States in order to launch the missiles. This was fundamentally different from the offer of IRBMs made to the NATO alliance in 1958. This agreement put the missiles under the authority of NATO, specifically SACEUR, with bilateral agreements with each nation that agreed to accept the weapons. The weapons offered to NATO were part of the joint defense plan for the alliance; the missiles offered to the British did not fall under NATO authority.

Eisenhower's Nuclear Calculus in Europe

In early 1958, the United States offered to NATO nations the ability to cooperate in the defense of the alliance by housing atomic material in their nations. This was part of the atomic stockpile agreement. The nations would not actually own the warheads. They formed a part of the broader defense plans of NATO, headed by SACEUR General Lauris Norstad. France, under René Coty, seemed receptive to such an agreement.[4]

Intermediate Range Ballistic Missiles were a part of the overall stockpile policy. The intent was to get these weapons deployed to European nations in order to bring the alliance closer together and prepare it for a combined nuclear weapons program. General Norstad's judgment of the French position, as described in a telegram by John Tuthill the Minister for Economic Affairs at the American Embassy, was largely positive. Tuthill conveyed to John Foster Dulles that Norstad looked for France to set the example for deploying IRBMs to Allied Command Europe (ACE). After the French agreements moved through the approval process in the North Atlantic Council, the U.S. would discuss IRBMs with Italy and other willing NATO nations. At the time, General Norstad referenced the Anglo-American bilateral agreement as a possible framework for a Franco-American agreement but made no promises about this.[5]

In a meeting between Ambassador Etienne de Crouy-Chanel, General Norstad, and French military Chief of the Defense Staff General Paul Ely concerning the proposed IRBM deployment to France, the discussion shifted to ownership of the missiles. Ambassador Crouy-Chanel communicated that the French position was that France eventually wanted some ownership over the stockpile. However, the French government did not want to make this a serious issue at the time. General Norstad agreed that the U.S. and France had to come some understanding about how these weapons worked in a future defense plan, whether through NATO or failing that a bilateral agreement covering the weapons between the two nations.[6]

General Ely asked how France could control these weapons. Norstad said that, under his plan, two or three squadrons would fall under French authority. There would be a U.S. officer on the French staff to serve as the liaison between the two governments. This was a similar arrangement to that of the Anglo-American agreement.[7]

General Ely continued by discussing the production of future weapons by Europe as a whole, including more advanced IRBMs that used solid fuel. General Norstad told Ely that the U.S. position was that a European IRBM program was the best solution. He reminded Ely that the United Kingdom already had a lead in that particular technology.[8]

8. Unintended Consequences

What General Norstad did not say was that the British were hesitant to abandon their own solid fuel IRBM for a combined European program. As discussed earlier, the British possession of an independent nuclear weapons program allowed the nation to have greater prestige in the alliance. If it abandoned its own independent program for a pan-European nuclear program it required losing some of its prestige and admit it could not continue to improve its independent nuclear program without European support due to the increased fiscal strain.

Another issue with using the Anglo-American IRBM agreement for a framework for a French accord was that it was still under development. Dulles, in response to Tuthill's telegram on January 10, 1958, reminded him that the U.S.-U.K. agreement was not final. Secretary Dulles told Tuthill that the Anglo-American IRBM agreement, because it was not final, would not be a good framework for a Franco-American pact. However, Dulles was in general agreement with Norstad's proposals concerning the developing situation concerning IRBMs in France.[9]

By the end of January 1958, France made its position clear about the IRBMs. French Ambassador Crouy-Chanel said his government wanted the IRBMs deployed to France. He told General Norstad that the government wanted to start to lay out the specifics of an agreement the following week.[10]

French cooperation in the Allied Command Europe IRBM program in early 1958 came with few conditions. The government did not state any specific needs or concessions on the part of the United States in order to get the approval for deploying these missiles inside of France. President Coty and Ambassador Crouy-Chanel wanted to conclude the agreement to deploy IRBMs as soon as possible and did not want to set up any roadblocks that delayed this.

Although the discussions concerning the NATO atomic stockpile and the deployment of IRBMs to France seemed to be going smoothly, there were some signs of trouble. The First Secretary of the French Embassy, Russell Fessenden, wrote to General Norstad about his concerns with the proposal. The French National Defense Committee had to meet to approve any agreements concerning the atomic stockpile or IRBMs. In order to accept the proposed NATO plan, the committee had to reverse its previous stance on this issue. Fessenden wrote that the French Foreign Office hoped that the committee could adopt a helpful policy concerning atomic issues. The office wanted to encapsulate the stockpile and IRBM proposals into one document in order to make this easier. However, the National Defense

Committee still had the approval authority; nothing could proceed until it gave its ascent.[11]

Another unsettling issue Fessenden brought up in his memo was an Associated Press story reporting that some members of the defense committee wanted to slow down the proposed atomic agreements between NATO and France. The news story claimed that some inside the committee hoped to get some concessions from the United States or NATO in order to grant approval of the atomic agreements. If this were true, the French IRBM program faced an uncertain future in the defense committee and could end up dividing a fragile government in France.[12]

The French atomic program was making steady progress in 1958. A group of French military officers led by General Buchalet came to the United States in February of that year. The group intended to study how to conduct atomic test, measure the data, and effectively analyze the results. The commission witnessed a U.S. nuclear test at the Nevada testing site. Buchalet told Horace Torbet, Director of Western European Affairs for the State Department, that his visit saved the French Government millions of dollars. Buchalet continued by stating that France hoped to use procedures developed by the U.S. instead of having to research and create the same techniques on their own.[13]

Atomic testing was not the only subject Buchalet discussed with Torbet. According to the general's conversation, Torbet believed that the French would have a successful atomic test soon, although he did not specify a date. One thing holding up the French testing was the lack of plutonium. Buchalet conveyed to Torbet that the weapons testing had to take a backseat to nuclear testing for energy purposes, since this did not destroy the radioactive material the way that testing bombs did.[14]

If France's atomic weapons program was successful, it gave French leaders more leverage in promoting France as a leading member of NATO. It also possibly improved France's ability to craft bilateral agreements similar to the Anglo-American pact concerning atomic weapons, assuming cooperation from the United States. An independent nuclear weapons program gave France more strength in arguing for concessions that were the same as the Anglo-American IRBM agreement in its bilateral agreement with the U.S. However, this meant that the weapons would not fall under NATO directly, detracting from the NATO stockpile plan that Eisenhower championed. It also made clearer the power of independent

8. Unintended Consequences

nuclear weapons programs in determining status in the alliance. This could lead other nations to want an independent weapons program of their own. However, as long as France did not have its own atomic weapons, it could not hope to be in the top-tier of the NATO alliance, unless the metric for judging within the alliance power changed.

While the French government seemed cooperative, under President Coty, the U.S. offer of IRBMs received a positive reception. Through the beginning of 1958, the French government accepted the proposal as it came. It did not offer many amendments, although there were rumors of problems for the agreement in the National Defense Committee, the French president, at the time, wanted to make this agreement final as soon as possible. However, the coming instability of the French government changed U.S. enthusiasm for the deployment of IRBMs to France. The rise of Charles de Gaulle to lead the new government destroyed any hopes of including France in the ACE IRBM deployment.

In addition to concerns about the impending successful test of a French atomic weapon, there were other concerns about France's position in the international arena. John Foster Dulles, in a telegram to the West German Chancellor, Konrad Adeneaur, covered some of the Secretary's chief worries. He wrote that the ability of the French government to maintain its influence in North Africa worried him. Dulles compared France's position in North Africa to that of its predicament in Vietnam in 1954. He did not think that the France was able to summon the will to continue to forcefully impose its will in the Maghreb. This meant that France had to accept its status as a post-colonial power.[15]

Dulles continued with his telegram by discussing the possible implications of French war weariness from its North African conflicts. If they continued to fight such a conflict, Dulles worried that that it fomented political instability in France. The possibility that the ruling French government had to reach out to French communists for support to remain in power disturbed him because it made communism more powerful in an influential Western European nation. This, Dulles feared, undermined NATO in Western Europe. He compared the threat of a Communist resurgence in France to the left-wing of the government bringing down the European Defense Community during the Indo-China conflict earlier in the decade.[16]

France, although a democracy and a part of NATO, had an influential communist political party in the nation and any instability could provide enough opportunity for it to become more powerful. Dulles' worries about the stability of the Coty government were indicative of the doubts about the possible divergence of U.S. and French interests. This cast doubts about the advisability of giving France nuclear weapons or storing them there under any agreement. If France fell under a communist government, or a government that included a significant communist presence, the rest of NATO then faced a French nation armed with atomic weapons that was possibly sympathetic to the Soviet Union.

This fear of instability in France came to fruition of April 1958. Prime Minister Felix Gaillard resigned after the bombing of a Tunisian village, which was a part of the French effort to secure its colonial holdings in North Africa. Christian Pineau, the French Foreign Minister, invited Armor Houghton and other State Department officials to a discussion about the implications of the recent fall of Gaillard's government. Pineau told the U.S. delegation that many in the French government felt that the U.S., after the Suez Crisis, abandoned the nation. Pineau continued by telling Houghton that Eisenhower's recent visit to Paris did help heal the rift somewhat but that there was still some resentment.[17]

Armory Houghton described the turmoil in France with the lack of a government in a telegram to the State Department on May 14, 1958. In the Maghreb, the Algerian situation, according to Houghton, could inflame support for the Communists. If the French were unable to bring the conflict to a quick resolution, it gave the communist party, the Labor Union Popular Front, an opportunity to increase its political influence. He wrote that the Communists continued to try to turn every event to their profit and continued to be a threat. By the end of year, de Gaulle provided stability by forming a government and leading France again.[18]

In August of 1959, President Eisenhower met with President de Gaulle, one of the topics they discussed was French participation in NATO. Eisenhower listened as de Gaulle explained his ideal organization for the European treaty organization. De Gaulle wanted to form a three-nation leadership group comprised of the U.S., Britain, and France. This group, de Gaulle argued, could provide the overarching strategy for NATO, since these three nations had global interests. Eisenhower thought that the idea potentially caused more problems than it resolved.[19]

Next, de Gaulle told Eisenhower of his concerns about French military independence in the NATO alliance. For de Gaulle, having French units subordinate to the Supreme Allied Commander was an affront to

8. Unintended Consequences

French sovereignty and detracted from its ability to defend itself effectively. De Gaulle explained that it was necessary for France to become a nuclear power. This nested with a previous decision that de Gaulle made to disallow any allied nuclear weapons on French soil unless France had veto authority over their use. Eisenhower could not accommodate this demand, nor could he actively support France becoming a nuclear power.[20]

When the two presidents met, Eisenhower was already aware of de Gaulle's problematic positions concerning NATO and nuclear weapons. Previous meetings between Secretary Dulles and de Gaulle provided important background to the meeting between Eisenhower and de Gaulle. Getting French cooperation with the NATO atomic stockpile program generally and the IRBM deployment specifically was important. However, de Gaulle's demands concerning French authority over the use of these weapons and ownership of them prevented any agreement between the two nations concerning these missiles.

De Gaulle's intentions for France domestically were not too troubling, at least as it concerned U.S. interests in the region. But the French leader's designs for NATO and reorganizing the alliance required a shift away from the two-tier structure established by the Anglo-American IRBM agreement. De Gaulle wanted a more prestigious position in the alliance for France. He did not think that NATO, in its contemporary form, adequately accounted for France's importance to the defense of Europe.

De Gaulle's desire to increase French prestige in the alliance and region ended an arms sharing agreement that was close to being finished. In late 1957 and early 1958, a nuclear agreement seemed imminent between the two nations. The proposed agreement fell under the NATO structure and introduced IRBMs under the auspices of Allied Command Europe. However, de Gaulle put an end to the discussions by demanding veto authority and more control over the weapons. As the French Empire collapsed so did its power and prestige. Nuclear weapons were a means to regain some of this lost dignity.

One of the problems that Eisenhower had to overcome was de Gaulle's distrust of NATO as a concept. In his memoirs, de Gaulle discussed NATO as a way for the United States to control the foreign policy as well as the territory of member states. While this compromise made sense when in the late 1940s by the mid 1950s the security situation was more dangerous. Both the U.S. and the Soviets had the capacity to destroy each other and de Gaulle worried that the central and western European states could find themselves in the middle of a nuclear exchange that they could not control. This was one of the reasons why de Gaulle wanted to change the structure of NATO.[21]

When Secretary Dulles met with de Gaulle in July 1958, he made it clear that the U.S. did not agree with the French president's demands concerning a reorganization of NATO. Dulles stressed that the U.S. wanted to make NATO an organization that represented all of its member nations. He also brought up the importance of IRBMs and their place in defending the alliance. These missiles allowed NATO member states to have more peace of mind concerning the Soviet nuclear threat and would be a stopgap response to the Soviet ICBM capability until the U.S. had an operational ICBM. Dulles described a plan that gave NATO, specifically SACEUR, more control over the use of nuclear weapons as a way to assuage concerns that the U.S. might not agree to the use of atomic weapons to protect Europe. None of these positions were agreeable to de Gaulle who made it clear that the only way to gain French support was to have nuclear weapons on French soil was to allow France to have control of the weapons.[22]

General Norstad brought up the issue of the lack of French cooperation in nuclear issues in October 1958 when he met with the new French Permanent Representative to NATO, Ambassador Geoffrey de Courcel. He asked the new representative what the obstacles for getting French agreement to the deployment of IRBMs were. De Courcel said that if NATO agreed to institute some of de Gaulle's ideas concerning its organization and granted France a more prominent role in the alliance, then the nuclear issues could find some resolution. De Courcel also blamed U.S. intransigence concerning the atomic stockpile but offered no details for this point of tension. If France could not agree to the atomic stockpile, Norstad told the French representative that it made it difficult to maintain U.S. air assets in the nation. If France rejected the deployment of any nuclear weapons in its borders it meant that U.S. aircraft deployed to French bases would be less secure. If these aircraft did not have access to nuclear weapons it was problematic to keep them in France because they lacked the ability to execute their mission. Such aircraft were only targets and not weapons.[23]

These issues came up again when the Permanent Representative de Courcel left his position in January 1959. De Courcel and General Norstad discussed common ground between France, Great Britain, and the United

8. Unintended Consequences

States. Africa was one area where the two agreed that there was some consensus. De Courcel said that de Gaulle did not need any formal agreement and that he wanted to deal with the U.S. and U.K. in good faith. Norstad reminded de Courcel that the problems between NATO and France had more to do with the heavy-handed manner that de Gaulle used in allied relations. These measures alienated France from the rest of the alliance and would not endear de Gaulle to Eisenhower or Macmillan.[24]

Neither Eisenhower nor Macmillan shared de Gaulle's estimation of the strategic situation. Although all three nations agreed that securing Africa was important, the problem was how best to do this. De Gaulle continued to press for direct French involvement through its traditional colonial centers of power. In order for the U.S. and the U.K. to support this meant that these nations would have to concede to French colonial holdings in North Africa. This would prevent President Eisenhower from supporting nationalist Arab groups in the region in favor of an imperial power imposing its rule on a subject people.

The NATO stockpile and atomic weapons also came up in this conversation. Norstad reminded the French representative that other NATO nations agreed to the deployment of atomic weapons under NATO control as well as the NATO atomic stockpile agreement but France continued to resist this proposal. General Norstad told de Courcel that if the French did not reverse their position, he had to recommend the withdrawal of the 9 U.S. Air Force squadrons deployed to France. In response, de Courcel told Norstad that France could not accept nuclear weapons deployed inside the nation without being in direct control of them. According to de Courcel this was especially true since France still lacked atomic weapons of its own. He told the general that France was "a Great Power" and "not Benelux," referring to the nations of Belgium, the Netherlands, and Luxembourg.[25]

De Courcel's position evinced the importance of nuclear weapons in determining the position of a nation in the alliance. He implied that the deployment of nuclear weapons outside of French control was galling, particularly because France did not have such weapons under its own control. The only nation in Europe with that capability was Great Britain. De Courcel's description of France as a superior nation was also telling. He used the term Benelux when referring to Belgium, Netherlands, and Luxemburg, implying that allowing NATO to deploy nuclear weapons in French territory relegated France to subordinate status in the alliance.

Eisenhower's Nuclear Calculus in Europe

The two-tier informal structure of the alliance in place in the late 1950s clearly frustrated de Gaulle. However, he did not have the leverage to change France's status in the organization. French prestige continued to suffer as the French president struggled to convince Eisenhower and Macmillan that a non-nuclear France was a vital member state.

One consistent problem between de Gaulle, Eisenhower, and Macmillan was the different perceptions of the strategic importance of Africa. De Gaulle continued to argue that Africa, particularly French holdings in the north, were vital to any defense of Western Europe. This interpretation, if accepted by Eisenhower and Macmillan, would mean that holding France in the alliance was vital to its effectiveness. De Gaulle looked to increase French prestige by creating a reason for a larger role in the alliance for France. However, this required that Eisenhower and Macmillan agreed with his perception of the strategic situation and France's importance in that framework.

Although the issue of possessing nuclear weapons was important, a corollary of this was also an important problem. De Gaulle did not see in the agreement the ability for France to ensure that an atomic strike carried out from France would not further jeopardize its security situation. As shown earlier, de Gaulle's proposed solution to this problem was French control over U.S. warheads, which was an impossible and an unreasonable policy position. By taking such a position, there was little room for Norstad to negotiate in good faith. It was impossible for him, or Eisenhower, to agree to give the French control over atomic warheads. Not even the Anglo-American IRBM agreement allowed this.[26]

The U.S. ambassador to France, Cecil Lyon referenced a conversation he had with Louis Jacquinot, the French Minister of State concerning de Gaulle. Lyon said that de Gaulle was mistaken concerning the lack of a French veto. The French minister asked who held the authority to use such weapons. Lyon replied that the Supreme Commander held the authority, but he suggested de Gaulle get an official brief on such matters from NATO officials. However, Lyon assured the minister that France had a veto over the use of such weapons.[27] Lyon was right, France did have a veto. However, the decision to use such weapons rested with General Norstad as SHAPE commander. This streamlined the decision making process but it also put NATO nations under the authority of an American general.

The problem of control of nuclear weapons came up again when the

8. Unintended Consequences

French Ambassador presented a series of proposed discussion points that de Gaulle wished to cover in an upcoming meeting between the U.S., the U.K., and France. De Gaulle thought it important to discuss a cooperative approach to world strategy and how a nuclear deterrent factored into it. Dulles replied that the U.S. held "its nuclear deterrent in trust for the free world."[28] This attitude was representative of the subordination of French interests to that of the United States. As long as France relied on the U.S. for its nuclear deterrent, even if the U.S. held this in trust, it meant that France was not truly independent to chart its own course, its policies had to align with its protector, the United States. De Gaulle did not think that the security gains were worth the sacrifice and de Gaulle voice such concerns to Dulles in their meeting in July 1958.[29]

These issues of sovereignty were not purely theoretical for de Gaulle. When the United States needed an airbase to move troops into Lebanon in 1958 in response to the creation of the United Arab Republic, it used the NATO base in Evreux in France to establish an aerial line of communication to Lebanon without seeking permission from the French government for this use first. De Gaulle saw this as a violation of French sovereignty and saw that such actions could possibly involve France in a war that it did not choose to join. Maintaining control of French weapons and security resources was vital for de Gaulle to ensure France determined its own path.[30]

One of the first manifestations of de Gaulle's frustration with NATO was the removal of the French Mediterranean Fleet from NATO. In early 1959, de Gaulle decided to take direct control of the fleet and end its affiliation with the alliance. General Norstad did not think that this detracted from the military power of the NATO naval presence; rather he thought that the French lost more in the fleet's removal. He believed that the political ramifications to the alliance would be more troubling. One thing Norstad did not want to do was to beg de Gaulle to bring his fleet back to NATO. General Norstad argued that the French needed NATO's assistance in the naval realm more than the alliance needed their contribution.[31]

General Ely, president of the French Chiefs of Staff Committee, met with General Norstad on March 6, 1959, to discuss the decision to remove the Mediterranean Fleet from NATO. Norstad told Ely that there were other remedies; he suggested that the French fleet could be put in the same status as the U.S. Sixth Fleet or operate directly under SACEUR.

General Ely did not respond positively to these suggestions and told Norstad that the decision to remove the fleet was not going to change.[32]

A subsequent conversation on March 11, 1959, between the officers covered a broad range of NATO related topics, particularly de Gaulle's frustration with the alliance. One of the first topics that came up was the French interests in North Africa. General Ely communicated de Gaulle's position. He stated that the French believed that if they left the region it invited communist influence into it. Ely noted that such a decision created the conditions for open revolt against the government in France and this only helped the communists. De Gaulle, according to Ely, saw the French withdrawal from Algeria as the beginning of the end for the free world. The differences in the strategic outlooks between de Gaulle and Eisenhower was one cause of their inability to come to an agreement about the IRBMs and nuclear cooperation between the two nations.[33]

General Norstad explained the U.S. policy for North Africa supported the creation of an Arab alliance. He told General Ely that by supporting independent Arab states the U.S. was not inviting Soviet influence in the region. Norstad continued by stating that the U.S. position clashed with the French interpretation of the situation both in Algiers and previously in Suez.[34]

Another issue implied in this conversation was that of decolonization. De Gaulle wanted to retain some influence in French colonies. Although he couched his argument, as presented by General Ely, purely in defensive terms, French prestige was the foundational issue. France, de Gaulle argued, was important because of its position in North Africa. Its colonial holdings, or its continued ties to former colonies, gave it a unique position in NATO. However, as Norstad explained, President Eisenhower did not think that focusing on colonial ties was an effective policy. Rather, newly independent Arab states made more viable partners in creating a regional group to resist Soviet incursion if they were truly independent. This undercut French prestige because it discounted France's colonial presence and power in the Middle East and within NATO.

One of the reasons that Italy as well as Turkey accepted the offer of IRBMs was that it increased their prestige within NATO. These weapons gave both of these states a more powerful voice in NATO atomic policy. The problem with France was that the offer of IRBMs did not increase French prestige, de Gaulle saw them as an admission that France was a junior partner in the alliance.[35]

8. Unintended Consequences

The subject of IRBMs came up during President Eisenhower's visit to Paris in 1959. De Gaulle and Eisenhower discussed why de Gaulle was unhappy with the framework offered by Eisenhower. De Gaulle said that if the Soviets attacked the U.S., Eisenhower could count on French support. However, given the ability of the Soviets to destroy the U.S., de Gaulle warned that he could not be sure of U.S. willingness to use military force if there was no direct Soviet attack on the U.S. De Gaulle did not see the benefit of tying his nation's hands. France, de Gaulle believed, had to have control over its atomic force. Eisenhower cautioned de Gaulle that France could not hope to rival the Soviet atomic arsenal. De Gaulle replied that, "in order for our deterrent to be effective, it is enough to be able to kill the enemy once, even if he possesses the means to kill us ten times over."[36]

General de Gaulle's resistance to the NATO atomic stockpile program and the Allied Command Europe IRBM program came largely as a result of the lack of concessions from President Eisenhower to align his view of French prestige with that of de Gaulle. Although Eisenhower was correct not to accommodate de Gaulle, he did not anticipate the obvious negative French reaction. De Gaulle argued that France deserved more importance in the alliance; it did not deserve to be told what would happen inside its own borders, especially in terms of atomic warfare. De Gaulle argued that France was a vital member of alliance because of its strategic importance in North Africa. He argued that this overrode the absence of a lack of French nuclear deterrent. The lack of a deterrent was also a problem that France was working on but required years to be able to compete with Britain.

Neither Eisenhower nor Macmillan wanted France to become a nuclear power. But there was little either could do to stop this from occurring. Eisenhower never offered the amount of technical help to de Gaulle that he offered to United Kingdom. He also did not agree to give IRBMs to France outside the NATO framework, as he did with the U.K. Nuclear weapons acted as a barometer for status in the alliance at this time. Although de Gaulle tried to convince the U.S. and U.K. of his nation's importance the alliance, he could not sway their interpretation of the strategic threat or the need to reorganize NATO to suit French needs.

Conclusion

The deployment of IRBMs to Western Europe, although a military issue, influenced the political realm of the NATO alliance. President Eisenhower's use of two different frameworks to deploy the missiles created a two-tiered structure in Western Europe. First, from the fact that both Britain and the U.S. were nuclear powers, and second this tiered configuration came from the disparate terms offered to NATO nations by the Eisenhower administration. The Anglo-American agreement did not incorporate the IRBMs into SACEUR in a formal manner. The offer to other NATO nations provided the missiles only through SACEUR and the NATO atomic stockpile. The deployment of Thor missiles to Britain helped heal the rift between the United Kingdom and the United States in the wake of the Suez Canal Crisis. The same agreement also alienated France and influenced de Gaulle's decision to remove France from the military alliance. These weapons also revealed the influence of the New Look defense policy. Although Eisenhower never removed a significant amount of U.S. troops from Europe, he clearly saw the addition of missiles to Europe as part of the groundwork for such an event in the future. The deployment of IRBMs demonstrated that the perceived military value of a weapons system could make up for any perceived deficiencies in its military effectiveness.

Judged by their political influence and efficacy the IRBMs, both Jupiter and Thor were a success. The deployment of these weapons helped bring the Anglo-American alliance closer. However, the unexpectedly quick development of the ICBM and advances in solid-fuel rockets soon made the Thor and Jupiter missiles obsolete. Although the weapons only remained operational for five years they were an important part of the early Cold War period.

Eisenhower's deployment of IRBMs to Western Europe was a small part of the Cold War. However, this event demonstrated the importance

Conclusion

of a nation possessing an independent deterrent or other strategically important asset. Although in the specifics of the deployment of IRBMs, the vital issue was possession of nuclear weapons. The fact that the British had their own atomic weapons program meant that Prime Ministers Eden and Macmillan could use their position to leverage an advantageous agreement. It also meant that the U.K. could operate as a more equal partner in the alliance than the French, who did not possess an independent strategic deterrent.

The New Look defense policy established atomic weapons and Massive Retaliation as the paramount form of national defense for both economic and defense reasons. Although the usual interpretation of the New Look defense policy focuses mainly on its economic rationale, there were significant military assumptions and reasons that formed the foundation of the defense policy. The Solarium Conference was not an economic forum; it was a defense oriented discussion. This meeting established the broad outlines of the New Look policy. Although Eisenhower certainly focused on the economic aspects of national defense, fiscal concerns did not eclipse the need to defend the United States from the threat of the Soviet Union.

President Eisenhower did worry about the economic implications of defense spending but he did not think that it was prudent to sacrifice national defense in order to realize economic outcomes. His defense program was able to reduce defense spending, primarily through reductions in Army force levels and Army budget reductions. This led to a mid-decade low in defense spending to approximately $30 billion dollars. However, Eisenhower was unable to sustain such a relatively low defense budget. By the end of his administration, defense allocations rose to $40 billion dollars. Much of this increase came in the Air Force budget, which by the end of the decade was almost half of the total defense budget.

The reason for the increased defense spending was another focus of the New Look policy. In order to reduce the burden of securing the nation from the Soviet Union, the Air Force, with its strategic force projection capability, took over the primary role in security. This made economic sense because Eisenhower hoped to reduce the amount of money that the U.S. spent funding large ground divisions deployed to Europe. However, this required spending more on Air Force assets, particularly atomic weapons, diminishing much of Eisenhower's defense savings. As a result of the supremacy of the Air Force, nuclear weapons formed the basis for

Conclusion

the New Look defense policy. The doctrine of Massive Retaliation was one example of the reliance on atomic weapons. President Eisenhower understood that atomic weapons fundamentally changed how the U.S. prepared to fight future wars. The U.S. had to have the ability to fight on the atomic battlefield and the Air Force had the capability to do this most effectively.

Eisenhower's conception of atomic warfare also explains the problems that the Army faced during the 1950s. Since the Army focused on deploying large ground forces to contentious regions in order to deter conflicts, it was an expensive means of preventing conflicts. This made it difficult for Army leaders, such as Chief of Staff General Maxwell Taylor, to justify a prominent role for their service in Eisenhower's construct of atomic warfare. Another problem the Army faced in making the case for a larger role in national defense was the issue of casualties in a nuclear war.

The atomic battlefield, in Eisenhower's understanding, would not be a friendly place for densely organized ground units. This is what made the Air Force such an attractive option. With manned strategic bombers and later guided missiles, the U.S. could effectively deter any conflict with the Soviet Union without deploying and sustaining large ground units around the Soviet Union. If a conflict did break out with the Soviet Union, Eisenhower had no doubt that countering it required a large nuclear barrage. This again played to the strengths of the Air Force. The Air Force could strike targets deep inside the Soviet Union and purportedly destroy much of the Soviet war making capability quickly. The promise of immediate efficacy contributed to the Air Force's budget success under the New Look.

Through the 1950s Eisenhower's conception of atomic warfare influenced defense policy. This, in turn, affected foreign policy as well. As the U.S. continued to increase its reliance on atomic weapons in deterring conflicts, it shifted the burden of fighting smaller-scale wars to its allies. The premise of the New Look defense policy's economic savings relied on the U.S. not getting involved in another limited conflagration, like the Korean War. The concentration on nuclear weapons and their subsequent prominence in defense issues made them a barometer of political importance in the NATO alliance.

By the middle of the 1950s there were only two nations with an independent nuclear capability in the NATO alliance, Great Britain and the United States. This created a de facto two-tier structure within the asso-

Conclusion

ciation that would influence how the U.S. interacted with the U.K. and other non-nuclear nations, particularly France. The Suez Canal Crisis created strain in the alliance between France, Great Britain, and the United States. Although significant for its ramifications in the Middle East, its impact on the European alliance was also important.

The Bermuda Conference, hosted in March 1957, was an effort for the U.S. and the U.K. to repair the relations between the two nations. President Eisenhower and Prime Minister Harold Macmillan met on the Caribbean island to discuss how to bring the two states closer together. Part of this rapprochement was Eisenhower's offer of IRBMs to the United Kingdom. Along with this promised deployment was the agreement to work for alterations in U.S. law concerning cooperation on atomic weapons technology.

The agreement between Eisenhower and Macmillan did affect a change in relations between the U.S. and the U.K. Left out of this agreement was France, which did not have its own nuclear weapons program. This was one of the instances where possession of nuclear weapons was crucial to the status of a nation inside the NATO alliance. The independent British nuclear deterrent was not the only reason for the IRBM program; it also impacted the character and form of the agreement that regulated the deployment of the missiles and the future nuclear Anglo-American cooperation.

Although the Bermuda agreement established the deployment of IRBMs, these missiles were not ready for full-scale production at the time of the accord. When Eisenhower made this offer in March 1957, he did not expect to expand the program to other NATO nations. The Soviet launch of *Sputnik* increased the intensity of the research and manufacture of guided missiles, particularly the ICBM and IRBM. At the time of the launch there was only one system that could hit Soviet military and industrial targets from Western Europe, the IRBM. ICBMs, according to estimates at the time, were still years from being ready. This made IRBMs the only weapon system that could quickly establish the United States and, by extension, its allies as formidable powers in the missile age.

In light of the *Sputnik* launch, President Eisenhower agreed to expand the deployment of IRBMs to any NATO nation willing to accept them. This raised the question of how to broaden the scope of the deployment of these missiles to the rest of Europe. The framework of the Anglo-American agreement required creating a series of bi-lateral agreements

Conclusion

with each nation in NATO, in effect negating much of the power of the alliance. President Eisenhower, instead, offered the weapons through the North Atlantic Council and the warheads through SACEUR. This ensured that the missiles worked within alliance to secure the broader security of Western Europe, and that nuclear weapons remained under U.S. control.

This concern about protecting the power of the alliance exposed Eisenhower's hesitation to encourage the proliferation of independent nuclear programs throughout Europe. Such a dispersed effort detracted from economic resources that the European nations needed to dedicate to building conventional forces, which the U.S. expected in order to withdraw some of its ground forces. The president did not see U.S. troops in Europe as part of the permanent U.S. force structure. Rather, he wanted them to assume some of the duties of defending U.S. allies until those states could provide for their own defenses. Once this occurred, the United States could drawdown some of its ground forces and maintain its strategic defense of Western Europe by using its nuclear weapons in the region and its ICBMs and strategic bomber force from the continental United States.

One of the nations affected by the expansion of the IRBM program to NATO was France. Although initially receptive to the deployment of IRBMs to its nation, the situation changed when Charles de Gaulle came to power. He wanted France to assume a larger role in the affairs of the alliance. Specifically regarding the IRBMs, he wanted an agreement that was similar to the Anglo-American pact concerning the weapons and future nuclear cooperation. De Gaulle refused to accept the proposed agreement that came through the auspices of SACEUR and the NATO Atomic Stockpile, because he felt it required France to acquiesce its sovereignty.

Much of the disagreement concerning the proposed deployment of IRBMs came from disparate evaluations of the France's position in the alliance. De Gaulle argued that France was vital to the organization because of its position in North Africa. French colonies in the Maghreb, according to de Gaulle, served to stop any Soviet incursion that looked to retrace the route of Nazi Germany in World War II. This made France a key part of securing Western Europe, at least according to French leaders.

Neither President Eisenhower nor Prime Minister Macmillan shared de Gaulle's estimation of French importance to the security of Europe. The difference between the two strategic assessments was one of the rea-

Conclusion

sons that France did not receive the same consideration when it came to deploying IRBMs to Britain. In addition to the conflict over strategic importance was the possession of nuclear weapons. In this situation, de Gaulle again overestimated his nation's importance.

The French nuclear weapons program successfully tested its first nuclear weapon in 1960; however, it did not have a viable weapons program until the middle of that decade. At the time of the initial IRBM deployment the French nuclear weapons program was an unknown entity. Both Eisenhower and Macmillan knew of its existence but were uncertain of how soon it could come to fruition. Neither wanted France to become a nuclear nation but both understood that there was little they could do to stop such an event. One important thing that Eisenhower could withhold from France was technical assistance.

President Eisenhower did not want France to spend its resources building its own nuclear arsenal, which he saw as redundant because of the presence of the U.S. deterrent. He did not want to offer technical help because this only encouraged de Gaulle to continue to divert his efforts from building a common European defense. This was quite different from Eisenhower's efforts to change U.S. legislation to afford more technical cooperation between the U.S. and the U.K.

Altering the command and control agreement of the IRBM agreement from the model used by the Anglo-American form was another way Eisenhower sought to use the IRBM deployment to realize a larger policy goal. The Anglo-American agreement was outside of NATO command and control. The Thors deployed to Britain would complement and coordinate with SACEUR but the prime minister and the president had to agree to fire the missiles. For the missiles offered under SACEUR, President Eisenhower could delegate the decision to launch the missiles to the U.S. commander in Europe. De Gaulle refused to accept France being placed in a subordinate position relative to Great Britain, or to giving up its sovereignty on issues of security. The changes in the IRBM agreement alienated France and set the stage for its eventual withdrawal from the military side of the NATO alliance.

The deployment of IRBMs to Europe had two important goals. The first was to affect a rapprochement between the United States and the United Kingdom in the wake of the Suez Canal Crisis. The second was to answer the domestic security concerns in light of *Sputnik* by expanding the deployment of IRBMs throughout Western Europe in order to increase

Conclusion

U.S. missile capability. Although the weapons left operational service by 1963, they had a dramatic impact on the relationship between France, the United Kingdom, and the United States. These weapons, although not militarily important, were significant because of their impact on the NATO alliance. This is indicative of how peacetime military deployments can have second and third order effects outside of the intended policy end state.

Chapter Notes

Introduction

1. Campbell Craig, *Destroying the Village: Eisenhower and Thermonuclear War* (New York: Columbia University Press, 1998).
2. Peter Roman, *Eisenhower and the Missile Gap* (Ithaca: Cornell University Press, 1995).
3. Philip Nash, *The Other Missiles of October: Eisenhower, Kennedy, and the Jupiters 1957–1963* (Ithaca: Cornell University Press, 1997).
4. Edward Kaplan, *To Kill Nations: American Strategy in the Air-Atomic Age and the Rise of Mutually Assured Destruction* (Ithaca: Cornell University Press, 2015).
5. Frederic Bozo, trans. Susan Emanuel, *Two Strategies for Europe: De Gaulle, the United States, and the Atlantic Alliance* (New York: Rowman & Littlefield, 2001).

Chapter 1

1. David Halberstam, *The Fifties* (New York: Ballantine Books, 1994), 87, 99.
2. Dwight David Eisenhower, *Mandate for Change: The White House Years, a Personal Account, 1953–1956* (New York: Doubleday, 1963), 95.
3. Eisenhower, *Mandate for Change*, 78.
4. Eisenhower, *Mandate for Change*, 97–98.
5. Dwight David Eisenhower and Robert Ferrell, ed., *The Eisenhower Diaries* (New York: Norton, 1981), 53.
6. Eisenhower, *The Eisenhower Diaries*, 175.
7. Michael Korda, *Ike: An American Hero* (New York: Harper Perinnial, 2008), 490–491.
8. Eisenhower, *The Eisenhower Diaries*, 324.
9. Eisenhower, *The Eisenhower Diaries*, 257–258.
10. Eisenhower, *Mandate for Change*, 446.
11. Dwight Eisenhower, *At Ease: Stories I Tell to Friends* (New York: Doubleday, 1967), 186.
12. Dwight Eisenhower, "Letter to General Alfred Gruenther," Folder November 1964, Box 6, DDE Diary Series, Eisenhower papers as President, Dwight David Eisenhower Presidential Library, Albilene (hereafter DDE Presidential Library), 2 (herefter Letter to Alfred Gruenther).
13. Francis, Howard Heller. Ed., *Economics and the Truman Administration* (Lawrence: University Press of Kansas, 1981), 5.
14. Letter to Gen. Alfred Gruenther, 1.
15. Letter from Secretary of Treasury Humphrey, 29 July 1953, DDE Papers as President, DDE Diary Series, Box 3, Folder December 52 through July 53(1), DDE Presidential Library 1; United States. Bureau of the Budget and United States. Office of Management and Budget. "Fiscal Year Ending June 30, 1955," *Budget of the United States Government* (January 21, 1954). https://fraser.stlouisfed.org/scribd/?item_id=19008&filepath=/files/docs/publicati-

ons/usbudget/bus_1955.pdf, accessed on August 24, 2017, 7.

16. Letter to George Whitney, 24 June 1953, DDE Papers as President, Box 3, Folder December 52 through July 53(2), DDE Presidential Library, 3 (hereafter Letter to George Whitney).

17. Memo from Secretary of the Treasury Humphrey, Dated 29 July 1953, DDE Papers as President, DDE Diary Series, Box 3, DDE Presidential Library, 1.

18. Letter to Alfred Gruenther, 4.

19. Bernard Brodie, "Nuclear Weapons: Strategic or Tactical?," *Foreign Affairs* 32 (January 1954): 223.

20. John Slessor, "Air Power and World Strategy," *Foreign Affairs* 33 (October 1954): 46.

21. Central Intelligence Agency, "Comparison of U.S. and Soviet Population and Manpower," (Washington, D.C.: Central Intelligence Agency, 1960), http://www.foia.cia.gov/docs/DOC_0000380594/DOC_0000380594.pdf (accessed 11 November 2012), 1.

22. Memorandum by Frank Pace, 1949, File 130, Papers of Harry S. Truman PSF: Subject File, 1940–1953: Bureau of the Budget File: Defense Production Act to FY 1952–1953, Harry S. Truman Presidential Library, Independence.

23. John Snyder to President Truman, June 28, 1949, Student Research File #14, file The Attempt to Achieve Stable Economic Growth During the Truman Administration [7 of 13]. Truman Presidential Library, Independence.

24. Dean Acheson, *Present at the Creation: My Years in the State Department* (New York: W.W. Norton, 1969), 420.

25. Paul Pierpaoli, *Truman and Korea: The Political Culture of the Early Cold War* (Columbia: University of Missouri Press, 1999), 26.

26. Edward A. Kolodziej, *Uncommon Defense and Congress, 1945–1963* (Columbus: Ohio State University Press, 1966), 167.

27. Dwight David Eisenhower, "Annual Message to the Congress on the State of the Union," Given on 2 February 1953, The American Presidency Project, http://www.presidency.ucsb.edu/ws/index.php?pid=9829 (Hereafter Eisenhower State of Union Address, 1953) (accessed on 5 December 2017) (hereafter Eisenhower State of the Union Address, 1953).

28. Eisenhower State of the Union Address, 1953.

29. Gallup Poll, July 1953. Retrieved April 16, 2010 from the iPOLL Databank, The Roper Center for Public Opinion Research, University of Connecticut. http://www.ropercenter.uconn.edu.www2.lib.ku.edu:2048/data_access/ipoll/ipoll.html.

30. Waldemar Kaempffert, "First Atomic Shell Fired from a Gun Opens Still Another Phase of Military Tactics," *New York Times*, May 31, 1953, http://select.nytimes.com/gst/abstract.html?res=F50F1EFA3D59107A93C3AA178ED85F478585F9 (accessed 2 October 2014).

31. *Foreign Relations of the United States*, 1952–1954 National Security Affairs, Vol II, part 1, p. 436 (All Foreign Relations of the United States citations after this will be FRUS [year, volume]).

32. Campbell Craig, *Destroying the Village: Eisenhower and Thermonuclear War* (New York: Columbia University Press, 1998) 45.

33. The other members of the Task Force were Tyler Wood, Rear Admiral H.P. Smith, Army Colonel G.A. Lincoln, Army Colonel C.H. Bonesteel, Navy Captain H.E. Sears, and John M. Maury. To lessen confusion, I will refer to the reports of the Task Forces in terms of their Chairmen.

34. The "X" Article titled "The Sources of Soviet Conduct" appeared in *Foreign Affairs* in July 1947.

35. George Kennan et al., "A Report to the National Security Council by Task Force "A" of Project Solarium on A Course of Action Which the United States Might Presently or in the Future Undertake with respect to the Soviet Power Bloc—Alterna-

Chapter Notes—2

tive "A" (1953), White House Office, National Security Council Staff: Papers 1948–1961, Box 39, Folder Project Solarium-Task Force "A" Report (1) DDE Presidential Library, 1 (hereafter cited as Task Force A Report).

36. Task Force A Report, 21–2.
37. Task Force A Report, 18.
38. Task Force A Report, 18.
39. Task Force A Report, 13–14.
40. Task Force A Report, 151–153.
41. The other members of Task Force B were John C. Campbell, Army Major General (RET) John R. Deane, Calvin Hoover, Air Force Colonel Elvin Ligon, Phillip Mosley, and James Penfield.
42. U.S. Air Force, "Major General James McCormack Jr.," http://www.af.mil/about-us/biographies/display/article/106328/major-general-james-mccormack-jr/, Accessed 27 October 2017.
43. Major General James McCormack et al., "A Report to the National Security Council by Task Force "B" of Project Solarium on A Course of Action which the United States might Presently or in the Future Undertake with Respect to the Soviet Power Bloc—Alternative "B," White House Office, National Security Council Staff: Papers 1948–61, Disaster File, Box 39, Folder Project Solarium—Task Force "B" Report, 1948–61 Disaster File, 1 (hereafter Task Force B Report).
44. Task Force B Report, 3–4.
45. Task Force B Report, 3–4.
46. Task Force B Report, 4.
47. Task Force B Report, 5–6.
48. Task Force B Report, 5.
49. Task Force B Report, 13–14.
50. Task Force B Report, 18.
51. Task Force B Report, 11–12.
52. The other members of Task Force C were Army Lieutenant General L.L. Lemnitzer, G.F. Reinhardt, Kilbourne Johnson, Army Colonel Andrew Goodpaster, Leslie Brady, and Army Colonel Harold Johnson.
53. R.L. Conolly et al., "A Report to the National Security Council by Task Force "C" of Project Solarium on Course of Action which the United States might presently or in the Future Undertake with Respect to the Soviet Power Bloc—Alternative "C," White House Office, Office of the Special Assistant for National Security Affairs: Records, 1952–62, Box 9, Folder Project Solarium, Report to NSC by Task Force "C" [1953] (hereafter Task Force C Report) (1–2).
54. Task Force C Report, 1–2.
55. Task Force C Report, 3.
56. Task Force C, i.
57. Task Force C, 8.
58. Oral History Interview with Bromley Smith by John Luter on 29 August 1972, part of the Columbia University Oral History Project, DDEL, OH-270, 33.

Chapter 2

1. Oral History Interview with Andrew Goodpaster, Ann Whitman, Raymond Saulnier, Elmer Staats, Arthur Burns, Gordon Gray by Hugh Helco and Anna Nelson, The National Academy of Public Administration, DDE Presidential Library, Filed as OH 508, 3.
2. Memorandum by Robert Cutler discussing Project Solarium, DDE Papers as President, NSC Series, Box 4, Folder Minutes of 155th Meeting of the NSC 16 July 1953, DDE Presidential Library, 3 (hereafter Cutler NSC Solarium Memo).
3. Cutler NSC Solarium Memo, 3.
4. Cutler NSC Solarium Memo, 2–3.
5. Cutler NSC Solarium Memo, 2.
6. James Lay, "A Report to the National Security Council by the Executive Secretary on Basic National Security Policy," White House Office, National Security Council Staff: Papers, 1948–61 Disaster File, Box 11, Folder NSC 162/2 (2), DDE Presidential Library (hereafter cited as NSC 162/2), 5–6.
7. NSC 162/2, 24–25.
8. Andrew Goodpaster, interview by Malcolm McDonald conducted on 10 April 1982, Oral History Number 477, DDE Presidential Library, Abilene (hereafter OH-477), 5.

Chapter Notes—3

9. Memorandum for Record by President Dwight D. Eisenhower written on 11 November 1953, DDE Papers as President, DDE Diary Series, Box 4, Folder October–December, 1953, DDE Presidential Library, 1 (hereafter Eisenhower Conversation 11 November 1953).

10. Eisenhower Conversation 11 November 1953, 1.

11. Gallup Poll (AIPO), October 1953. Retrieved April 16, 2010 from the iPOLL Databank, The Roper Center for Public Opinion Research, University of Connecticut. http://www.ropercenter.uconn.edu.www2.lib.ku.edu:2048/data_access/ipoll/ipoll.html.

12. Adrian Lewis, *The American Culture of War: The History of U.S. Military Force from World War II to Operation Iraqi Freedom* (New York: Routledge, 2007), 70.

13. Foreign Affairs Survey, April 1954. Retrieved April 16, 2010 from the iPOLL Databank, The Roper Center for Public Opinion Research, University of Connecticut. http://www.ropercenter.uconn.edu.www2.lib.ku.edu:2048/data_access/ipoll/ipoll.html

14. Campbell Craig describes this idea more fully in *Destroying the Village: Eisenhower and Thermonuclear War* (New York: Columbia University Press, 1998).

15. Carl Von Clausewitz, *On War*, trans. and ed. Michael Howard and Peter Paret (Princeton: Princeton University Press, 1976), 81.

16. Richard Leighton, *History of the Office of the Secretary of Defense Vol. II, Strategy, Money, and the New Look, 1953–1956* (Washington, D.C.: Historical Office, Office of the Secretary of Defense, 2001) 535–537.

17. FRUS (1955–1957, National Security Policy, vol. 19), document number 30.

18. Department of Defense, *Selected Manpower Statistics Fiscal Year 2003* (Washington, D.C.: Department of Defense, 2003), 43–44 (hereafter Selected Manpower Statistics).

19. Selected Manpower Statistics, 43–44.

20. Selected Manpower Statistics, 43–44

21. Ingo Trauschweizer, *The Cold War U.S. Army: Building Deterrence for Limited War* (Lawrence: University Press of Kansas, 2008), 242, 243, 245–249.

22. U.S. Army Center for Military History, "Statistical Data on Strength and Casualties for Korean War and Vietnam" updated 30 May 2011, http://www.history.army.mil/documents/237ADM.htm (accessed 21 February 2012).

23. FRUS (1955–57, National Security Policy vol. 19), document number 53.

Chapter 3

1. Andrew Goodpaster, "Memorandum of Conference with the President May 24, 1956" Digital National Security Archive, document number NH00088, http://gateway.proquest.com/openurl?url_ver=Z39.88-2004&res_dat=xri:dnsa&rft_dat=xri:dnsa:article:CNH00088, p. 1 (hereafter Conference with President 24 May 1956).

2. Conference with President 24 May 1956, 2.

3. Maxwell Taylor, *The Uncertain Trumpet* (New York: Harper, 1959), 3–4.

4. Conference with the President 24 May 1956, 2–3.

5. Conference with the President 24 May 1956, 2.

6. Conference with the President 24 May 1956, 3.

7. Campbell Craig argues that Eisenhower did change his point of view and focused more on limited wars during the middle of his administration. However, Eisenhower's defense budgets do not show such a change in policy. Campbell Craig. *Destroying the Village: Eisenhower and Thermonuclear War* (New York: Columbia University Press, 1998).

8. Dwight Eisenhower, "State of the Union Address 6 January 1955," The American Presidency Project. http://www.presidency.ucsb.edu/ws/index.php?pid=10416 (accessed 5 December 2017) (hereafter State of the Union Address 1955).

Chapter Notes—3

9. State of the Union Address 1955.
10. State of the Union Address 1955.
11. State of the Union Address 1955.
12. State of the Union Address 1955.
13. For fiscal year 1955, the federal budget was 68 billion dollars; the defense budget was 42 billion while non-defense spending was almost 26 billion. Information from the historical budget information from the White House webpage found at http://www.whitehouse.gov/omb/budget/Historicals (accessed 29 September 2012).
14. Dwight David Eisenhower, "Annual Message to the Congress on the State of the Union." Given on 6 January 1955, The Anerican Presidency Project, https://www.presidency.ucsb.edu/node/233954 (hereafter Eisenhower State of the Union Address, 1955) (accessed on 17 November 2018)
15. James Lay, "A Report to the National Security Council by the Executive Secretary on Basic National Security Policy," White House Office: National Security Staff Papers, 1948–1961: Disaster File Series, Box 1, DDE Presidential Library (DDE Library), 7 (hereafter NSC 162/2).
16. James Lay, "287th Meeting of the NSC 7 June 1956," DDE Papers as President, NSC Series, Box 7, DDE Presidential Library, Papers as President, NSC Series Box 7.
17. Gleason Everett, *288th Meeting of the NSC 15 June 1956*. DDE Papers as President, NSC Series, Box 7, DDE Presidential Library, Papers as President, Whitman File NSC Series box 7.
18. James Lay, *Memo Declaring Policy of U.S. Regarding Atomic Weapons*. White House Office; NSC Staff Papers: Ex Secretary Series Box 5, Folder Policy Regarding Atomic Weapons (2), DDE Presidential Library, 1.
19. Lewis Strauss, *Memo for Executive Secretary of National Security Council: Report of Status of Atomic Energy Program on June 30, 1955*. White House Office NSC Staff Papers, Executive Secretary Sub Series Box 1, DDE Presidential Library.
20. FRUS (1955–1957 National Security Policy, vol. 19) document number 120.
21. FRUS (1955–1957 National Security Policy, vol. 19) document number 120.
22. Robert Osgood, *Limited War: The Challenge to American Strategy* (Chicago: The University of Chicago Press, 1957), 1.
23. Bernard Brodie, *Strategy in the Missile Age* (Princeton: Princeton University Press, 1959).
24. NSC 162/2, 1.
25. NSC 162/2, 4.
26. Osgood Caruthers, "Victory Seen by Russia," *New York Times*, January 19, 1961, p. 1.
27. Matthew Ridgway, "My Battles in War and Peace" *Saturday Evening Post*, vol. 228, no. 20 (January 21, 1956): 17–48, 45–46.
28. Ridgway, 48.
29. Ridgway, 48.
30. Ridgway, 48.
31. Ridgway, 48.
32. Maxwell Taylor, Speech to Executives' Club of Chicago, 7 October 55. Digital National Defense Library. https://digitalndulibrary.ndu.edu/cdm4/document.php?CISROOT=/taylor&CISOPTR=233&REC=2 (accessed 30 August 10), p.33 (hereafter cited as Executives' Club Speech).
33. Speech to Executives' Club of Chicago, 30.
34. Maxwell Taylor, "Remarks by General Maxwell Taylor at His First Meeting with the Army Staff After Assuming the Duties of Chief of Staff, United States Army," 7 July 1955. Digital National Defense University Library, https://digitalndulibrary.edu/cdm4/document.php?cisroot=/taylor&cisoptr=367&rec=7, p. 1 (hereafter Cited as Speech to the Army Staff) (Accessed on 30 August 2010).
35. James Lay, *257th Meeting of the NSC*, DDE Library, Papers as President, NSC Series Box 7, 7.
36. Speech to Executives' Club of Chicago, 21.
37. For a detailed description of the Pen-

tomic Army see Andrew Bacevich, *The Pentomic Era: The U.S. Army Between Korea and Vietnam* (Washington, D.C.: National Defense University Press, 1986).

38. Douglas Kinnard, "Eisenhower and the Defense Budget," *The Journal of Politics*. Vol. 39 issue 3 August 1977, 604.

39. Thomas White, "The Strategy of United States Air Power," *Annals of American Academy of Political and Social Science*. 1955, 25.

40. Gallup Poll (AIPO), November 1952. Retrieved Aug-23-2011 from the iPOLL Databank, The Roper Center for Public Opinion Research, University of Connecticut. http://www.ropercenter.uconn.edu.www2.lib.ku.edu:2048/data_access/ipoll/ipoll.html (hereafter November 1952 Gallup Poll).

41. November 1952 Gallup Poll.

42. FRUS (1955–1957, vol. 19) document number, 34.

43. FRUS (1955–1957, vol. 19) document number 67.

44. FRUS (1955–1957, vol. 19) document number 67.

45. Richard Steward, ed., *American Military History, Volume II: The United States Army in a Global Era, 1917–2003* (Washington, D.C.: Center for Military History, 2005), 257–8.

46. Center of Military History, United States Army. *History of Strategic Air and Ballistic Missile Defense. Volume II: 1956–1972* (Washington, D.C.: Center for Military History, 2009), 35.

47. FRUS (1955–1957, vol. 19) document number 67.

48. FRUS (1955–1957 National Security Policy, vol. 19) document number, 3.

49. FRUS (1955–1957 National Security Policy, vol. 19) document number, 3.

50. FRUS (1955–1957 National Security Policy, vol. 19) document number, 3.

51. FRUS (1955–1957 National Security Policy, vol. 19) document number, 70.

52. FRUS (1955–1957 National Security Policy, vol. 19) document number 71.

53. James Marchio, "Risking General War in Pursuit of Limited Objectives: U.S. Military Contingency Planning for Poland in the Wake of the 1956 Hungarian Uprising," *Journal of Military History* Vol. 66, Issue 3, July 2002. pp. 783–812, 807–8.

54. Marchio, 791–2.

55. James Gavin, *War and Peace in the Space Age* (New York: Harper & Brothers, 1958), 136–139.

56. FRUS (1955–1957, National Security Policy, vol. 19) document number, 61.

57. Dwight Eisenhower, Robert Ferrell, ed., *The Eisenhower Diaries* (New York: W.W. Norton, 1981), 307.

58. Eisenhower, *The Eisenhower Diaries*, 307.

59. James Lay, NSC 5501, DDE Records as President, White House Central Files (Confidential File), 1953–1961, Box 45, Folder National Security Council (3), DDE Presidential Library, 1 (hereafter NSC 5501).

60. NSC 5501, 2.

Chapter 4

1. Samuel Huntington, "Interservice Competition and the Political Roles of the Armed Services" *The American Political Science Review* vol. 55, Issue 1, pp 40–52, 47.

2. W.C. Stanton 7 June 1956 RG 319 Army Staff chief of R&D relating to Joint Army-navy ballistic Missile committee 1955–1956 box 12 folder 30.1, p. 1.

3. Brain Linn, *Elvis's Army: Cold War GIs and the Atomic Battlefield* (Cambridge: Harvard University Press, 2016), 230–232.

4. Bob Ward, *Dr. Space: The Life of Werhner Von Braun* (Annapolis: Naval Institute Press, 2005), 80.

5. Gavin, 153–154.

6. Huntington, 47.

7. Huntington, 47.

8. Cecil Smith, RG 319, Army Chief of R&D relating to Joint Army-Navy Ballistic Missile committee 1955–1956 Redstone Box 12 folder 30.1, 1. National Archives and Records Administration II, College Park MD (hereafter NARA II).

Chapter Notes—4

9. Huntington, 41.
10. Michael Armacost, *The Politics of Weapons Innovation: The Thor-Jupiter Controversy* (New York: Columbia University Press, 1969), 46–47.
11. "Chronology of Significant Events in IRBM and ICBM Program," Miscellaneous and Satellite Report on Significant Events Appendix," White House Office, Office of the Staff Secretary, Subject Series, Department of Defense Subseries, Box 7, DDE Presidential Library, pages a-b.
12. Dwight D. Eisenhower, "30 March 1956 Diary Entry," DDE Papers as President, DDE Diary Series, Box 13, Folder March 1956, DDE Presidential Library.
13. Armacost, 53.
14. Armacost, 51.
15. Richard Damms, "James Killian, the Technological Capabilities Panel, and the Emergence of President Eisenhower's 'Scientific-Technological Elite" *Diplomatic History* Vol. 24, Issue 1, Malden: Blackwell Publishers, 58.
16. Armacost, 50–1.
17. Damms, 58.
18. Damms, 68.
19. Ward, 80–98.
20. Ward, 98.
21. Ward, 98.
22. Norman Polmar and Robert Norris, *The U.S. Nuclear Arsenal: A History of Weapons and Delivery Systems Since 1945* (Annapolis: Naval Institute Press, 2009) p 168.
23. Andrew Goodpaster. Memo of Conversation with the President 8 October 1957, White House Office, Office of Staff Secretary, Subject Series, Department of Defense subseries, box 1, Folder Department of Defense Volume II (August-October 1957), DDE Presidential Library, 2.
24. Roger Lanius and Dennis Jenkins, eds., *To Reach the High Frontier: A History of U.S. Launch Vehicles* (Lexington: The University Press of Kentucky, 2002),239.
25. Armacost, 87–88.
26. Launis, 239.
27. John Eisenhower, Memorandum of Conversation with the President 16 August 1957, White House Office, Office of the Staff Secretary, Subject Series, Department of Defense Subseries, Box 1, Folder Department of Defense Volume II (2) August 1957.
28. Neil Sheehan, *A Fiery Peace in a Cold War: Bernard Schriever and the Ultimate Weapon* (New York: Vintage Books, 2009), 317–319.
29. Chronology of Significant Events in IRBM and ICBM Programs, 12–14.
30. Launis, 48–49.
31. Charles Wilson, Memo to Secretary Bruker from SECDEF Wilson IRBM Program. Digital National Security Archive. http://gateway.proquest.com/openurl?url_v er=Z39.88-2004&res_dat=xri:dnsa&rft_dat =xri:dnsa:article:CNH01058 accessed (23 Sep 11), 1–2.
32. FRUS (1955–1957 National Security Policy, vol. 19), document number 139.
33. John Eisenhower, Memorandum of Conversation with the President 20 August 1957, White House Office of the Staff Secretary for National Security Affairs, Subject Series, Department of Defense Subseries, Box 1, Department of Defense Volume II (1) August 1957, DDE Presidential Library.
34. James M. Gavin, *War and Peace in the Space Age* (New York: Harper Brothers, 1958), 77–78.
35. Polmar and Norris, 186–188.
36. Gavin, 260–261.
37. Charles Wilson, Memo for JCS Concerning Readjustment of IRBM Program, White House Office, Office of the Staff Secretary for National Security Affairs, Subject Series, Department of Defense Subseries, Box 6, Folder Missiles and Satellites August 1957 Volume I (2), DDE Presidential Library.
38. Andrew Goodpaster, Memorandum of Conversation with the President 8 October 1957, White House Office, Office of the Staff Secretary for National Security Affairs, Subject Series, Department of Defense Subseries, Box 1, Folder Department of Defense

Chapter Notes—4

Volume II August through October 1957, DDE Presidential Library (hereafter Goodpaster Memo of Conversation with the President 8 October 1957).

39. Maxwell Taylor, Memorandum for the Secretary of Defense Concerning the Army Redstone Modernization Program, dated 2 August 1957, White House Office, Office of the Staff Secretary for National Security Affairs, Subject Series, Department of Defense Subseries, Box 6, Folder Missile and Satellites 1957 Volume II August through October 1957, DDE Presidential Library.

40. George Kistiakowsky, Progress Report for Dr. Killian on the State of Guided Missile Programs, White House Office, Office of the Staff Secretary for National Security Affairs, Subject Series, Department of Defense Subseries, Box 8, Folder Science and Technology Assistant to the President (2), DDE Presidential Library (hereafter Progress Report for Dr. Killian on Guided Missiles).

41. Chronology of significant events in IRBM and ICBM programs, 10–11.

42. Progress Report for Dr. Killian on Guided Missiles, 5.

43. Chronology of Significant events in the IRBM ICBM programs, 11–16.

44. Bob Ward, *Dr. Space: The Life of Wernher Von Braun* (Annapolis: The Naval Institute Press, 2005).

45. Chronology of significant events in IRBM and ICBM programs, 10–15.

46. "Andrew Goodpaster, Summary of Conversation in Governor Adam's Office 16 November 1957, White House Office, Office of Staff Secretary for National Security Affairs, Subject Series, Department of Defense Subseries, Box 6, Folder Missiles and Satellite September through December 1957 Volume I (3), DDE Presidential Library, 2 (hereafter Cited as Conversation in Governor Adam's Office 26 November 1957).

47. Conversation in Governor Adam's Office 26 November 1957, 3.

48. Conversation in Governor Adam's Office 26 November 1957, 3–4.

49. Conversation in Governor Adam's Office 26 November 1957, 2.

50. Conversation in Governor Adam's Office 26 November 1957, 1.

51. James Lay, NSC 151/2 Note by the Executive Secretary to the National Security Council on Disclosure of Atomic Information to Allied Countries, White House Office, Office of the Special Assistant Series, Presidential Subseries, Box 1, Folder President Papers 1953 (2), DDE Presidential Library, 35 (hereafter NSC 151/2 Disclosure of Atomic Information).

52. Andrew Pierre, *Nuclear Politics: The British Experience with an Independent Strategic Force, 1939–1970* (London: Oxford University Press, 1972), 26–27.

53. Pierre, 21.

54. Pierre, 45.

55. Pierre, 45.

56. Mcmahon Act, http://www.osti.gov/atomicenergyact.pdf, 13 (Accessed 14 October 11).

57. Pierre, 63.

58. Viscount Waverly, "Report of the Committee on the Future Organisation for the Atomic Energy Project" 23 July 1953, British National Archives Online Collection.

59. Harold MacMillan, "Letter to RAB from Macmillan in the Ministry of Defence" 21 March 1955, British National Archives CAB/21/4053 Online Collection.

60. Norman Polmar and Robert S. Norris, *The U.S. Nuclear Arsenal: A History of Weapons and Delivery Systems Since 1945* (Annapolis, MD: Naval Institute Press), 44.

61. William Strath, "The Defense Implications of Fall-Out from a Hydrogen Bomb: Note by the Home Defence Committee" 22 March 1955, British National Archives Online Collection.

62. British Cabinet Meeting Conclusion 7 July 1954 including Confidential Annex, British National Archives Online Collection, 6 (hereafter 7 July 1954 British Cabinet Meeting).

63. 7 July 1954 British Cabinet Meeting, 3.

Chapter Notes—5

64. Harold MacMillan, "Guided Weapons for the Army" 2 March 1955, CAB/129/74/12, British National Archives, http://discovery.nationalarchives.gov.uk/details/r/D7657724 (accessed 23 October 2018).

Chapter 5

1. Mohamed Heikal, *Cutting the Lion's Tail: Suez Through Egyptian Eyes* (New York: Arbor House, 1987), 120–127.
2. Heikal, 127.
3. For an in depth treatment of Eisenhower's reaction to the crisis see Cole Kingseed's *Eisenhower and the Suez Crisis of 1956*. For an effective treatment of the impact of the crisis on British imperialism see William Roger Louis's collection of essays in *Ends of British Imperialism: The Scramble for Empire, Suez and Decolonization*. For a general discussion of the crisis from the British perspective see Chester Cooper's *The Lion's Last Roar: Suez, 1956*.
4. Charles Wilson, "Military and Other Requirements for Our National Security," White House Office, Office of the Staff Secretary, Subject Series, Department of Defense Subseries, Box 6, Folder Military Planning, 56–57 (2), DDE Presidential Library, 4–5 (hereafter cited as Wilson Security Memo February 1956).
5. Wilson Security Memo 1956, 6.
6. Arthur Radford, "Memorandum for the Secretary of Defense," White House Office, Office of the Staff Secretary, Subject Series, Department of Defense Subseries, Box 6, Folder Military Planning 56–57(2), DDE Presidential Library (hereafter Radford memo to Sec Def 12 March 1956).
7. Dwight Eisenhower, Robert Ferrell, ed., *The Eisenhower Diaries* (New York: W.W. Norton, 1981), 329–330.
8. Everett Gleason, "Minutes of the 289th Meeting of NCS" DDE Papers as President, National Security Council Series, Box 6, Folder 289th Meeting of NSC 29 June 1956, DDE Presidential Library, 6–7 (Hereafter 289 Meeting of NSC).
9. 289 Meeting of NSC, 7.
10. Eisenhower, 329–330.
11. Eisenhower, 330.
12. Eisenhower, 330.
13. Peter Boyle, ed., *The Eden-Eisenhower Correspondence, 1955–1957* (Chapel Hill: University of North Carolina Press, 2005), 162–3.
14. Boyle, 162–3.
15. Boyle, 162–3.
16. William Roger Louis, *Ends of British Imperialism: The Scramble for Empire, Suez and Decolonization* (New York: Taurus, 2006), 689–692.
17. Boyle, 164.
18. Boyle, 164.
19. Kathleen Teltsch, Special to the *New York Times* (1956, October 3). "Lloyd Is Hopeful Over Suez in U.N.: Briton Here to Seek Backing for International Control Lloyd Hopes U.N. Solves Case Complicating Factor Seen Lloyd Wants Peaceful Solution," *New York Times* (1923—Current File),1. Retrieved December 16, 2011, from Proquest Historical Newspapers, *New York Times* (1851–2007) w/ Index (1851–1993) (Document ID: 84885656).
20. FRUS (1955–1957, Suez Crisis Vol. 16) Document Number 300.
21. FRUS (1955–1957 Suez Crisis, Vol. 16) Document Number 300.
22. Dwight Eisenhower, *Waging Peace: The White House Years* (London: Heinmann, 1966),71–73.
23. Boyle, 178.
24. Boyle, 176–7.
25. Boyle, 176–7.
26. Andrew Goodpaster, "Memorandum of Conference with the President 30 October 1956, DDE Papers as President, DDE Diary Series, Box 19, DDE Presidential Library, 3–4 (hereafter Conference with President 30 October 1956).
27. Conference with President 30 October 1956, 3.
28. Martin Gilbert, *Israel: A History* (New York: Harper Perennial, 1998), 315–322.

29. Gilbert, 320–21.
30. Dwight Eisenhower, "Phone Call Between Eisenhower and Dulles," DDE Papers as President, DDE Diary Series, Box 18, Folder Phone Call, DDE Presidential Library, 2 (hereafter Call between Eisenhower and Dulles 30 October 1956).
31. Call between Eisenhower and Dulles, 30 October 1956, 4.
32. Eisenhower, *Waging Peace*, 58–62.
33. Eisenhower, *Waging Peace*, 62–64.
34. John Foster Dulles, Telephone Conversation with Lester Pearson 30 October 1956, John Foster Dulles Papers, Telephone Conversation Series, Box 5, DDE Presidential Library 1.
35. Eisenhower, *Waging Peace*, 77–78.
36. Dwight Eisenhower, Letter to Lew Douglas 3 November 1956, DDE Papers as President, DDE Diary Series, Box 20, DDE Presidential Library, 1.
37. Dwight Eisenhower, Letter to Dr. Eli Ginzberg 5 November 1956, DDE Papers as President, DDE Diary Series, Box 20, DDE Presidential Library, 1.
38. Eisenhower, *Waging Peace*, 89–90.
39. Andrew Goodpaster, Memorandum of Conference with the President, 5 November 1956, Papers as President, DDE Diary Series, Box 19, DDE Presidential Library, 2.
40. Eisenhower, *Waging Peace*, 91.
41. Andrew Goodpaster, Memorandum for Record 6 November 1956, DDE Papers as President, DDE Diary Series, Box 19, DDE Presidential Library, 3–4.
42. Eisenhower, *Waging Peace*, 124.
43. FRUS (1955–1957 Western Eruope and Canada, vol. 27) document number 253.
44. FRUS (1955–1957 Western Europe and Canada, vol. 27) document number 254.
45. FRUS (1955–1957 Western Europe and Canada, vol. 27) document number 256.
46. FRUS (1955–1957 Western Europe and Canada, vol. 27) document number 256.
47. FRUS (1955–1957 Western Europe and Canada, vol. 27) document number 256.
48. FRUS (1955–1957 Western Europe and Canada, vol. 27) document number 274.
49. United States Delegation to the Bermuda Conference, Memorandum of Conversation 22 March 1957, DDE Papers as President, International Meetings Series, Box 3, DDE Presidential Library, 2 (hereafter Bermuda Conference Meeting 22 March 1957).
50. Bermuda Conference Meeting 22 March 1957, 3.
51. Bermuda Conference Meeting 22 March 1956, 5.
52. Bermuda Conference Meeting, 22 March 1956, 10.
53. United States Delegation to the Bermuda Conference, Memorandum of Conversation 22 March 1957 (afternoon session), DDE Papers as President, International Series, Box 3, DDE Presidential Library, 6–7 (hereafter Bermuda Conference Afternoon Session 22 March 1957 Meeting).
54. FRUS (1955–1957 Western Europe and Canada, vol 27) document number 292.

Chapter 6

1. Special to the *New York Times*, "Device Is 8 Times Heavier than One Planned by U.S: Its Direction in Doubt Weight of 'Moon' a Surprise to U.S. Assumptions on 'Moon.'" *New York Times* (1923—Current File), October 5, 1957, http://www.proquest.com.www2.lib.ku.edu:2048/ (accessed December 21, 2011) (hereafter Special to the *New York Times*).
2. Ward, 98.
3. Ward, 98–99.
4. Sputnik, *Science*, New Series, Vol. 126, No. 3277 (October 18, 1957), pp. 739–740, http://www.jstor.org.www2.lib.ku.edu:2048/stable/1754428 (accessed 19 October 2012).
5. Special to the *New York Times*.

Chapter Notes—6

6. David Halberstam, *The Fifties* (New York: Random Hosue, 1993),624–5.

7. Gallup Poll (AIPO), October 1957. Retrieved Oct-19–2012 from the iPOLL Databank, The Roper Center for Public Opinion Research, University of Connecticut. http://www.ropercenter.uconn.edu.www2.lib.ku.edu:2048/data_access/ipoll/ipoll.html.

8. Gallup Poll (AIPO), November 1957. Retrieved Oct-19–2012 from the iPOLL Databank, The Roper Center for Public Opinion Research, University of Connecticut. http://www.ropercenter.uconn.edu.www2.lib.ku.edu:2048/data_access/ipoll/ipoll.html.

9. Halberstam, 625.

10. Andrew Goodpaster, "Memo of Conference with President on 8 October 1957," DDE Papers as President, DDE Diary Series, Box 27, Folder Staff Notes October 1957 (2), DDE Presidential Library (hereafter Memo of Conference with the President 8 October 1957), 2.

11. Memo of Conference with the President 8 October 1957, 2.

12. Memo of Conference with the President 8 October 1957, 2.

13. Special to the *New York Times*, "7 Astronauts Watch Space Capsule Shot," *New York Times* (1923—Current File), December 20, 1960. 1, http://search.proquest.com/docview/115087853?accountid=14556 (accessed 29 October 2012).

14. 8 October 1957 Conference with the President, 1–2.

15. L.A. Minnich, "Cabinet Meeting Minutes 11 October 1957", DDE Papers as President, DDE Diary Series, Box 27, Folder October 1957 Staff Notes (2), DDE Presidential Library (hereafter Cabinet Meeting 11 October 1957), 4.

16. Cabinet Meeting 11 October 1957, 4.

17. Cabinet Meeting 11 October 1957, 3.

18. Cabinet Meeting 11 October 1057, 2.

19. Dwight D. Eisenhower, *The White House Years: Waging Peace, 1955–1961* (New York: Doubleday, 1965), 483.

20. "CIA Collection Activities Against the Soviet Guided Missile Program"[Includes Attachment], Top Secret Chess; Eider, Memorandum, Excised Copy, January 16, 1958, 3 pp. From the Digital National Security Archives, http://gateway.proquest.com/openurl?url_ver=Z39.88–2004&res_dat=xri:dnsa&rft_dat=xri:dnsa:article:CHN01009 (accessed 28 June 12).

21. Andrew Goodpaster, "Memorandum of Conversation with the President 11 October 1957," DDE Papers as President, DDE Diary Series, Box 27, Folder Staff Notes October 1957 (2), DDE Presidential Library, 1–2.

22. Andrew Goodpaster, "Memorandum of Conference with the President 22 October 1957," DDE Papers as President, DDE Diary Series, Box 27, Folder October 1957 Staff Notes (2) DDE Presidential Library (hereafter Conference with the President 22 October 1957), 1.

23. Conference with the President 22 October 1957, 2.

24. Conference with President 22 October 1957, 1.

25. Bernard Baruch, "Memorandum," DDE Papers as President, DDE Diary Series, Box 27, Folder October 1957, DDE Presidential Library, 1.

26. Hanson Baldwin, "Missiles for Britain: Where U.S. Program Stand Now," The Week in Review, *New York Times*, March 30, 1957.

27. Andrew Goodpaster, "Memorandum of Conference with the President, 25 October 1957," DDE Papers as President, DDE Diary Series, Box 27, Folder October Staff Notes (1), DDE Presidential Library, 1–2.

28. Andrew Goodpaster, "Memorandum of Conference with the President, 26 October 1957," DDE Papers as President, DDE Diary Series, Box 27, Folder Staff Notes 1957 (1), DDE Presidential Library (hereafter Conference with the President 26 October 1957), 1–2.

29. Conference with the President 26 October 1957, 2.

30. Conference with the President 26 October 1957, 2.

31. Conference with the President 26 October 1957, 2.
32. Andrew Goodpaster, "Memorandum of Conference with the President 28 October 1957," DDE Papers as President, DDE Diary Series, Box 27, Folder October 1957 Staff Notes (1), DDE Presidential Library, 1–2.
33. Andrew Goodpaster, "Memorandum of Conference with the President 29 October 1957," DDE Papers as President, DDE Diary Series, Box 27, Folder October 1957 Staff Notes (1), DDE Presidential Library, 1–2.
34. Andrew Goodpaster, "Memorandum of Conference with the President 30 October 1957," DDE Papers as President, DDE Diary Series, Box 27, Folder October 1957 Staff Notes (1), DDE Presidential Library, 3–4 (hereafter Conference with the President 30 October 1957).
35. Conference with the President 30 October 1957, 3–4.
36. Andrew Goodpaster, "Memorandum of Conference with the President 4 November 1957," DDE Papers as President, DDE Diary Series, Box 27, Folder November 1957 Staff Notes, DDE Presidential Library (hereafter Conference with the President 4 November 1957), 1.
37. Conference with the President 4 November 1957 2–3.
38. Conference with the President 4 November 1957, 1–2.
39. Conference with the President 4 November 1957, 2.
40. *New York Times*, October 11, 1957.
41. Andrew Goodpaster, "Memo for Record 6 November 1957," DDE Papers as President, DDE Diary Series, Box 28, Folder November 1957 Staff Notes, DDE Presidential Library, 1, 4.
42. Andrew Goodpaster, "Memorandum of Conference with the President 7 November 1957," DDE Papers as President, DDE Diary Series, Box 28, Folder November 1957, Staff Notes DDE Presidential Library (hereafter Conference with the President 7 November 1957), 2.
43. Conference with the President 7 November 1957, 1–2.
44. Conference with the President 7 November 1957, 1–2.
45. Dwight Eisenhower, "Letter to CAPT Hazlett" DDE Papers as President, DDE Diary Series, Box 28, Folder Diary November 1957, DDE Presidential Library, 1–2.
46. Dwight Eisenhower, "Telephone Call to Defense Secretary Charles Wilson 21 November 1957," DDE Papers as President, DDE Diary Series, Box 29, Folder Phone Calls November 1957, DDE Presidential Library, 1.
47. Andrew Goodpaster, "Memorandum of Conference with the President 22 November 1957," DDE Papers as President, DDE Diary Series, Box 28, Folder November 1957 Staff Notes, DDE Presidential Library, 1.
48. Roger Lanius and Dennis Jenkins, eds., *To Reach the High Frontier: A History of U.S. Launch Vehicles* (Lexington: University Press of Kentucky,2002), 7.
49. L.A. Minnich, "Bipartisan Congressional Meeting Minutes 3 December 1957," DDE Papers as President, DDE Diary Series, Box 29, Folder Staff Notes December 1957, DDE Presidential Library (hereafter Bipartisan Meeting 3 December 1957), 3.
50. Bipartisan Meeting 3 December 1957, 3.
51. Bipartisan Meeting 3 December 1957, 3.
52. Bipartisan Meeting 3 December 1957, 4.
53. Bipartisan Meeting 3 Dec 1957, 3–4.
54. Bipartisan Meeting 3 December 1957, 8.

Chapter 7

1. *Defence: Outline of Future Policy*. DDE Library, Norstad Papers, Box 78, Folder Sir Frank Roberts (3), 3 (hereafter *Defence: Outline of Future Policy*).
2. *Defence: Outline of Future Policy*, 3.
3. *Defence: Outline for Future Policy*, 3.

Chapter Notes—7

4. "Agreement Between the Government of the United Kingdom of Great Britain and Northern Ireland and the Government of the United States of American for Co-Operation on the Uses of Atomic Energy for Mutual Defence Purposes," http://www.nti.org/media/pdfs/56_4.pdf?_=1316627913 (accessed on 27 January 2012).

5. *Defence: Outline for Future Policy*, 9.

6. Benson Timmons, "Working Group on NATO: Political Authority for Use of Atomic Weapons" Norstad Papers, Box 85, Folder Atomic Nuclear Policy 57–59 (2), DDE Presidential Library (hereafter Working Group on NATO: Political Authority for Use of Atomic Weapons), 1–2.

7. Working Group on NATO: Political Authority for use of atomic weapons, 2–3.

8. Working Group on NATO: Political Authority for use of atomic weapons, 2–3.

9. Working Group on NATO: Political Authority to use Atomic Weapons, 2.

10. FRUS (1958–1960 Western Europe vol. 7, part 2) document number 336.

11. FRUS (1958–1960 Western Europe, vol. 7, part 2) document number 336.

12. Robert Murphy, "Report to the President and Prime Minister: Procedure for the Committing to the Attack of Nuclear Retaliatory Forces in the United Kingdom," DDE Papers as President, Dulles Herter Series, Box 10, Folder June 1958, DDE Presidential Library (hereafter Report to President and Prime Minister Concerning Use of Atomic Weapons), 1.

13. Amory Houghton, "Telegram from U.S. Embassy Paris 11 February 1958" DDE Library, Norstad Papers, Box 89, Folder IRBM (3), DDE Presidential Library, 1.

14. Frank Roberts, "North Atlantic Council British White Paper Statement Prior to Publication 12 February 1958," Norstad Papers, Box 78, Folder Sir Frank Roberts (3), DDE Presidential Library (hereafter Frank Roberts Statement to NAC), 2.

15. Frank Roberts Statement to NAC, 2.

16. Frank Roberts Statement to NAC, 2.

17. "Report on Defence: Britain's Contribution to Peace and Security," Norstad Papers, Box 50, Folder UK 57–59 (5), DDE Presidential Library (hereafter Report on Defence: Britain's Contribution to Peace and Security), 4.

18. Report on Defence: Britain's Contribution to Peace and Security, 1.

19. Report on Defence: Britain's Contribution to Peace and Security, 1.

20. Report on Defence: Britain's Contribution to Peace and Security, 2.

21. Report on Defence: Britain's Contribution to Peace and Security, 4.

22. Report on Defence: Britain's Contribution to Peace and Security, 6.

23. Frank Roberts Statement to NAC, 2.

24. Andrew Bacevich, *The Pentomic Era: The U.S. Army Between Korea and Vietnam* (Washington, D.C.: National Defense University Press, 1986).

25. FRUS (1958–1960 Western Europe, vol. 7, part 2) document number 338.

26. FRUS (1958–1960 Western Europe, vol. 7, part 2) document number 338.

27. North Atlantic Treaty Organization, "The North Atlantic Treaty," http://www.nato.int/cps/en/natolive/official_texts_17120.htm (accessed 21 January 2012).

28. FRUS (1958–1960 Western Europe, vol. 7, part 2) document number 336.

29. John Foster Dulles, "Proposed Response to Prime Minister Macmillan 21 February 1958," DDE Papers as President, Dulles Herter Series, Box 10, Folder February 1958 (1), DDE Presidential Library (hereafter Dulles Proposed Response to MacMillan), 1.

30. Dulles Proposed Response to MacMillan 21 February 58, 1–2;

31. FRUS (1958–1960 Western Europe, vol. 7, part 2) document number 339.

32. FRUS (1958–1960 Western Europe, vol. 7, part 2) document number 344.

33. FRUS (1958–1960 Western Europe, vol. 7, part 2) document number 346.

34. FRUS (1958–1960 Western Europe, vol. 7, part 2) document number 347.

35. Ray Thurston, "Memo Concerning

Chapter Notes—8

British Offer to Buy IRBMs 28 August 1958," Norstad Papers, Box 89, IRBM (3), DDE Presidential Library, 1.

36. Benson Timmons, "Memorandum Concerning Transfer of Corporal Warheads 5 SEP 1958," Norstad Papers, Box 85, Folder Nuclear Policy 57–59 (2), DDE Presidential Library, 1.

37. Joseph Wolf, "Regarding Deptel 775 UK Proposal to Purchase Thors and ALO 834," Norstad Papers, Box 89, IRBM (3), DDE Presidential Library (hereafter Memo Concerning U.K. Proposal to Purchase Thors), 1.

38. Memo Concerning U.K. Proposal to Purchase Thors, 1.

39. Memo Concerning U.K. Proposal to Purchase Thors, 1.

40. Memo Concerning U.K. Proposal to Purchase Thors, 1.

41. Memo Concerning U.K. Proposal to Purchase Thors, 2.

42. Memo Concerning U.K. Proposal to Purchase Thors, 2.

43. Memo Concerning U.K. Proposal to Purchase Thors, 2.

44. Lauris Norstad, "Statement to North Atlantic Council Concerning General Operational Requirement for ACE IRBM Weapon System," Norstad Papers, Box 89, IRBM (3), DDE Presidential Library (hereafter Norstad Statement to NAC Concerning IRBM), 1.

45. Norstad Statement to NAC Concerning IRBM, 1.

46. Norstad Statement to NAC Concerning IRBM, 2–3.

47. Norstad Statement to NAC Concerning IRBM, 3.

48. Norstad Statement to NAC Concerning IRBM, 3.

49. Norstad Statement to NAC Concerning IRBM, 4–5.

50. Norstad Statement to NAC Concerning IRBM, 4.

51. Walworth Barbour, "Telegraph to State Department 14 August 1959," Norstad Papers, Box 85, Folder Nuclear Policy 57–59 (1), DDE Presidential Library (hereafter Barbour Telegraph to State Department), 1.

52. Barbour Telegraph to State Department, 1.

53. Barbour Telegraph to State Department, 2.

54. Barbour Telegraph to State Department, 2.

Chapter 8

1. Kenneth Perkins, "Pressure and Persuasion in the Policies of the French Military in Colonial North Africa," *Military Affairs*. Vol. 40 Iss. 2, April 1976, 1226.

2. Perkins, 1228.

3. Bozo, 5–6.

4. John Tuthill, "Telegram from Thurston to SECSTATE," Norstad Papers, Box 87, Folder France Problems 58–59 (3), DDE Presidential Library (hereafter Telegram from Thurston to SECSTATE).

5. Telegram from Thurston to SECSTATE, 1–2.

6. John Tuthill, "Telegram 10 January 1958" Norstad Papers, Box 87, Folder France Problems 58–59 (3), DDE Presidential Library (hereafter Telegram 10 January 1958).

7. Telegram 10 January 1958, 1.

8. Telegram 10 January 1958, 1.

9. John Foster Dulles, "Telegram from Dulles to Paris," Norstad Papers, Box 87, Folder France Problems 58–59 (3), DDE Presidential Library, 1.

10. Amory Houghton, "Telegram to SECSTATE 23 January 1958," DDE Library, Norstad Papers, Box 87, Folder France Problems 58–59 (3), 1.

11. Russell Fessenden, "Fessenden Memorandum for Record 31 January 1958," Norstad Papers, Box 87, Folder France Problems 58–59 (3), DDE Presidential Library (hereafter Fessenden Memorandum for Record 31 January 1958).

12. Fessenden Memorandum for Record 31 January 1958, 1.

13. FRUS (1958–1960 Western Europe, vol. 7 part 2) document number 3.

14. FRUS (1958–1960 Western Europe, vol. 7 part 2) document number 3.
15. FRUS (1958–1960 Western Europe, vol. 7 part 2) document number 4.
16. FRUS (1958–1960 Western Europe, vol. 7 part 2) document number 4.
17. FRUS (1958–1960 Western Europe, vol. 7 part 2) document number 5.
18. FRUS (1958–1960 Western Europe, vol. 7 part 2) document number 6.
19. Dwight D. Eisenhower, *Waging Peace: The White House Years* (London: Heinemann, 1965), 426–427.
20. Eisenhower, *Waging Peace*, 427–428.
21. Charles de Gaulle, George Weidenfeld trans, *Memoirs of Hope: Renewal and Endeavor* (New York: Simon & Schuster, 1970), 199–201.
22. FRUS (1958–1960 Western Europe, vol. 7 part 2) document number 34.
23. Cecil Lyon, "Telegram to SECSTATE from Paris," DDE Library, Norstad Papers, Box 87, folder France Problems 58–59 (3), 1.
24. Armory Houghton, "Washington 2479: Conversation Between Outgoing Permrep and Amory Houghton," DDE Library, Norstad Papers, Box 87, folder France Problems 58–59 (3), 1 (hereafter Washington 2479).
25. Washington 2479, 1.
26. FRUS (1958–1960 Western Europe, vol. 7 part 2) document number 34.
27. Cecil Lyon, "Conversation Between Lyon and Jacquinot," DDE Library, Norstad Papers, Box 87, folder France Problems (3), 1–2.
28. John Foster Dulles, "Telegram by Dulles About Conversation with U.S. Ambassador to France," DDE Library, Norstad Papers, Box 87, France Problems 58–59 (3), 1.
29. Bozo, 12–13.
30. Bozo, 14–15.
31. Randolph Burgess, "Telegram to SECSTATE About Removal of French Fleet from NATO 28 February 59," DDE Library, Norstad Papers, Box 87, folder France Problems 58–59 (2), 1 (hereafter Telegram to SECSTATE 28 February 1959).
32. Cecil Lyon, "Telegram SECSTATE Concerning French Removal of Fleet from NATO, 6 March 59," DDE Library, Norstad Papers, Box 87, Folder France Problems 58–59 (2), 1.
33. Nauris Norstad, "Conversation Between Generals Norstad and Ely," Norstad Papers, Box 87, France Problems 58–59 (2), 2 (hereafter Conversation between Norstad and Ely).
34. Conversation between Norstad and Ely, 2.
35. Dionysios Chourchoulis, *The Southern Flank of NATO, 1951–1959: Military Strategy or Political Stablilization* (Lanham, MD: Lexington, 2015), 207–208.
36. De Gaulle, 214–215.

Bibliography

Archival Sources
Alfred M. Gruenther Papers
Ann Whitman File
British National Archives Online, the Cabinet Papers
C.D. Jackson Papers
Command and General Staff College, Combined Arms Center Research Library, Archive, Ft. Leavenworth, KS
Digital National Defense University Archives
Digital National Security Archives
Dwight D. Eisenhower Papers
Dwight D. Eisenhower Presidential Library, Abilene, KS
Herbert Brownell Papers
Lauris Norstad Papers
Maxwell D. Taylor Papers
National Archives, College Park, MD
Oral Histories: Bowie, Robert; Goodpaster, Andrew; Smith Bromley
Pre-Presidential
Records of the Army Staff— RG 319
Records of the Department of State— RG 59
Records of the Joint Chiefs of Staff— RG 218
Records of the Office of the Secretary of Defense— RG 330
Records of the Secretary of the Army— RG 335
White House Central File
White House Office, National Security Council Staff
White House Office, Office of Staff Secretary
White House Office, Office of the Special Assistant for National Security Affairs: Records
Military Journals Consulted
Army Information Digest
Military Review

Dissertations and Thesis
Appleby, Charles. "Eisenhower and Arms Control, 1953–1961: A Balance of Risks." Ph.D. Diss., Johns Hopkins University, 1987.

Bibliography

Greenwald, Bryon. "Scud Alert!: The History, Development, and Military Significance of Ballistic Missiles on Tactical Operations." Command and General Staff College, 1995.
Jussel, Paul. "Intimidating the World: The United States Atomic Army, 1956–1960." Ohio State University, 2004.
Skelton, John. "The Forbidden Weapon—The Employment of Army Tactical Nuclear Weapons." Command and General Staff College, 1990.

Published Primary Documents

Boyle, Peter, ed. *The Eden-Eisenhower Correspondence, 1955–1957*. Chapel Hill: University of North Carolina Press, 2005.
Eisenhower, Dwight D. *Eisenhower: The Prewar Diaries and Selected Papers, 1905–1941*. Edited by Daniel D. Holt and James Leyerzapf. Baltimore: Johns Hopkins University Press, 1998.
_____. *The White House Years: Mandate for Change*. New York: Doubleday, 1963
_____. *The White House Years: Waging Peace, 1956–1961*. London: Heinemann, 1965.
Ferrell, Robert, ed. *The Eisenhower Diaries*. New York: W.W. Norton and Company, 1981.
Foreign Relations of the United States. Washington, D.C.: Government Printing Office.
Hagerty, James C. *The Diary of James C. Hagerty: Eisenhower in Mid-Course, 1954–1955*. Bloomington: Indiana University Press, 1983.

Books and Articles

Abbott, Philip. "King Utopus, and the Fifties Decade in America." *Presidential Studies Quarterly* 32, no. 1 (March 2002): 7–29.
Acheson, Dean. *Present at the Creation: My Years at the State Department*. New York: W.W. Norton, 1969.
Adan, Avraham. *On the Banks of the Suez*. San Francisco: Presidio Press, 1980.
Aliano, Richard. *American Defense Policy from Eisenhower to Kennedy*. Columbus: Ohio State University, 1975.
Allen, Craig. *Eisenhower and the Mass Media: Peace, Prosperity, and Prime-Time TV*. Chapel Hill: University of North Carolina Press, 1993.
Ambrose, Stephen. *Eisenhower: Soldier, General of the Army, and President Elect*. New York: Simon & Schuster, 1983.
_____. *Eisenhower: The President*. New York: Simon & Schuster, 1984.
_____. *The Military and American Society* New York: Free Press 1972.
Ambrose, Stephen E., Caleb Carr, Thomas Fleming, and Victor Hanson. *The Cold War: A Military History*. Edited by Robert Cowley. New York: Random House, 2006.
Amme, Carl. *NATO Without France: A Strategic Appraisal*. Stanford: Hoover Institute on War, Revolution, and Peace. 1967.
_____, and Fredrick Logevall. *America's Cold War: The Politics of Insecurity*. Cambridge, MA: Belknap Press of Harvard University, 2009.
_____, and Sergey S Radchenko. *The Atomic Bomb and the Origins of the Cold War*. New Haven, CT: Yale University Press, 2008.

Bibliography

Anderson, Patrick. *The Presidents' Men: White House Assistants of Franklin D. Roosevelt, Harry S. Truman, Dwight D. Eisenhower, John F. Kennedy, and Lyndon B. Johnson.* [Anchor Books ed.]. Doubleday, 1969.

Armacost, Michael. *The Politics of Weapons Innovation: The Thor-Jupiter Controversy.* New York: Columbia University Press, 1969.

Armstrong, Hamilton Fish. "Postscript to E.D.C." *Foreign Affairs* 33, no. 1 (October 1954): 17–27.

Baar, James. *Combat Missilemen.* New York: Harcourt, Brace and Company, 1960.

———. *Polaris!* New York: Harcourt, Brace and Company, 1960.

Bacevich, Andrew. *The New American Militarism: How Americans Are Seduced by War.* New York: Oxford University Press, 2006.

———. *The Pentomic Era.* Washington, D.C.: National Defense University Press, 1986.

Ball, S.J."Military Nuclear Relations Between the United States and Great Britain Under the Terms of the Mcmahon Act, 1946–1958." *The Historical Journal* 38, no. 2 (June 1, 1995): 439–454.

Barnaby, Frank, and Douglas Holdstock. *The British Nuclear Weapons Programme, 1952–2002.* New York: Routledge, 2003.

Baucom, Donald R. *The Origins of SDI, 1944–1983.* Lawrence: University Press of Kansas, 1992.

Baylis, John. *Ambiguity and Deterrence: British Nuclear Strategy 1945–1964.* New York: Oxford University Press, 1996.

Beede, Benjamin R. *Military and Strategic Policy: An Annotated Bibliography.* New York: Greenwood Press, 1990.

Biddle, Tami Davis. *Rhetoric and Reality in Air Warfare: The Evolution of British and American Ideas About Strategic Bombing, 1914–1945.* Princeton, NJ: Princeton University Press, 2004.

Bischoff, Gunter, and Stephen Ambrose. *Eisenhower: A Century Assessment.* Baton Rouge: Louisiana State University Press, 1995.

Botti, Timothy. *The Long Wait: The Forging of the Anglo-American Nuclear Alliance, 1945–1958.* New York: Greenwood Press, 1987.

Bowie, Robert. *The North Atlantic Nations: Tasks for the 1960s—A Report to the Secretary of State August 1960, Nuclear History Program Occasional Paper # 7.* Baltimore: University of Maryland, 1991.

Bozo, Frederic, trans. Susan Emanuel. *Two Strategies for Europe: De Gaulle, the United States, and the Atlantic Alliance.* New York: Rowman & Littlefield, 2001.

Brands, Henry. "Johnson and Eisenhower: The President, the Former President, and the War in Vietnam." *Presidential Studies Quarterly* 15, no. 3 (Summer 1985): 589–601.

Brandt, Willy. "The Means Short of War." *Foreign Affairs* 39, no. 2 (January 1961): 196–207.

Brennan, Donald, ed. *Arms Control, Disarmament, and National Security.* New York: George Braziller, 1961.

Brewer, Susan A. *Why America Fights: Patriotism and War Propaganda from the Philippines to Iraq.* New York: Oxford University Press, 2011.

Brodie, Bernard. "Military Demonstration and Disclosure of New Weapons." *Foreign Affairs* 5, no. 3 (April 1953): 281–301.

Bibliography

_____. "Nuclear Weapons: Strategic or Tactical?" *Foreign Affairs* 32, no. 2 (January 1954): 217–229.
Brodie, Bernard, and Fawn M. Brodie. *From Crossbow to H-Bomb: The Evolution of the Weapons and Tactics of Warfare*. Bloomington: Indiana University Press, 1973.
_____. *Strategy in the Missile Age*. Princeton, NJ: Princeton University Press, 1965.
Brodie, Bernard. The Heritage of Douhet. Santa Monica: RAND Corporation, 1965.
Brownlee, James F. *The Defense We Can Afford*. Committee for Economic Development, 1958.
Buchan, Alastair. "The Reform of NATO." *Foreign Affairs* 40, no. 2 (January 1962): 165–182.
Carpenter, Charles A. *Dramatists and the Bomb: American and British Playwrights Confront the Nuclear Age, 1945–1964. Contributions in Drama and Theatre Studies No. 91*. Westport, CT: Greenwood Press, 1999.
Center for Military History. *History of Strategic Air and Ballistic Missile Defense*. Washington, D.C.: Center for Military History, U.S. Army, 2009.
Chourchoulis, Dionysios. *The Southern Flank of NATO, 1951–1959: Military Strategy or Political Stabilization*. Lanham, MD: Lexington Books, 2015.
Cirincione, Joseph. *Bomb Scare: The History & Future of Nuclear Weapons*. New York: Columbia Press University, 2007.
Clark, Ian, and Nicholas J. Wheeler. *The British Origins of Nuclear Strategy 1945–1955*. New York: Oxford University Press, USA, 1989.
Cleave, William R. Van. *Tactical Nuclear Weapons: An Examination of the Issues*. London: Crane Russak & Co., 1978.
Coffman, Edward. "The Course of Military History in the United States Since World War II." *The Journal of Military History* 61, no. 4 (October 1997): 761–775.
Collins, J. Lawton. "NATO: Still Vital for Peace." *Foreign Affairs* 34, no. 3 (April 1956): 367–379.
Condit, Doris. *History of the Office of the Secretary of Defense: The Test of War, 1950–1953*. Washington, D.C.: Historical Office, Office of the Secretary of Defense, 1988.
Cook, Don. *Charles De Gaulle*. New York: G.P. Putnam's Sons, 1983.
Cordle, Daniel. *States of Suspense: The Nuclear Age, Postmodernism and United States Fiction and Prose*. Manchester: Manchester University Press, 2008.
Cox, Donald. "A Dynamic Philosophy of Airpower." *The Journal of Military History* 21, no. 3 (Autumn 1957): 132–138.
Craig, Campbell. *Destroying the Village: Eisenhower and Thermonuclear War*. New York: Columbia University Press, 1998.
Creveld, Martin Van. *The Art of War* (Smithsonian History of Warfare) : War and Military Thought, 2005.
Croft, Stuart. "European Integration, Nuclear Deterrence and Franco-British Nuclear Cooperation." *International Affairs* (Royal Institute of International Affairs 1944–) 72, no. 4 (October 1, 1996): 771–787.
Cuddy, Edward. "Mr. Johnson's War. or Mr. Eisenhower's?" *The Review of Politics* 65, no. 4 (Autumn 2003): 351–374.
Damms, Richard. "James Killian, the Technological Capabilities Panel, and the Emergence of President Eisenhower's 'Scientific-Technological Elite.'" *Diplomatic History* 24, no. 1 (2000): 57–78.

Bibliography

Deibel, Terr ed. *Containment: Concept and Policy Vols. 1 and 2* Washington, D.C.: National Defense University Press, 1986.

DeWeerd, H.A."Britain's Changing Military Policy." *Foreign Affairs* 34, no. 1 (October 1955): 102–116.

Dickson, Paul. *Sputnik: The Shock of the Century.* New York: Walker, 2001.

Dingman, Roger. "Atomic Diplomacy During the Korean War." *International Security* 13, no. 3 (winter, -1989 1988): 50–91.

Divine, Robert. *The Sputnik Challenge: Eisenhower's Response to the Soviet Satellite.* New York: Oxford University Press, 1993.

Dockrill, Saki. *Eisenhower's New Look National Security Policy, 1953–1961.* New York: St. Martin's Press, 1992.

Donnelly, William. "The Best Army That Can Be Put in the Field in the Circumstances: The U.S. Army, July 1951- July 1953." *The Journal of Military History* 71, no. 3 (July 2007): 809–847.

Duchin, Brian. "The Most Spectacular Legislative Battle of That Year: President Eisenhower and the 1958 Reorganization of the Department of Defense." *Presidential Studies Quarterly* 24, no. 2 (Spring 1994): 243–262.

Eisenhower, David. *Going Home to Glory: A Memoir of Life with Dwight D. Eisenhower, 1961–1969.* New York: Simon & Schuster, 2010.

Eisenhower, Dwight. *At Ease: Stories I Tell to Friends.* New York: Doubleday, 1967.

Eisenhower, Dwight David. *Crusade in Europe.* Baltimore: Johns Hopkins University Press, 1997.

Eisenhower, John. *General Ike: A Personal Reminiscence.* New York: Free Press, 2004.

Fairchild, Byron. *History of the Joint Chiefs of Staff: The Joint Chiefs of Staff and National Policy 1957–1960* Vol. 7, Washington D.C.: Office of Joint History, 2000.

Fautua, David. "The 'Long Pull' Army: NSC 68, the Korean War, and the Creation of the Cold War U.S. Army." *The Journal of Military History* 61, no. 1 (January 1997): 93–120.

Fox, William T.R. *NATO and the Range of American Choice.* New York: Columbia University Press, 1967.

Fursenko, Aleksandr, and Timothy Naftali. *Khrushchev's Cold War: The Inside Story of an American Adversary.* New York: W.W. Norton & Company, 2007.

Gaddis, John Lewis. *George F. Kennan: An American Life.* New York: Penguin, 2011.

_____. *Strategies of Containment: A Critical Appraisal of Postwar American National Security Policy.* New York: Oxford University Press, 1992.

_____. *We Now Know: Rethinking the Cold War History.* New York: Oxford University Press, 1998.

Gallois, Pierre M. "New Teeth for NATO." *Foreign Affairs* 39, no. 1 (October 1960): 67–80.

Gantz, Kenneth F., ed. *The United States Air Force Report on the Ballistic Missile: Its Technology, Logistics, and Strategy.* Garden City, NY: Doubleday, 1958.

Garthoff, Raymond. *Assessing the Adversary: Estimates by the Eisenhower Administration of Soviet Intentions and Capabilities.* Washington D.C.: Brookings Institute, 1991.

Gat, Azar. *A History of Military Thought: From the Enlightenment to the Cold War.* New York: Oxford University Press, 2002.

Bibliography

———. *War in Human Civilization.* New York: Oxford University Press, 2008.
Gavin, James M. *War and Peace in the Space Age.* New York: Harper, 1958.
Gellhoed, Bruce. *Charles E. Wilson and Controversy at the Pentagon, 1953–1957.* Detroit: Wayne State University Press, 1979.
Giglio, James N. *The Presidency of John F. Kennedy.* Lawrence: University Press of Kansas, 2006.
Gooch, John, ed. *Airpower: Theory and Practice* London: Frank Cass, 1995.
Greenstein, Fred. *The Hidden-Hand Presidency: Eisenhower as Leader.* New York: Basic, Books, 1982.
Halberstam, David. *The Fifties.* New York: Ballantine Books, 1994.
Hamburg, Roger. "Massive Retaliation Revisited." *The Journal of Military History* 38, no. 1 (February 1974): 17–23.
Herf, Jeffrey. *War by Other Means: Soviet Power, West German Resistance, and the Battle of the Euromissiles.* New York: Free Press, 1991.
Herspring, Dale R. *The Pentagon and the Presidency: Civil-Military Relations from FDR to George W. Bush.* Lawrence: University Press of Kansas, 2006.
Hoag, Malcolm W. "NATO: Deterrent or Shield?" *Foreign Affairs* 36, no. 2 (January 1958): 278–292.
Hogan, Michael J., and Thomas G. Paterson, eds. *Explaining the History of American Foreign Relations.* 2nd ed. Cambridge, MA: Cambridge University Press, 2004.
Howard, Michael. "Britain's Defenses: Commitments and Capabilities." *Foreign Affairs* 39, no. 1 (October 1960): 81–91.
Humphrey, Hubert H. "The Senate in Foreign Policy." *Foreign Affairs* 37, no. 4 (July 1959): 525–536.
Hunt, Michael H. *Ideology and U.S. Foreign Policy.* 2nd ed. New Haven, CT: Yale University Press, 2009.
Huntington, Samuel. *The Soldier and the State: The Theory and Politics of Civil Military Relations.* Cambridge: Belknap Press, 1985.
Inglis, Fred. *The Cruel Peace: Everyday Life in the Cold War.* New York: Harper, 1991.
Jackson, Michael. "Beyond Brinkmanship: Eisenhower, Nuclear War Fighting, and Korea, 1953–1968." *Presidential Studies Quarterly* 35, no. 1 (March 2002): 52–75.
Jansen, Bruce. *Sixteen Trillion Dollar Mistake: How the U.S. Bungled Its National Priorities from the New Deal to the Present.* New York: Columbia University Press, 2001.
Jansson, Bruce S. *The Sixteen-Trillion-Dollar Mistake.* New York: Columbia University Press, 2002.
Kaempffert, Waldemar. "First Atomic Shell Fired from a Gun Opens Still Another Phase of Military Tactics." *New York Times,* May 31, 1953. http://select.nytimes.com/gst/abstract.html?res=F50F1EFA3D59107A93C3AA178ED85F478585F9. [accessed 2 October 2014].
Kahn, Herman. *On Thermonuclear War.* Princeton, NJ: Princeton University Press, 1961
Kaplan, Edward. *To Kill Nations: American Strategy in the Air-Atomic Age and the Rise of Mutually Assured Destruction.* Ithaca, NY: Cornell University Press, 2015.

Bibliography

Kaplan, Fred. *The Wizards of Armageddon: This Is Their Untold Story*. New York: Touchstone, 1983.

Kaplan, Lawrence S. *NATO and the Policy of Containment. Problems in American Civilization*. Boston: Heath, 1968.

———. *NATO 1948: The Birth of the Transatlantic Alliance*. Lanham, MD: Rowman & Littlefield, 2007.

Kennan, George F. "Peaceful Coexistence: A Western View." *Foreign Affairs* 38, no. 2 (January 1960): 171–190.

Khrushchev, Nikita S. "On Peaceful Coexistence." *Foreign Affairs* 38, no. 1 (October 1959): 1–18.

King, James E., Jr. "Nuclear Plenty and Limited War." *Foreign Affairs* 35 (Winter, 1957): 238.

Kingseed, Cole C. *Eisenhower and the Suez Crisis of 1956*. Baton Rouge: Louisiana State University Press, 1995.

Kinnard, Douglas. "Eisenhower and the Defense Budget." *The Journal of Politics* 39, no. 3 (August 1977): 596–623.

Kintner, William, and Reinhardt, George. *Atomic Weapons in Land Combat*. Harrisburg: Military Service Publishing Company, 1953.

Kissinger, Henry. *Nuclear Weapons and Foreign Policy*. New York: Harper, 1957.

Kissinger, Henry A. "Force and Diplomacy in the Nuclear Age." *Foreign Affairs* 34, no. 3 (April 1956): 349–366.

———. "Military Policy and Defense of the 'Grey Areas.'" *Foreign Affairs* 33, no. 3 (April 1955): 416–428.

———. "Missiles and the Western Alliance." *Foreign Affairs* 36, no. 3 (April 1958): 383–400.

———. "Nuclear Testing and the Problem of Peace." *Foreign Affairs* 37, no. 1 (October 1958): 1–18.

———. "Reflections on American Diplomacy." *Foreign Affairs* 35, no. 1 (October 1956): 37–56.

———. "The Search for Stability." *Foreign Affairs* 37, no. 4 (July 1959): 537–560.

Knorr, Klaus. "Nuclear Weapons: 'Haves' and 'Have-Nots.'" *Foreign Affairs* 36, no. 1 (October 1957): 167–178.

Knorr, Klaus, ed. *NATO and American Security*. Princeton, NJ: Princeton University Press, 1959.

Kolodzeij, Edward. *The Uncommon Defense and Congress, 1945–1963*. Columbus: Ohio State University Press, 1966.

Kroenig, Matthew. *Exporting the Bomb: Technology Transfer and the Spread of Nuclear Weapons*. Ithaca, NY: Cornell University Press, 2010.

Lafeber, Walter. *America, Russia, and the Cold War, 1945–2002 9th Edition*. Boston: McGraw-Hill, 2002.

Latham, Michael. *Modernization as Ideology: American Social Science and "Nation Building" in the Kennedy Era*. Chapel Hill: University of North Carolina Press, 2000.

Launius, Roger, and Dennis Jenkins, eds. *To Reach the High Frontier: A History of U.S. Launch Vehicles*. Lexington: University Press of Kentucky, 2002.

Ledbetter, James. *Unwarranted Influence: Dwight D. Eisenhower and the Military-Industrial Complex*. New Haven, CT: Yale University Press, 2011.

Bibliography

Leffler, Melvyn. *For the Soul of Mankind: The United States, the Soviet Union, and the Cold War.* New York: Hill and Wang, 2008.

_____. *A Preponderance of Power: National Security, the Truman Administration, and the Cold War.* Stanford: Stanford University Press, 1992.

Leighton, Richard. *Strategy, Money, and the New Look: 1953-1956.* Washington D.C.: Historical Office of the Secretary of Defense, 2001.

Lewis, Adrian R. *The American Culture of War: A History of U.S. Military Force from World War II to Operation Iraqi Freedom.* 2nd ed. Routledge, 2007.

Maddock, Shane. "The Fourth Country Problem: Eisenhower's Nuclear Nonproliferation Policy." *Presidential Studies Quarterly* 28, no. 3 (Summer 1998): 553–572.

_____. *Nuclear Apartheid: The Quest for American Atomic Supremacy from World War II to the Present.* Chapel Hill: University Press of North Carolina, 2010.

Mahnken, Thomas. *Technology and the American Way of War Since 1945.* Columbia University Press, 2010.

Marchio, James. "Risking General War in Pursuit of Limited Objectives: U.S. Military Contingency Planning for Poland in the Wake of the 1956 Hungarian Uprising." *The Journal of Military History* 66, no. 3 (July 2002): 783–812.

Marks, Fredrick. *Power and Peace: The Diplomacy of John Foster Dulles.* Westport: Praeger, 1993.

Mastny, Vojtech. *A Cardboard Castle? An Inside History of the Warsaw Pact, 1955–1991.* Budapest: Central European University, 2005.

Mataxis, Theodore. *Nuclear Tactics: Weapons, and Firepower in the Pentomic Division, Battlegroup, and Company.* Harrisburg: The Military Service Publishing Company, 1958.

Mayer, Michael. *The Eisenhower Presidency and the '50s.* New York: Houghton Mifflin, 1998.

McClenahan, William. *Eisenhower and the Cold War Economy.* Baltimore: Johns Hopkins University Press, 2011.

McDougall, Walter A. *The Heavens and the Earth: A Political History of the Space Age.* New York: ACLS History E-Book Project, 2008.

Mosely, Philip E. "Soviet Foreign Policy: New Goals or New Manners?" *Foreign Affairs* 34, no. 4 (July 1956): 541–553.

Moskin, J. Robert. *M R. Truman's War: The Final Victories of World War II and the Birth of the Postwar World.* Lawrence: University Press of Kansas, 2002.

Nash, Philip. *The Other Missiles of October: Eisenhower, Kennedy, and the Jupiters, 1957–1963.* Chapel Hill: University of North Carolina Press, 1997.

Neufeld, Jacob. *The Development of Ballistic Missiles in the United States Air Force, 1945–1960.* Washington, D.C.: Office of Air Force History, 1990.

Neufeld, Michael. "The End of the Army Space Program: Interservice Rivalry and the Transfer of the Von Braun Group to NASA, 1958–1959." *The Journal of Military History* 69, no. 3 (July, 2005).

Newhouse, John. *De Gaulle and the Anglo-Saxons.* New York: Viking Press, 1970.

Nichols, David. A. *Eisenhower 1956: The President's Year of Crisis—Suez and the Brink of War.* New York: Simon & Schuster, 2011.

Nitze, Paul H. "Atoms, Strategy and Policy." *Foreign Affairs* 34, no. 2 (January 1956): 187–198.

Bibliography

Osgood, Kenneth. *Total Cold War: Eisenhower's Secret Propaganda Battle at Home and Abroad.* Lawrence: University Press of Kansas, 2006.

Osgood, Robert. *Limited War, the Challenge to American Strategy.* Chicago: University of Chicago Press, 1958.

Pach, Chester, and Elmo Richardson. *The Presidency of Dwight D. Eisenhower.* Lawrence: University Press of Kansas, 1991.

Paret, Peter. *Makers of Modern Strategy: From Machiavelli to the Nuclear Age.* Princeton, NJ: Princeton University Press, 1986.

Paterson, Robert H. *Britain's Strategic Nuclear Deterrent: From Before the V-Bomber to Beyond Trident.* New York: Routledge, 1997.

Patterson, Bradley. "Teams and Staff: Dwight Eisenhower's Innovations in the Structure and Operations of the Modern White House." *Presidential Studies Quarterly* 24, no. 2 (Spring 1994): 277–298.

Patterson, Gardner, and Edgar S. Furniss, Jr. *NATO: A Critical Appraisal.* Princeton, NJ: Princeton University Press, 1957.

Paul, T.V. *The Tradition of Non-Use of Nuclear Weapons.* Stanford: Stanford Security Studies, 2009.

Pearson, Lester B. "After Geneva: A Greater Task for NATO." *Foreign Affairs* 34, no. 1 (October 1955): 14–23.

Peeters, Paul. *Massive Retaliation: The Policy and Its Critics.* Chicago: Henry Regnery Co., 1959.

Pierre, Andrew J. *Nuclear Politics: British Experience with an Independent Strategic Force, 1939–70.* Oxford University Press, 1972.

Pieterse, Jan. "The Development of Developmental Theory: Towards Critical Globalism." *Review of International Political Economy* 3, no. 4 (Winter 1996): 541–564.

Pleven, René. "France in the Atlantic Community." *Foreign Affairs* 38, no. 1 (October 1959): 19–30.

Podvig, Pavel, ed. *Russian Strategic Nuclear Forces.* Cambridge, MA: MITPress, 2004.

Polmar, Norman, and Robert S. Norris. *U.S. Nuclear Arsenal: A History of Weapons and Delivery Systems Since 1945.* Washington, D.C.: Naval Institute Press, 2009.

Powell, Robert. *Nuclear Deterrence Theory: The Search for Credibility.* New York: Cambridge University Press, 2008.

Przeworski, Adam, and Fernando Limongi. "Modernization: Theories and Facts." *World Politics* 49, no. 2 (January 1997): 155–183.

Rearden, Steven. *History of the Office of the Secretary of Defense: The Formative Years, 1947–1950.* Washington, D.C. 1984.

Reese, David. *The Age of Containment: The Cold War.* New York: St. Martin's Press, 1967.

Ritter, Scott. *Dangerous Ground: America's Failed Arms Control Policy, from FDR to Obama.* New York: Nation Books, 2010.

Roberts, Geoffrey. *Stalin's Wars: From World War to Cold War, 1939–1953.* New Haven, CT: Yale University Press, 2008.

Rockefeller, Nelson A. "Purpose and Policy." *Foreign Affairs* 38, no. 3 (April 1960): 370–390.

Roland, Alex. "Technology, Ground Warfare, and Strategy: The Paradox of American

Bibliography

Experience." *The Journal of Military History* 55, no. 4 (October 1991): 447–468.
Roman, Peter. *Eisenhower and the Missile Gap*. Ithaca, NY: Cornell University Press, 1995.
Rose, John. *The Evolution of U.S. Army Nuclear Doctrine, 1945–1980*. Boulder, CO: Westview Press, 1980.
Rublee, Maria Robin. *Nonproliferation Norms: Why States Choose Nuclear Restraint*. Athens: University of Georgia Press, 2009.
Sagan, Scott D. *Moving Targets. Nuclear Strategy and National Security*. Princeton, NJ: Princeton University Press, 1989.
Schnabel, Jones. *History of the Joint Chiefs of Staff: The Joint Chiefs of Staff and National Policy, 1945–1947*. Washington, D.C.: Office of the Chairman of the Joint Chiefs of Staff, 1996.
Schwartz, David N. *Nato's Nuclear Dilemmas*. Washington, D.C.: Brookings Institute Press, 1983.
Scott, Len, and Stephen Twigge. *Planning Armageddon: Britain, the United States and the Command of Nuclear Forces, 1945–1964*. Newark: Harwood Academic Press, 2000.
Sheehan, Neil. *A Fiery Peace in a Cold War: Bernard Schriever and the Ultimate Weapon*. New York: Random House, 2009.
Sigal, Leon. *Nuclear Forces in Europe: Enduring Dilemmas, Present Prospects*. Washington, D.C.: Brookings Institution, 1984.
Slessor, John. "British Defense Policy." *Foreign Affairs* 35, no. 4 (July 1957): 551–563.
Smith, Bruce L.R. *American Science Policy Since World War II*. Washington, D.C.: Brookings Institution Press, 1990.
Snead, David. *Gaither Committee: Eisenhower & Cold War*. Columbus: Ohio State University Press, 1998.
Spaak, Paul-Henri. "New Tests for NATO." *Foreign Affairs* 37, no. 3 (April 1959): 357–365.
Stares, Paul B. *The Militarization of Space, U.S. Policy, 1945–1984*. Ithaca, NY: Cornell University Press, 1985.
Stocker, Jeremy. *Britain and Ballistic Missile Defence, 1942–2002*. New York: Routledge, 2004.
Stockholm International Peace Research Institute. *Tactical Nuclear Weapons: European Perspectives*. London: Crane, Russak, 1978.
Strang, Lord. "Germany Between East and West." *Foreign Affairs* 33, no. 3 (April 1955): 387–401.
Strauss, Franz-Josef. "Soviet Aims and German Unity." *Foreign Affairs* 37, no. 3 (April 1959): 366–377.
Taylor, Maxwell. *The Uncertain Trumpet*. New York: Harper & Brothers, 1959.
Trachtenberg, Marc. *A Constructed Peace: The Making of the European Settlement, 1945–1963*. Princeton, NJ: Princeton University Press, 1999.
____*History and Strategy*. Princeton, NJ: Princeton University Press, 1991.
Tudda, Chris. *The Truth Is Our Weapon: The Rhetorical Diplomacy of Dwight D. Eisenhower and John Foster Dulles*. Baton Rouge: Louisiana State University, 2006.
Vernon, Raymond. "Foreign Trade and National Defense." *Foreign Affairs* 34, no. 1 (October 1955): 77–88.

Bibliography

Wallace, William. "British Foreign Policy After the Cold War." *International Affairs* (Royal Institute of International Affairs 1944-) 68, no. 3 (July 1, 1992): 423–442.

Ward, Bob. *Dr. Space: The Life of Wernher Von Braun.* Annapolis, MD: Naval Institute Press, 2009.

Watson, Robert J., Historical Office, and Office of the Secretary of Defense. *History of the Office of the Secretary of Defense, Volume IV: Into the Missile Age 1956–1960.* Washington, D.C.: Government Printing Office, 2011.

Wigley, Russel. *The American War of War: A History of U.S. Military Strategy and Policy.* Bloomington: Indiana University Press, 1973.

Williams, Appleman. *Tragedy of American Diplomacy.* New York: W.W. Norton, 2009.

Williamson, Murray. *Military Innovation in the Interwar Period.* New York: Cambridge University Press, 1996.

Wohlstetter, Albert. "The Delicate Balance of Terror." *Foreign Affairs* 37, no. 2 (January 1959): 211–234.

_____ "Nuclear Sharing: NATO and the N+1 Country." *Foreign Affairs* 39, no. 3 (April 1961): 355–387.

Wolfers, Arnold. "Superiority in Nuclear Weapons: Advantages and Limitations." *Annals of the American Academy of Political and Social Science* 29 (November 1953): 7–15.

Wolfers, Arnold, ed. *Alliance Policy in the Cold War.* Baltimore: Johns Hopkins Press, 1959.

Zaloga, Steven. *The Kremlin's Nuclear Sword: The Rise and Fall of Russia's Strategic Nuclear Forces, 1945–2000.* Washington, D.C.: Smithsonian Books, 2002.

Zeman, Scott, and Michael Amundson. *Atomic Culture: How We Learned to Stop Worrying and Love the Bomb.* Boulder: University Press of Colorado, 2004.

Zubok, Vladislav, and Contantine Pleshakov. *Inside the Kremlin's Cold War: From Stalin to Khrushchev.* Cambridge, MA: Harvard University Press, 1996.

Zuckerman, Solly. "Judgment and Control in Modern Warfare." *Foreign Affairs* 40, no. 2 (January 1962): 196–212.

Index

Adeneaur, Konrad 153
Algeria 95, 148, 149, 154, 160
Allied Command Europe (ACE) 150–153
Aswan Dam 87–88
Atomic Energy Commission 20, 24, 126
Auriol, Vincent 148

Barbour, Walworth 145, 146
Baruch, Bernard 116
Brodie, Bernard 43–44
Brucker, Wilbur 68
Bulganin, Nikolai 98–99

Central Intelligence Agency 18, 20, 51, 87, 96
Connolly, Robert 26–29
Coty, René 126, 148, 150, 151, 153, 154
Courcel, Geoffrey de 156–157
Crouy-Chanel, Etienne de 150–151
Cutler, Robert 29, 50
Czechoslovakia 87

De Gaulle, Charles 2, 3, 5, 9, 105, 139, 146, 162, 166–167; decolonization 160; French need for atomic weapons 149; French role in NATO 91, 149, 157–160; IRBM deployment 161; meeting with John Foster Dulles 156; meeting with President Eisenhower 154–155, 161; president of France 148–149, 153–162, 166–167
Douglas, Dillon 95
Douglas, Lew 98,
Dulles, Alan 20, 87
Dulles, John Foster 6–7, 30–32, 73, 75, 87–88, 92–97, 100, 103, 115, 117, 125–126, 138–139, 150–151, 153–156, 159

Eden, Anthony 9, 104, 163; post-Suez Anglo-American relations 99; Suez Crisis 84–98
Egypt 28, 84–99, 104

Eisenhower, Dwight D. 1–10, 15, 17, 55, **56**, **60**, 63, 67, **108**, **110**, 162–167; Bermuda Conference 100–105; differences with the U.S. Army leadership 37–41, 45–52, 68–69, 123; Hungarian rebellion 97–98; impact of Clausewitz 14, 31; Indochina 31–32; IRBM 55, 60–82, 107, 115–117, 123–127, 129–147, 148–161; Korean War 11, 16; NATO 115–120, 126–128, 129–147, 148–161; New Look Defense Policy 19–21, 25, 27, 28–31, 33–36, 41–45, 61–62, 65; Project Solarium 22–28; relations with France 83–84, 92, 94–95, 97–99, 148–161; relations with the U.K. 77–79, 81–82, 83–86, 88–105, 115–117, 127–128, 129–147, 149; Soviet threat 12, 18, 53–54, 62, 119–125; Sputnik 106–128; Suez Canal crisis 84–105; Technology Capabilities Panel (Killian Report) 63–65; understanding of war 12–14
Ely, Paul 150, 159–160
European Defense Community 153

Fessenden, Russel 151–152
Forrestal, James 58–59
France 2, 5–6, 133; Anglo-Franco-American relations 8–9; Franco-American reconciliation post-Suez 99–100; French reaction to US-UK IRBM Agreement 148–168; implications of US-UK IRBM Agreement 139, 142; post-war decolonization and international prestige 90–97; Suez Canal crisis 84–85; US-French nuclear cooperation 126–127, 129, 131; US-UK efforts to limit nuclear weapons access 103–105, 111, 145–146

Gaillard, Felix 154
Gavin, James 52, 57, 65, 66, 69, 70
Goodpaster, Andrew 28, 30, 50, 116, 171, 172, 175, 176, 177, 178, 179, 180, 184

195

Index

Hagen, John 107, 109
Hagerty, James 50, 99
Hoover, Herbert 99
Humphrey, George 17, 49, 87
Hungary 51, 96-98

Indochina *see* Vietnam
International Geophysical Year 106
Italy 61, 142, 150, 160

Kennan, George 19, 21, 22, 23, 24, 29
Khrushchev, Nikita 1, 44, 96, **110**
Killian, James 63, 71, 72, 75, 112
Korean War 4, 8, 11-17, 19-22, 32-36, 164

Lebanon 159
Lewis, Strauss 126
Lloyd, Selwyn 103

Macmillan, Harold 5, 115, 130, 163, 165, 166, 167; Bermuda Conference 100-105; differences with Charles de Gaulle 156-158; fiscal concerns 79; non-proliferation 145-146, 149, 161; nuclear test ban 132-133; nuclear weapons 81; purchase of Thor missiles 140; US-UK cooperation 139; US-UK IRBM Agreement 130-131, 137-138
Martin, Edwin 101
McBride, Robert 140
McCormack, James 23-26
McElroy, Neil 73, 75, 114, 116, 120, 125, 127
Medaris, John 60, 64
Mollet, Guy 97-99

National Aeronautics and Space Administration 57, 73, 106, **107**, 112
National Security Council 14, 19-20, 28-32, 37, 40, 42, 49, 52, 53, 87, 101, 123, 170, 171, 173, 174, 184
New Look Defense Policy 1-10, 14, 25, 30-35, 39, 43-47, 51, 54, 67-68, 116-118, 125, 129-130, 131-134, 137, 142, 162-164
non-proliferation of nuclear weapons 5, 103, 147, 166; combined European research program to limit proliferation 143-144; combined US-UK efforts to limit European nuclear weapons proliferation 145; limited nuclear weapons proliferation 103; nuclear test ban 133-134
North Atlantic Council 101, 136, 143, 166

Osgood, Robert 43-44

Pearson, Lester 97
Perkins, George 117-118

Project Vanguard 106-109, 119-120

Quarles, Donald 102, 111-113

Radford, Arthur 31, 42, 86, 99
retaliation 6, 8, 36, 43-44, 53
Rhee, Sygman 11
Ridgway, Matthew 31, 39, 44, 45, 46, 55, 57
Royal Air Force 79, 133, 136, 137, 138

Sandys, Duncan 100
Sprague, Robert 123-124
Sputnik 1, 3, 10, 165, 167; comparison to US launches 64, 67, 74; impact on British strategy 135-136; implications for Eisenhower Administration 13, 71-76, 82, 106-128, 129
Stalin, Josef 23
Strategic Air Command 123, 133, 138, 164
Strauss, Lewis 126, 127
Union of Socialist Soviet Republics 1-4, 6-10, 28, 31-32, 39-41, 51-52, 61, 67, 81-82, 84-86, 104, 145, 154, 160-161, 163-166; Hungarian Uprising 97; Israel 84, 86, 93, 94, 95, 97, 98; McMahon Act 77, 126, 139-144; New Look Defense Policy 43-49; Project Solarium 21-27; Soviet support to Egypt 87-88; Sputnik 73, 76, 106-128, 129; Suez Canal crisis 92-99; Supreme Allied Commander Europe 5, 119, 126, 154; thermonuclear capability 11, 80, 131; threat 11-20, 29-30, 34-36, 37-38, 42-43, 45-46, 53, 62-64, 70-73, 75, 79, 133-136, 156

Taylor, Maxwell 2, 37-39, 46-51, 55, 70-71, 81, 123, 164
Timmons, B.E.L. 140-141
Torbet, Horace 152
Truman, Harry 9, 14-16, 18, 19, 21, 23-24, 28, 33, 78
Turkey 61, 160
Tuthill, John 150-151

U 2 109-110
United Kingdom 2, 4, 5, 6, 8, 9, 10, 14, 161, 162, 163, 164, 165; Bermuda Conference 100-105, 127, 165; decolonization 90-91; Eisenhower experience in WWII 12-13; European implications of US-UK relationship 115; limiting nuclear weapons to France 104, 149; NATO relations 154, 156-157; nuclear program 118; participation in the Combined European Missile Program 149-151; post-Suez IRBM discussion 99-101; post-war nuclear strategy 79-82; Sput-

Index

nik 106, 110-111, 114-115, 126-127; Suez Canal crisis 83-99; US sale of Thor missiles 140; US-UK IRBM Agreement and deployment 71-72, 129-147, 165, 167-168; US-UK IRBM Agreement as framework for Franco-American IRBM Agreement 151; US-UK nuclear cooperation 61-62, 127

United Nations 89, 92, 93, 94, 97

U.S. Air Force 2, 4, 7, 31, 33, 34, 37, 39-41, 44, 48-54, *59*, *66*, 101-102, 107, 109, 111, 114, 123, 138, 157, 163-164; Atlas 62; development of IRBM 55, 56, 58-75; Thor 7, 55, *56*, 58, *59*, 62, 65, 67, 70-75, 114, 133, 140, 142-143, 147, 162, 167; Thor-Able 72; Titan 62

U.S. Army 2, 4, 7, 9, 15, 18, 30, *56*, *57*, *66*, 107-109, *107*, *108*, 112, 114, 120, 123, 137, 163-164; Corporal Missile 45, 81, 140; development of IRBMs 55-81, 71; impact of New Look 33-37, 37-41, 43-54; Jupiter Missile 2, 7, 52, 55-59, *56*, *57*, 62, 64-75, *66*, 81, 106-109, *108*, 112, 114, 119-120, 133, 143, 162; Jupiter-S 67; Mercury-Redstone 112; Pentomic Division 47, 117, 137; Pershing Missile *57*; Redstone Missile 57-58, 60, 65, *66*, 68-71, *108*, 112

U.S. Congress 17, 44, 55, 58, 59, 77, 112, 113, 125, 126, 139

U.S. Navy Polaris Missile 3, 30, 34, 37, 39, 41, 52-53, 65-67, 70-72, 114

Universal Military Training 58-59

V- 2 13, 57
Vietnam 19, 27, 31-32, 91, 148, 153
von Braun, Werhner 57, 64, *66*, 67, 68, 73, *107*, 107, *108*, 109, 174, 176, 191, 194

Western European Union 103
White, Thomas 49
Wilson, Charles 30, 61, 62, 64, 68, 70, 85, 86, 100, 120

Yugoslavia 28

www.ingramcontent.com/pod-product-compliance
Lightning Source LLC
Chambersburg PA
CBHW032100300426
44116CB00007B/829